Blount County
Tennessee

COUNTY COURT RECORDS

1808–1811

WPA RECORDS

Heritage Books
2024

HERITAGE BOOKS

AN IMPRINT OF HERITAGE BOOKS, INC.

Books, CDs, and more—Worldwide

For our listing of thousands of titles see our website
at
www.HeritageBooks.com

A Facsimile Reprint
Published 2024 by
HERITAGE BOOKS, INC.
Publishing Division
5810 Ruatan Street
Berwyn Heights, MD 20740

1937

International Standard Book Number
Paperbound: 978-0-7884-8995-2

W.P.A. RECORDS

The WPA Records are, for the most part, carbon copies of the original that was typed on onion skin paper during the Depression. Since these records were typed on poor machines by people who did not type in some cases and at the same time, they were read by persons not always sure of the older handwritten materials, the results are often less than perfect.

We have made every attempt to make as clear a copy as can be made from these older papers. Sometimes there are water stains and burned edges around the paper. This is the results of a fire at the home of one of the workers, Mrs. Penelope Allen, who was over most of the project. Sometimes, the index will be misleading in that they index by the middle name when a list of names are given in one family, i.e. "... the children of John Smith are, John, Jr., Mary Warren, and Oscar Sims. The indexer would list a Warren and a Sims in the index, when they should be Smith. Mountain Press has acquired a rather large number of finished and un-finished manuscripts. Many of these latter manuscripts are being typed and index now.

The WPA Records are now very scattered between the Tennessee State Library, various Public and Private Libraries and other collections. Some day, there is a hope that all of these can be collected and stored in one place. In spite of their many mistakes and problems, these are still the most complete collection of Tennessee records found anywhere.

TENNESSEE

RECORDS OF BLOUNT COUNTY

COURT RECORDS

1808 - 1811

HISTORICAL RECORDS PROJECT
Official Project No. 165-44-6999

COPIED UNDER WORK'S PROGRESS ADMINISTRATION

MRS. JOHN TROTWOOD MOORE
STATE LIBRARIAN & ARCHIVIST, SPONSOR

MRS. ELIZABETH D. COPPEDGE
DIRECTOR OF WOMEN'S & PROFESSIONAL PROJECTS

MRS. PENELOPE JOHNSON ALLEN
STATE SUPERVISOR

MRS. MARGARET HELMS RICHARDSON
PROJECT SUPERVISOR

COPIED BY
MISS DORA H. BORING

TYPED BY
MRS. FLEDA L. LOWE

September 22, 1937

BLOUNT COUNTY

COURT MINUTES
1808-1811

INDEX

Note: page numbers in this index refer to those of the original volume from which this copy is made. These numbers are carried in the left hand margin of this copy.

Eagleton, David, 10, 157, 158, 161, 310

Eagleton, John, 352, 353, 366, 386, 371

Earhart, Micheal, 383

Earhart, Nicholas, 146

Eddington (Edington) David, 20, 33

Eddington, James, 112, 113

Eddington, John, 45, 65, 80, 81, 122, 124 146, 162, 168, 240, 267

Eddington, Polly, 246

Edmonds, John, 187, 267, 277, 280, 289, 302, 305, 318

Edmondson, David, 235

Edmondson, James, 30, 375

Edmondson, John, 19

Edmondson, William, 121

Edwards, Amos, 247, 313

Edwards, Greenbury, 149, 151, 390

Edwards, Morgan, 82, 383

Eggins, Edward, 70, 194

Egnew, Andrew, 241

Eldon, Joseph, 246

Elliott, Hugh, 208

Elliott, Thomas, 249

Elliott, Wyat, 332

Embra, Elihu, 36, 200

England, Thomas, 39

Egglely, David, 186, 187

Epherson, William, 8

Erwin, (Ervin) Benjamin, 143, 206, 210

Erwin, George, 346

Etherton, Thomas, 11

Evins, (Erwin) Andrew, 82, 247, 342

Evins, Charles, 342

Ewing, Andrew, 127

Ewing, George, 3, 12, 20, 40, 43, 57, 58, 82, 89, 92, 93, 95, 101, 120, 127, 143, 180, 194, 195, 203, 221, 237, 245 246, 250, 251, 256, 259, 267 267, 318, 324, 327, 341, 365, 394, 395

Ewing, James, 81, 90, 114, 127, 144

Ewing, John, 9, 90

Ewing, Nathan, 305

Ewing, William, Wm., 30, 137, 269

F

Fagg, William, 5, 6, 7, 88, 103, 117, 142, 150, 158, 191, 223,

Farmer, Nathan, 383

Farr, John, 209

Ferguson (Forguson) Andrew, 152, 188, 359

Ferguson, Robert, 48, 157, 158

Finley, Alexander, 100

Finley, George, 126

Finley, John, 18, 197, 212, 261, 264, 265, 280, 303, 314, 372,

Finley, Robert, 138, 186

Finley, Saml., 33, 55, 54, 74, 100, 139, 163, 166, 210, 394

Finley, Sam William, 98, 302, 320, 339

Fitsgerald, Patrick, 131

Flanagan, Saml., 46, 54, 77

Fleet, Manuel, 58

Fletcher, David, 28

Ford, Alexander, 38, 39, 40, 63, 79, 199, 212, 318, 355

Ford, Benjamin, 18

Fout, Philip, 338

Fox, George, 88

Francis, William, 352

Franks, Henry, 59, 101, 105, 116, 122, 126, 206, 220, 223, 224, 228

Frazier, Samuel, 23, 38, 41, 42, 302m, 314, 316, 348

Freshier, (Fresher-Frusher) George, 57

Freshier, Jacob, 112, 334

Frew, Archibald, 13, 49, 137

Fryer, John, 5

Fulkner, James, 118

G

Gamble, Agnes, 135

Gamble, Alexander, 112, 113, 317

Gamble, Andrew, 20, 231, 247, 256, 342

Gamble, Henry, 111

Gamble, Jas., 116

Gamble, John, 146, 187, 205, 237, 324

Gamble, Josiah, 21, 67, 92, 169, 351

Gamble, Moses, 141x 144, 173

Gamble, Nancy, 184

Gamble, Ro, 123xx3 327

Gamble, Thos., 1, 156, 197, 218, 231

N

Neel (Nail) John, 16, 110, 156, 379
Nelson, Joseph, 37
Nicol, John, 63, 136, 159, 167, 176, 231, 270, 327, 333, 341, 388, 389, 391, 393, 396
Nicol, Josiah, 13, 61, 67, 231, 270, 289
Niman, (Nyman) Jacob, 59
Niman, Margaret, 222
Niman, Micheal, 74, 250, 251
Noblet, Thomas, 3
Norwell, Nathanial, 58, 82, 93
Norwood, Henry, 309
Norwood, John, 254, 287, 283 353
Norwood, Samuel, 153
Null, John, 355, 375

O

O'Conner, Terrance, 5
O'Conner, Thomas, 201, 289
O'Dell, Benj., 3
Oliver, William, 28
Owens, Thomas, 114, 225, 315

P

Parker, Benj., 347
Parks, Josiah, 113
Parks, Joseph, 113
Parks, Robert, 101, 186
Parrott, Henry, 55, 240, 310, 311
Parsons, Enoch, 5, 16, 33, 43, 47, 55, 61, 62, 72, 79, 80, 81, 82, 84, 94, 95, 136, 176, 203, 213, 216, 223, 237, 277, 329, 330, 337, 342, 358, 394, 395
Parsons, Josiah, 37, 49, 207, 241
Pate, Joseph, 166
Pate, Mathew, 187
Pate, Stephen, 187
Patterson, Alexander, 37, 90, 195, 198, 218, 301, 321 391
Patton, Anthony, 72
Patty, Josiah, 11, 19, 113, 113, 121, 168, 218, 321

Patty, Zarabelle, 218
Paul, James, 72, 117, 132, 142, 212 214,
Paxton, William, 42, 235
Payne (Pain) Francis, 106
Payne, Josiah, 231, 254, 269, 282, 305
Pearce, James, 47, 67, 53, 54, 55, 98, 129, 290, 306, 310, 337,
Pearce, John, 94
Pearce, Josiah, 231
Peary, (Peery) George, 92
Penry, James, 220
Peary, Leon, 84, 133
Peary, William, 90, 112, 158, 175,
Pearson, Robert, 67
Peck, Adam, 11, 45, 67, 70, 112, 146
Peck, Jacob, 98, 380, 317, 341, 367
Phillips, Abraham, 81, 82, 174
Phillips, David, 4, 57
Pickle, David, 10
Porter, Charles, 141
Porter, James, 13, 16, 36, 378
Porter, Saml., 19
Porter, P. H., 60
Posey, Joseph, 224
Posey, Hezikiah, 326, 328
Powel, Thomas, 92
Prater, Benj., 8
Pride, Benj., 16
Pride, Burton, 48, 74, 147, 202, 249, 320
Pride, Thomas, 123
Pride, Wisley, 9
Pride, Wm., 16, 203
Preston, George, 230
Prigmore, Ephriam, 18
Prush, Jacob, 369
Pugh, Hugh, 321
Purries, John, 257

R

Ramsey, Richard, 1, 2, 158, 168, 174, 278
Rankin, John, 65, 68, 80, 96, 121, 161, 198, 204, 376, 379
Rankin, Thomas, 333
Rawson, Joseph, 110
Ray, Jesse, 146
Ray, Robert, 21

BLOUNT COUNTY, TENNESSEE

COUNTY COURT RECORDS, BOOK No. 2

1808 - 1811

1. Delinquents

	Acres	White	
Josiah Payne	883	1	
Sam'l D. Sanson		1	Ditto
George Dillard Pd.		1	3 Blacks
Valentine Mayo	264	1 1	"
Jacob Franks	164	" "	
Wm Grave	137	1 "	"
Hugh Cunningham	317	1 "	"
John Hickland	726	2 Black	
Thos Gamble	100	1 White " P	

1A. At a Court of Pleas and Quarter Sessions began and held for the County of Blount at the Court House in Maryville on the fourth Monday of February 1808.-

Present

John Tedford, Andrew Bogle and John Gardiner Esquires etc.-

Samuel Cowan Esquire high Sheriff of the County aforesaid returned Writ of Venire facias to him directed Executed on the following persons, to wit,

1. Richard Ramsey		18. Edom Dickson
2. William Scott		19. David Wilson
3. John Sharp		20. Joseph Henderson
4. Andrew Thompson		21. Peter Bowerman
5. John Thornbury		22. John Ish
6. John B. Cusack		23. Alexander McCullock
7. James Weir, Jr.		24. James McNutt
8. Charles Logan		25. Henery McCully
9. John Craig, Exc'd.		26. Benjamin Rodgers
10. Silas George		27. William Durham
11. John T. Garnor		28. Archibald Jonston
12. Robert McTear, Exc'd.		29. Robert Hughs
13. Adam Curry		30. John Gautt
14. William Maclin		31. John Duncan
15. Robert Tedford		32. Isiah Bowerman
16. Josiah Hutton, Exc'd.		33. Hugh Kelsoe, Exc'd.
17. Edom Dickson		34. Thomas Henderson

2. Out of which the following Persons were elected a Grand Inquest for the County of Blount

1. Robert Tedford	6. Silas George	11. Edom Dickson
2. Richard Ramsey	7. Robert Hughs	12. John Duncan
3. Thomas Henderson	8. Humphrey Montgomery	13. Daniel Wilson
4. Henery McCully	9. Arch Jonston	14. Peter Bowerman
5. William Durham	10. Benjamin Rodgers	15. Charles Logan

Were sworn received their Charge and retired to inquire of their Presentments

Traverse Jury

1. John Gantt	5. James Weir Jr.	9. James McNutt
2. William Scott	6. John Ish	10. William Maclin
3. Adam Henry	7. John B. Cusack	11. Alexander McCullock
4. Joseph Henderson	8. Andrew Thompson	12. John T. Garnor
		13. Isaiah Bowerman

An Assignment an a plat and certificate of Survey from Joseph Dobson to John Wilson was proven in Open Court by William McClung and Brice Blair the subscribing Witnesses thereto.-

An assignment of a plat and certificate of Survey from Michael Bowerman to Azariah Williams was proven in open Court by James Allen and Thomas Noblet the subscribing witnesses thereto.-

3.
Monday 22nd of February.___ Term 1808.

Present

Samuel Hendley George Ewing and Robert Boyd, Esqr. &C.

Benjamin Odle)
vs   Coveat.
Henery Weirs)   This day came the parties by their attornies and thereupon came a Jury "to wit."

1. John Gantt	5. James Weir Jr.	9. James McNutt
2. William Scott	6. John Ish	10. William Maclin
3. Adam Kuns	7. John B. Cusack	11. Daniel Richey
4. Joseph Henderson	8. Andrew Thompson	12. Daniel Durham

who being elected tried and sworn the truth to speak upon their Oaths do say

Which Jury after having retired some time to make up a verdict in this case came back into Court and said they cannot agree. By and with the consent of the parties on both sides it is agreed that they make a miss Trial.-

4.
An assignment of a Plat and Certificate of survey from Gavin Jonston by his attorney Joseph Ghormley to Thomas Noblet was drawn in open court by James Walker and Joseph Anderson the subscribing witness thereto.-

An assignment of a Plot and Certificate of Survey from John Richard to James Bates was proven in open court by Alexander B. Gamble & Willson

White two of the subscribing witnesses thereto

A relinquishment of a certain tract of land from David Philips unto William Hugh was proven in open court by Stephen Stafford and Samuel Cameron the subscribing witnesses thereto.-

An assignment of a Plat and certificate of survey from Alexander Moore to Hugh Kelsoe was proven in open Court by Hugh Montgomery and William Hutton the subscribing witnesses thereto.-

An assignment of a Plat and Certificate of survey from John Mordock to Henery Stephenson was proven in open court by William Durham and William Griffits the subscribing witnesses thereto

An assignment of a Plat and Certificate of survey from Alexander Moore to John Licans was proven in open court by Hugh Montgomery & Hugh Kelsoe the subscribing witnesses thereto

An Assignment of a Plot and Certificate of survey from James Anderson to Thomas Wooden was proven in open Court by John McCallister & William Griffits the witnesses thereto

5. David Russell   )
          vs   ) Atto.
    William Reckampecker) In this case on motion of the Plaintiff by E.
                         Parsons his attorney it appears that the attachment was returned levied on a tract of land joining lines with James Boyd & Others as the property of said Reckampecker. You are therefore summoned that you expose said Land to sale agreably to Law to satisfy said Plaintiff his Debt & costs

    John McGhee   )
          vs   ) Atto.
    Wm Reckampecker) In this case it appears on motion of Enoch Parsons
                         that an Attachment from John Gardiner Esqr vs the Defendant to the amount of Six Dollars & William Legg Constable returned said Attachment levied on a Tract of Land joining lines with James Boyd & others as the property of said Reckampecker._
        Therefore it is considered by our said Court that said Land be exposed to sale agreably to Law to satisfy said Debt & costs.-

An Assignment of a Plot of Land & Certificate of Survey from Fleet Mamiel to John Fryer Jun was proven in open Court by Paxton Mamiel & Samuel Donaway the subscribing witnesses thereto.-

An assignment of a Plot & Certificate of survey from John McCartney to George P. Hogg was proven in open Court by Thomas Maxwell and Torrence O. Conner the subscribing witnesses thereto.-

6.   Love & Co.)
          vs   ) Order of sale
    John McKnight) In this case on motion of the Plaintiff that an Execution Issued from John Gardiner Esqr to William Fagg Constable on the Defendant to the amount of $48.75 cents Debt

& the Cost and said Constable returned said Execution levied on a tract of Land as the property of said McKnight

Therefore it is considered that said land be exposed to sale agreably to Law to satisfy Exectiondr & Costs

King & Montgomery)
  vs   ) Order of Sale
John McKnight) In this case on motion of the Plaintiff it appears
         that an Execution issued from John Gardiner Esqr to the Constable commanding him to make the sum of $22.42 Cents & the Costs of that fi fa and the Constable retußned levied on a Tract of Land as the property of said McKnight

It is therefore considered that said land be exposed to sale agreably to Law to satisfy said Execution & costs.

An assignment of a Plot and Certificate of Survey from William Griffits to Benjamin Bailey was proven in open Court by Daniel Durham and John B. Cusack the subscribing witnesses thereto

7. Law & Co.)
   vs   ) Order of Sale
John McKnight) In this case it appears that an Execution from John
        Gardiner Esqr in favor of the Plaintiff vs the Defendant the amount $49 Debt & Costs & William Fagg the officer to whom it was directed redd'd levied on a Tract of Land as the property of the Defendant.-

It is therefore considered by our said Court that said Land be exposed to sale agreably to law to satisfy said Debt & Costs.-

Law & Co.)
  vs   ) Order of Sale
Hunter & Reed) In this case It appears that an Execution Issued
       from John Gardiner Esqr. in favor of the Plaintiff vs the Defendants to the amount of $16.95 Cents Debt & the Costs of the Execution & William Fagg Constable to whom it was directed return'd levied on a Tract belonging to the Defendants.

It is therefore considered by our said Court that land be exposed to sale agreably to Law to satisfy said Debt & Costs

Boyd   )
  vs   ) Order of Sale
Hunter & Reed) In this case on motion of the Plaintiff it appears that an Execution issued from John Gardiner Esqr. in favor of the Plaintiff vs the Defendants to the amount of $19.25 Cts. Debt & the Costs & William Fagg the Constable to whom it was directed returned Levied on a certain Tract of land as the property of the Defendant.

It is therefore considered by our said Court that said Land be exposed to sale agreably to Law to satisfy said Debt & Costs.-

8. An assignment of a Plot and Certificate of survey from Thomas Wooden to William Griffitts was proven in open court by John McCallister and William Brown the subscribing witnesses thereto.

An assignment of a Plot and certificate of Survey from John Murfy to Fleet Manuel was proven in open Court by Samuel Donaway & Paxton Manuel the subscribing witnesses thereto,

An assignment of a Plat and Certificate of survey from Michael Sailor to Samuel Richardson was proven in open Court by Paxton Manuel and Samuel Donaway the subscribing witnesses thereto.

An Assignment of a Plat and Certificate of Survey from Paxton Manuel to John Irwin was proven Court by Samuel Donaway & Fleet Manuel the subscribing witnesses thereto .

An Assignment of a Plat and Certificate of Survey from Louis Tarwater to Frederick Rush was proven in open Court by Samuel Donaway Paxton Manuel the Subscribing witnesses thereto.

An Assignment of a plat and Certificate of survey from Samuel Rowland to Frederick Rush was proven in open court by Samuel Dunnaway the & Steph Wise the subscribing witnesses thereto.

An Assignment of a plat & Certificate of Survey from Benjamin Pratter to William Epherson was proven in open Court by Wilson White & Samuel Dickey the subscribing witnesses thereto.

9.   An Assignment of a Plot & Certificate of Survey from Stephen Anderson to William Irwin was proven in open Court by Moses Keywood & Brice Blair the subscribing witnesses threrto.-

An Assignment of a Plot and Certificate of survey from Ahimaas Reagen to John Reagen was proven in open Court by Wilson White and Richard Kirby the witnesses thereto thereto.

An Assignment of a Plot and Certificate of survey from Alexander Malcom to John Malcom was proven in open Court by Silas George and William Crow the subscribing witnesses thereto.

An Assignment of a Plot an Certificate of Survey from Edom Dickson to Jonathan Dean James Allen and Thomas Noblet the subscribing witnesses thereto

An Assignment of a Plot and Certificate of survey from William Stover to Aaron ----? was proven in open Court by William Davis & George Snider the subscribing witnesses thereto.

An Assignment of a Plot and Certificate of survey from William Logan to Samuel Thompson was proven in open court by David Thompson & Wilsey Pride the subscribing witnesses thereto.

An Assignment of a Plat and Certificate of Survey from Samuel Thompson to Robert Thompson was proven in Court by William Logan & Welsey Pride the suvscribing witnesses thereto.

10.   Robert Eaken   )
          vs   )
      Robert McCully) In this case John Walker who was special bail for the
                       Defendant surrendered the principal in exchange of
      himself
                       And William Baker came into Court and undertook that said
      Robert McCully should pay the costs & condemnation against him or sur-

rneder himself into prison or that he would pay the costs for him or surrender him.

An Assignment of a Plat and certificate of Survey from John Stephens to Barney Chchran was proven in open court by David Eagleton & Thomas Maxwell the subscribing witnesses thereto.-

An Assignment of a Plat and Certificate of survey from James Knox to William McSharon was acknowledged in Open Court by the subscriber thereto.

An Assignment from John Chemens to James Gilmore for a Plat and Certificate of survey was proven in open Court by John Anderson & Samuel Cowan the witnesses thereto.

An Assignment of a Plat and certificate of survey from David Parkle to James Williams was proven in Open Court by Daniel Durham & Archabald Jonston the subscribing witnesses.

An Assignment of a Plat and Certificate of survey from James Watson to Paul Cochran was proven in Open Court by John Gardiner & Robert Gray the subscribing witnesses thereto.

11. An Assignment of a Plat and Certificate of survey from Thomas Etherton to William Cannon was proven in Open Court Josiah Patty & George Cannon the subscribing witnesses thereto.

An Assignment of a Plat and Certificate of Survey from John Allison to Nehemiah Benham was proven in open court by John Johnston & William Forrister the subscribing witnesses thereto.

An Assignment from John Malcom to William Crow was proven in open Court by Silas George and Alexander Malcom the subscribing witnesses thereto.

And a reassignment from said William Crow to Henery Creswell was proven in Open Court by Alexander Malcom and Silas George the witnesses thereto.

This day came John Brabson Deputy Marshall for the District of East Tennessee and acknowledged a Deed of Conveyance for four hundred acres of land to Adam Peck for the purpose therein mentioned
Wherefore it is condidered by our said court that said Deed be admitted to Registration as the Law directs.

An Assignment from William Walker to William Gray for a Plat and Certificate of Survey was proven in Open Court by Josiah Patty & Robert Young the Witnesses thereto.

12. An Assignment of a Plat and certificate of survey from Elizabeth Steel to James Schrimsher was proven in open court by John Williams and Robert Steel the witnesses thereto.

The last Will and Testament of Edward Higgins Ded'd. was proven in court by John Montgomery & John McGhee the subscribing witnesses thereto.

William McLegg was by the Court appointed Constable who entered into bond and took the Oath of Office.

Court adjourned untill tomorrow 9 Oclock.

Tuesday Morning 23rd February 1808

Court Met according to Adjournment

Present

Samuel Hendley George Ewing & Robert Boyd Esqrs Justices etc.

An Assignment of a Plat and Certificate of Survey from John McNutt to Adam McCormac was proven in Open Court by Barcley McGhee and Enoch Parsons the witnesses thereto.

An Assignment of a Plat and certificate of survey from James Wilson to John McGhee was proven in open Court by John Mowry & William Morton the Witnesses thereto.

13.   Ordered that Mary Stephens be allowed One Dollar for Week for keeping an orphan child named Griffitts until next Term.-

An Assignment of a Plat and Certificate of Survey from James Culton to Robert Lowe was proven in open Court by John Dunlap and James McCollom the witnesses thereto.

Albert McClure was by the Court appointed constable who entered into Bond and took the Oath of office.-

An Assignment from Samuel Hendley to Thomas Henderson of a Plat and Certificate was proven in Open Court by Enoch Parsons & Robert Houston the subscribing witnesses thereto.-

An Assignment of a Plat and Certificate of survey from William Moore to Henery Dunlap was proven in Open Court by John Dunlap & James McCollom the witnesses thereto.

An Assignment of a Plat and Certificate of Survey from Hezekiah Posey to Archibald Frew was proven in open Court by William Montgomery & James P. H. Porter the witnesses thereto.

An Assignment of a Plat and certificate of Survey from Edward Buvkhannan to Robert Henderson was proven in Open Court by David Caldwell Adam Dimmond the witnesses thereto.-

14.   Ordered by the Court that John Woods Jonathan L. Harris & John Gardiner Esqrs be commissioned to settle with the Executors of the Estate of Jonathan Mathews dec'd.

An Assignment of a Plat and Certificate of survey from John B. Cusack to Adam Dinsmore was proven in Open Court by David Caldwell &

Robert Henderson the subscribing witnesses thereto.

An Assignment of a plat and Certificate of Survey from Robert Cowan to Michael Higgins was proven in Open Court by James Sloan & John Williams the subscribing witnesses thereto.

An Assignment of a Plat and Certificate of Survey from Reuben Berryman to xxxx Arthur Moore was proven in Open Court by Shedrick Moore & Jacob Moore the subscribing witnesses thereto.

An Assignment of a Plat and Certificate of Survey from William Finley to James McTear was proven in Open Court by James Cook & Martin McTear the subscribing witnesses thereto.

An Assignment of a Plat and Certificate of Survey from Margaret Williams to William Colman was proven in Open Court by James McTear & John Rankin the subscribing Witnesses thereto.

An Assignment of a Plat and Certificate of Survey from Stuart Montgomery to John Jonston was proven in Open court by George Weir & William Montgomery witnesses thereto.

15.   An Assignment of a Plat and Certificate of Survey from Absolom Cook to James Sxx Young was proven in Open Court by John Sharp & Barclay McGhee the subscribing witnesses thereto.

An Assignment of a Plat and Certificate of Survey from George Wallace by Samuel Hendley his Attorney to John Hamontree was proven in open Court by John Wilkinson & John Gardiner the witnesses thereto.

An Assignment of a Plat and Certificate of Survey from James McTear &xWilliamxFindleyxxkx to James Cook was proven in open Court by Martin McTear & William Findley the witnesses thereto.

An Assignment from John Smith Assignee to Dempsey Hicks was proven in Open Court by James Henery & George Snider the subscribing witnesses thereto.

An Assignment of a plat and certificate of Survey from James Hogg to Elizabeth Houston Admx & John & James Houston Administrators of Samuel Houston Dec'd was proven in open Court by James Gillespie & William Setcherthe subscribing Witnesses thereto.

An Assignment of a Plat and Certificate of Surveyfrom James Hubbert to Reuben Berryman was proven in Open Court by David Cusack & James Henery the Witnesses thereto.-

16.   An Assignment from Edward Burnett for a plat and Certificate of Survey to Benjamin Pride was proven in Open Court by William Pride and John Burnett the Witnesses thereto

An Assignment of a Plat and Certificate of Survey from William Cagle to Jacob Moore was proven in Open Court by Enoch Parsons & James P. H. Porter the subscribing Witnesses thereto.

An Assignment of a Plat and Certificate of Survey from George Hogg to John McCartney Jun was proven in Open Court by James Logan & Thomas Maxwell Witnesses thereto

John McCallister)
         vs   ) Atta.
Alexander and Thomas Coulter) In this case John Ish and James Coulter came into Court and confessed that the Defendants should pay the costs and condemnation or surrender /himself or they would pay the costs and condemnation or surrender him.-

John McGhee)
       vs   )
James Wilson) In this case John Neel who was special Bail for the Defendant came into court and surrendered the principal in discharge of himself.
                    and the Deft confessed Judgment for costs.

17.   Wednesday 24th 1808 February Term

          Court met according to adjournment

                    Present

          William Lowry, James Gillespie, and John Gardiner Esqrs, Justices

          A Morgage for two Negro Slaves named Moses and Buck from John Lowry to Isaia Mankin was acknowledged in Open Court by John Lowry the subscriber thereto and ordered to be registered.-

          Ordered by Court that Isaiah Bowman be fined fifty cents for contempt shown to this Court summoned.

                    Wednesday 24th 1808 February Term

                    Present

          Samuel Hendley William Lowry John Tedford and Robert Boyd Esqrs.

18.   William Lackey)
            vs   ) Case
      James Morgan) This day came the parties by their attornies and thereupon came a Jury to wit

1. Alexander McCullock   5. David Cusack   9. David White
2. John ~~Scarnkey~~   6. George Stephens   10. John Wilson
        Thornberry   7. John Rankin   11. David B. Wallace
3. John Finley   8. Samuel Thompson   12. John McConnald
4. Joseph Rogers
who being elected tried and sworn the truth to speak upon issue joined upon this Oath Do say the Defts did not promise and assume upon himself in manner & form as the Plaintiff in pleading hath alledged
          Therefore It is considered by our said Court that the Plaintiff take nothing by his bill but for his false clamour be in mercy etc and the Defendant go thereof Without day and recover against the Plaintiff his costs by him in this behalf expended.-

An Assignment of a Plat and certificate of Survey from Washington
Allen to Ephriam Prigmore was proven in Open Court by Saml Eaken and
Benjamin Ford the Witnesses thereto

19.   An Assignment of a Plat and Certificate of Survey Charles McCormac
to John Edmondson was proven in Open Court by Josiah Patty & Henery
Whitenbarger the subscribing Witnesses thereto.

An Assignment of a Plat and Certificate of Survey from Larkin Bolin
to Thomas Davis was proven in Open Court by Adam Dunlap and John Gardiner the subscribing witnesses thereto.

An Assignment of a Plat and Certificate of Survey from James Ham-
let to Thomas Davis was proven in Open Court by Adam Dunlap & John Garnor the Witnesses thereto.

An Assignment of a Plat and Certificate of Survey from Jamesx Ham
Samuel Porter to Elijah Hicks was proven in Open Court by William Kibble
and Abraham Bayles the witnesses thereto.-

20.   An Assignment of a Plat and Certificate of Survey from David Eddington to William Williams was proven in Open Court by James Sloan &
Jonathan Appler the witnesses thereto

William Lowry George Ewing Robert Boyd and Andrew Bogle Esqrs
Justices Present, Etc.

Matthew Wallace)
         vs   )   Case
Robert Moore   )   This day came the parties by their Attornies and
                           thereupon came a Jury to wit

1. John L. Garner   5. Warnor Martin   9. Andrew Kenneday
2. William Houston   6. James Taylor   10. John Carroth
3. Jonathan Trippett   7. Andrew Gamble   11. James Baity
4. John David   8. John Woodey   12. Samuel Eaken

Who being elected tried and sworn the truth to speak etc Which Jury
after retiring some time return and say they cannot agree and by the
consent of the council and each side they make a miss Trial.

An Assignment of a Plat and Certificate of Survey from Samuel Por
ter to Elihu Hicks was proven in open court by William Kibble and
Absolom Bayless the witnesses thereto.-

21.   An Assignment of a Plat and Certificate of Survey from William
Williams to William B was proven in Open Court by John Wilson and
Samuel Findley the witnesses thereto.-

An Assignment of a Plat and Certificate of Survey from Robert
Ray to William H. Ray was proven in open Court by James Law & Robert
Gray the subscribing witnesses thereto.-

An Assignment of a Plat and Certificate of Survey from David Eddington to

Josiah Gamble)
   vs   ) Coveat
Silas George) In this case on motion of the Deft Attorney for the Plain-
             tiff to give security for the prosecution of this case
          It is ordered that if he does not before or at next Court
this Coveat be Dismissed.

Robert Eaken)
   vs   ) Covt.
John McGhee) Rule to show cause why the Deft should give Security
           in this case

William Findley)
    vs   )
McTear   ) On Petition of Defendant it is ordered that writs of
           Certioraria & Supersidias do issue to Constable----
------ & Esq --------.

22.   An Assignment of a Plat and Certificate of Survey from James Logan to John Glass was proven in open Court by John Wilson and Thomas
Maxwell the Witnesses thereto.-

     Court adjourned till tomorrow morning 9 Oclock

     Thursday 25th 1808

     Court met according to adjournment

        Present

     John Gardiner, John Allison, and Robert Boyd Esqrs, Justices, etc

     An Assignment of a Plot and certificate of Survey from William Wal-
ker to Michael Bowerman was proven in open Court by Samuel Cowan and
Andrew Cowan the witnesses thereto.-

     An Assignment of a Plat and certificate of Survey from William
Montgomery to (torn) was proven in open court by (torn) & Reuben
Charles the witnesses thereto.

23.   Robert Dial   )
      vs   ) Certioraria
   William Steward) This day came the parties by their Attornies and
             thereupon came a Jury "Viz"

1. Thomas Hardin	5. Alexander McCullock	9. John B. Cusack
2. Samuel Frazier	6. William Walker	10. John Ish
3. John Thornbury	7. Isiah Bowman	11. James Weir
4. John F. Garnor	8. James McNutt	12. Joseph Henderson

Who being elected tried and sworn the truth to speak upon the matter of
controversy upon their Oaths Do say they find for the Plaintiff and assess his damage to thirty five Dollars forty one and a fourth Cents
     Rule for new Trial discharged
     It is therefore considered by Court that the plaintiff recover

        Grand Jury discharged

An Assignment of a Plat and Certificate of Survey from George Weir to David Young was proven in open Court by James Schrimsher and John Williams Witnesses thereto.

24. Robert Dial)
    vs)
William Steward) In this case Andrew Miller was summoned as a Witness for the Plaintiff as appears by the return of the subpeona and being solemnly called came not but made default and on motion of the Plaintiff by his Attorney It is considered and adjudged by the Court that he pay the Plaintiff aforesaid for default the sum of 125 Dollars unless at next Court he can show good cause to the contrary.

Ditto)
    vs)
Ditto) In this case James P Chisholm was summoned a Witness for the Plaintiff as appears by the return of the subpeona and being solemnly called came not but made default and on motion of the Plaintiff by their Attorney it is considered and adjudged by the Court that he pay to Robert Dyal for Default the sum of 125 Dollars unless at next Court they can show good cause to the contrary.

Joseph Doherty)
    vs) Coveat
David Thompson) In this case the Plaintiff is put under a Rule to show cause why he should give Security for the Prosecution of this Case.

25. A Deed of Conveyance from Alexander Kelly to John Hackett and James Cosby containing 500 acres of Land was acknowledged in Open Court by Alexander Kelly the subscriber thereto.

           Present

    Andrew Bogle, Robert Boyd & James Gillespie

James Moore)
    vs)
John Keys) This day came the parties by their Attornies and thereupon came a Jury "to wit."

1. Aaron Baity	5. Joseph Coldwell	9. Adam Kunns
2. George Stephens	6. Robert Gillespie	10. John Baity
3. Thomas McCullock	7. David Black	11. John Gillespie
4. Archabald Maxwell	8. John Gault	12. Alexander Sharp

Who being elected tried and sworn the truth to speak upon the issue joined upon their Oaths Do say the Defendant is guilty in manner and form of the Trespass and that without any Justification as in the Plaintiffs Declaration stated assess the plfts damages to $34 & costs.

Therefore It is considered by our said Court that the Plaintiff recover against the Def't aforesaid his damages aforesaid as by the Jury aforesaid assessed & his Costs by him in this behalf expended & the said Deft is in mercy &c.

Rule for new Trial overruled. This Judg't made absolute.

26.   Lowry & Waugh)
          vs   )
Robert I. Henry) In this case ordered that Did. Pot. Issue to take
                   Deposition in behalf of both parties to the City of
Baltimore on the second Monday and tuesday of April next.

    Henery & Lindenberger)
          vs   )
Lowry & Waugh   ) In this case it is ordered that Did/ Pot. Issue
                   Depositions in behalf of both parties to be taken
on the second monday & tuesday of April next.

    State   )
      vs   )
Ambros Bryan) In this case Cadwell Hynds who was bound in a Recognizance
                 to appear at this court and prosecute in behalf of the
State vs said Bryan, and was solemnly called came not but made default
              It is therefore considered by Court that he forfeit his re-
cognizance aforesaid Discharged.

    State   )
      vs   )
James Montgomery) In this case Morris Baker who was bound in recognizance
                 to appear at this Court and prosecute in behalf of
the State vs Montgomery and being solemnly called came not but made default It is thereby considered by Court that he forfeit accordingly.

27.   An Assignment of a Plat and certificate of Survey from Alexander
Patterson to William Kendrick was proven in Open Court by Isaac Charles
and James Kendrick the Witnesses thereto.

      An Assignment of a Plat and Certificate of survey from John Craig
to Samuel Findley was proven in Open Court by Jonathan Appler and John
M. Crawford the Witnesses thereto.

      An Assignment of a Plat and Certificate of Survey from Mordecai
Mitchel to James Anderson was proven in Open Court by Alex Kelly and
William Walker the Witnesses thereto.

      An Assignment of a Plat and Certificate of Survey from John Wil-
liams to William Williams was proven in Open Court by James Schrimsher
and David Cook the Witnesses thereto.

28.   A Bill of Sale from Joseph Weir to James Weir for a Negro Girl was
acknowledged in Open Court by Joseph Wier the subscriber thereto.

      An Assignment of a Plat and Certificate of survey from Martin
Rorex to Alexander McGhee was proven in Open Court by John Gould &
William Moore the witnesses thereto.

      An Assignment of two Plots and Certificates of Surveys from
Abraham Wier to William Aylet was proven in open Court by Joseph B.
Lassley and Andrew Thompson the Witnesses thereto.

      An Assignment of a Plat and certificate of Survey from William
Davis to John Adams Wolf was proven in open Court by John Wilkinson

and Robert McCully Witnesses thereto.

Robert Eaken)
    vs   ) Sci. Fac.
Robert McCulley) Rule to show cause why a Writ of Error should be gran-
              ted when argued was refused.

     An Assignment of a Plat and Certificate of survey from David Row-
land and David Fletcher to William Scott was proven in open Court by
James Boyd & William Oliver the Witnesses thereto.

     Court adjourned till tomorrow morning 9 Oclock.

29.   Friday 26 February Term, 1808

     Friday Morning Court met according to adjournment

          Present

     John Gardiner Samuel Hendly & Robert Boyd Esqrs Justices Etc.

Hachell)
  vs)
Houston) Commission to Virginia for Plft with giving 20 days notice.

Robert Forrester)
    vs   )
Daniel Boatright) On motion of the Plaintiffx in this case and it
                appears to the Court that a Writ of Capias ad satis-
facundure had been returned to John Griffin Deputh Sherriff of Ruther-
ford County a sufficient time before August Term 1807 to be returned
to said Firn which was returnable to the same and that he failed to
return said Writ
          It is therefore considered and adjudged by said court
that Judgment be entered against Oludias Benge high Sherriff of said
County according to the Act of Assembly in such case made and Provided
for the sum of seventy three dollars and ninety three 8 1/3 cents and
the Execution issue for the same.

     Isiah Bowman who was fined fifty cents at this Term is released
from same on payment of Costs.

39.   An Assignment of a Plat and Certificate of Survey from William
Wallace to Nicholas Avory was proven in Open Court by Joel Morreson
and William Morreson the Witnesses thereto.

     An Asdgment of a Plat afid Certificate of Survey from James
Edmondson to William James was proven in Open Court by Robert Hooks
and William Ewing Witnesses thereto.

     William Lowry, William Gillespie ------ Franks Esqrs Justices

State   )
  vs   )
William Barnes) This day came as well E. Parsons who prosecutes in
              behalf of the State as the Defendant in his proper

person and thereupon came a Jury to wit,

1. Thomas Clerk	5. Adam Kenny	9. John B. Cusack
2. James Moore	6. Joseph Henderson	10. James McNutt
3. John Gault	7. James Weir	11. Alexander McCullock
4. Isiah Bowman	8. John Ish	12. John F. Garnor

Who being elected tried and sworn the truth upon the Issue in the verse upon their Oaths do say the Defendant is guilty in manner and form as charged in the Bill of Indictment

31.   An Assignment of a Plat and Certificate of Survey from John Cowan to Jonathan Trippet was proven in open Court by John Lowry & William Harris the witnesses thereto.

State   )
  vs   )
John Glass)   Same Jury as in the case State vs Barnes being sworn the
              truth to speak upon the issue in traverse Do say the De-
fendant is not guilty in manner and form as charged in the Bill of Indictment
              It is therefore

State   )
  vs   )
John Wilson)   Same Jury as in the last case being sworn do say the
               Defendant is not guilty as charged in the bill of In-
dictment
              It is therefore considered

32.   James Wyley John Waugh and Franks named in the Commission of the Peace for this county took the oath to support the Constitution of the United States and Oath to support the Constitution of the State of Tennessee and also took the Oath of a Justice of Peace.

                                                                      pay
        Ordered that any additional county Tax be Levyed as follows to have Jurors to wit on each hundred acres of land 12½ cts on each white pole 12½ cents on each Town Lot 25 cents on each Stud Horse the half season of one mare untill order be made.

State   )
  vs   )
James McNeely)   Same Jury as in the last case except John Thornbury
in lieu of Alexander McCullock who being elected tried and sworn the
truth to speak upon the issue in traverse Do say the Defendant is not
Guilty of the affray in manner & form as charged in the Bill of Indictment.
              It is therefore considered by

        An Assignment of a Plat and certificate of Survey from Alexander Logan to William Montgomery was proven in Open Court by James McNutt Alexander McCulloc the Witnesses thereto

33.   Abraham Wallace was appointed Guardian to Mary Wallace entered in-to Bond with Jonathan L. Harris & William Wallace his Securities

        William Montgomery Account for $36 Isd. for keeping Rebecka Lucher was allowed by Court.

Ordered by Court that James Wyley Esqr take in the taxeable Poles & property in Capt. Rupes Company

Enoch Parsons)
    vs)
David Eddington &)
William McCallister) Order of Sale In this Case on Motion of the
                plaintiff it appears that he obtained an Execution
before John Gardiner for $6.62½ Cents & Costs which Execution run to Sam
C. Fineley and he returned Levied on the Land that William Brown lives
on as the property of Eddington
          It is therefore considered by Court that said Land be ex-
posed to Sale to satisfy said Debt & Costs.

Ordered
34.
On the Petitiin of Leah Reagan for a Dower in the land of William Reagan
Decd. it was granted her and ordered that a Jury go upon upon the Land
and lay the same and Robert Houston is to make a survey of the same and
return a Plat to our Next court.

Court adjourned till tomorrow morning 9 Oclock

Saturday 27th 1808 February Term

Court met according to adjournment

PResent

William Lowry, Andrew Bogle and John Gardiner Esqrs Justices, etc.

King & Montgomery make a return of their machine for the years 1806 &
1807 with 40 Sous Sous

William Griffin a n Orphan Child who was bound at last court to
James S. Montgomery was returned by said Montgomery with his Indentury
And said orphan was rebound to William Taylor who entered into Indentury
as the Law Directs.

35.
Ordered by Court that Alexander Hartt be allowed $7 50 cents for
his attention paid to an Orphan Child named Joseph Griffen to be
drawn when moneysufficient shall come into the hands of the Treasurer

Ordered by Court that James S. Montgomery be allowed 1$ 50 Dents
for his attention paid to an orphan Child named Joseph Griffen.

Ordered by Court that William L. Taylor be allowed twenty Dollars
for the first year he will keepan Orphan Child that was this day bound
to him.

Ordered that John Wallace County Register be allowed $7.50 for
transcribing his books.

Ordered by Court that John Lowry Senr be allowed $7.50 foS compar-
ing the Register Books.

B. McGhee   )
   vs   )   Coveat
Joseph Tedford) Ordered that there be a Survey in this case to show
                   the interference of the Plaintiffs Coveat with the
Chaim of the said Joseph and the part in dispute and that John Williamson be and is appointed Surveyor and that he return two fair Plats of
the Survey he is hereby ordered to make

36.   A Bill of Sale from Thomas England to Benjamin Wallace was proven
in Open Court by Jonathan L. Harris the Witnesses thereto.

McCames Heirs)
   vs   )
Nicholas Hairhart)   Coveat
Minis & Houston   )   Ordered by Court that Survey be granted in the a-
                   bove Case and that Survey be granted in the above
case and that said Surveyors be directed to survey the said tract of
Land agreebly to the Original conditional lies where such there are
and also to ascertain the interferance of such of the above tract as
surveyed for the Defendants order to Issue to Josiah Patty Surveyor.-

Ordered by Court that ten Dollars be appropriated for the use of
Ichabolt Barnes until Next court
That Benjamin Wallace be allowed to draw the same.

The Settlement of the Estate of Jonathan Mathews Decd. returned &
filed.

An Orphan Child named Drew Richardson was bound to John B. Cusack
who entered into Indenturys as the Law directs.

Ordered by Court that the order binding Joab Therman to James P.H
Porter be rescinded and that James Logan take him on the same term to
have horse saddle & bridle and two years schooling which the Law directs.

Ordered by Court that the Clerk be allowed $60 for his exofficious
for the year 1807/

37.   Ordered by Court that the Sherriff be allowed $70 for his Exoffi-
cious Services for the year 1807.

Ordered by Court that the Soliciter be allowed $12.50 Cents for
each court from February Term 1807.

An Assignment of a Plat and Certificate of Survey from Joshua Parsons to Joseph Nelson was proven in Open Court by Robert McCulley &
James W. Lackey witnesses thereto.

An Assignment of a Plat & Certificate of Survey from William Lackey to David Vaught was proven in Open Court by William Green & James
Hall witnesses thereto.

Barcley McGhee)
   vs   )   Coveat
Joseph Tedford)On motion of the Defendants Attorney for perpetuating

testimony.

Ordered by Court that John Gardiner John Waugh and Jonathan L. Harris Esqr be commissioners to take same.

Ordered by Court that when a rule is entered to give Security for prosecution a Coveat at one court the Plaintiff shall have the next Monday or Tuesday to meet the Team.

Frazies

38.   Samuel Ryer return his machine for the year 1806 34 Sous & 1807 40 Sous

J. Lowry Jr)
      vs   )
David White)   Ordered by Court that Did; Pot; issue to Virginiato take
                  the Depositions of George Woods & others with giving twen-
ty Days notice.

Robert Hanna)
      vs   )
Lowry's Heirs)   Ordered by Court that Did; pot; issue to Virginia to take
                    the Depositions of George Woods and others to be read
in behalf of the Defendants with fiving 20 days notice.

An Inventory of the Estate of Robert Eaken Senr Decd returned & filed.

Lowry & Waugh   )
      vs   )
John Keys and Alexander   )
Ford & John Sherrell his   )
Securities   )   On motion of John Lowry Atto It appears the
                                 Plaintiffs in this case obtained An Execu-
tion against P. Fitsgerald for the sum of Sixteen Dollars and fifty cents principal & fifty Cents costs which Executi n run to the hands of John Keys Constable and he failing to return the money and Execution as the Law directs.

It is therefore considered by our courts that the Plaintiff recover against the said Keus and Alexander Ford & John Sherrell his Securities their Debts & costs aforesaid & their costs by them in be- half expended and the said Defendants are in mercy etc.

39.   John McCollister   )
              vs   )   In this case on motion of William Brown
      John Keys and Alexander)   atto. It appears that said McCallister ob-
      Ford and John Sherrell)   tained and Execution against George Sloan and
      his Securitie s   )   Samuel Hogg for the sum of fifty Dollars and
                                  one Dollar Sixty eight & three fourths Cents
Costs which Execution run to the hands of John Keys Consatable to col- lect the same and he failing to pay the money and return the Execution as the Law directs.

It is therefore considered by our Court that the Plaintiffs recover vs the said John Keys and Alexander Ford and John Sherrell his Security his Debt & Costs aforesaid and also his money by him in this behalf expended and the said Defendants are in mercy &c but the plain- tiff claims but $16.38½ cts.

County Treasurer
xxxxxxxxxxxxxxxx

County Treasurer)
          vs)
Joel Wallace and)   In this case on motion of E Parsons it appears that
Securities   )   an Execution issued to Jonathan L. Harris vs William
                    Trent and Thomas England for swearing which Excn went
into the hands of Joel Wallace Constable and it appears that he collec-
ted the money due thereon which was Six Dollars & fifty six and a half
Cents and he failed to pay the said money as the Law directs.

It is therefore considered by Court that Treasurer aforesaid recover ag't the said Joel Wallace and his Securities the sum a-
foresaid and the Costs in this behalf expended & the said Defendants are
in mercy &c.

40.   Nathaniel Barnes   )
               vs   )
      John Keys & Alexander Ford   )
      & John Sherrell his securities)   on motion of E. Parsons it appears
                                        that an Execution for $35.43 Cents
issued to John Keys Constable and he failing to return the money and &
the Execution as the law directs on the oath of Squire Gardiner.

It is therefore considered by Court that the Plaintiff
aforesaid recover agt. the sd John Keys and Alexander Ford & John Sherrell his Securities his Debt aforesaid & his Costs by him in this behalf expended &c.

William McCegg Holbert McClure are appointed constables to attend
at our next Court

Court adjourned till Court in Course

41.   At a court of pleas and Quarter Sessions began & held for the
County of Blount at the Court House in Maryville on the fourth Monday
of May 1808.

          Present

John Woods, Stephen Stafford and George Ewing, Esqrs

Samuel Cowan Esqr Sheriff of the County afforesaid returned our
Writ of Venire Facias to him directed executed on the following persons, Viz.

1. Saml McCammons	13. Alexander Tedford	25. William Gillespie
2. William Logan	14. John McGhee, Jr.	26. William Young
3. Joseph Bogle, Senr	15. Josiah Danforth	27. James Taylor
4. James Simms	16. William Henry	28. John Snider
5. John Reid	17. Saml Weir, Jr.	29. Joseph Black
6. Joseph Walker	18. Robert McNutt	30. Robert Sterling
7. William Wize	19. Adam Soffley	31. Jonathan Weir
8. Robert Hammell	20. Saml. Frazier	32. Benj. Wallace
9. Robert McGhil	21. James T. Steel	33. Moses Hughs
10. James Hall Senr	22. Alexander McCauley	34. John Simpson
11. Alexander McCollom	23. James Knight	35. John Bible
12. William McClung	24. John Glass	

42.   Out of which Venire the following persons were elected a Grand

Inquest to enquire for the body of the County of Blount, Viz.

1. William McClung	6. Saml. Frazier	11. John Snider
2. Benjamin Wallace	7. William Gillespie	12. Josiah Danforth
3. William Henery	8. Joseph Bogle	13. Robert McNutt
4. William Wise	9. Alexander McOollom	14. Robert McGill
5. Jonathan Wier	10. Robert Hammell	15. James Simms

Were sworn received their Charge and retired to enquire of their presentments

The Subpeona for William McCegg & Holbert McClure Constable to attend this Court returned Execution

John Gardiner Esqr produced a License to practice in the several Courts of Law and Equity in this State took the necessary oaths and was admitted to practice in this court accordingly.

Holbert McClure Consatble sworn to attend the Grand Inquest.

The resignation of Oliver Alexander Rainger of this county returned & filed.

An Assignment of a plat and Certificate of Survey from Nathl Matson to Wm Mc--? was proven in open court by Thomas McCullock & David Dearmond the witnesses thereto.

A Bill of sale from Andrew Miller to James William Payton to Nicholas Boyers for a Negro Titt Girl named Mary was proven in open Court by David Russell the witness thereto.

43.   A Bill of sale from Andrew Miller to James Hall was proven in open Court by Hugh Kelsoe and James Hall.

E. Parsons Assinee &c)
     vs   )
Adam Waffle   )   The defendant Adam Waffle and Jonathan Trippett
                        came into open Court and confessed Judgment to
the Plaintiff for the sum of one hundred & Eight Dollars for principal
and interest untillthis time. It is therefore considered by the Court
that the said Enoch Passons recover against the said Adam & Jonathan
the sum aforesaid with Costs and they are in Mercy &c. the plaintiff
stays Execution untill the first day of February next.

William Griffith was appointed Guardian to John and James Mathews
Infants

Court adjourned till tomorrow morning 9 Oclock.

44.   Tuesday 245h May Term, 1808

Court met according to adjournment

Present

Saml Hendly, George Ewing & James Mathews Gillespie Esqr.

A Deed of Conveyance from David Campbell to Samuel Law Mercht for land lying on Pistol Creek was proven by James Montgomery a subscribing witness thereto and he swore that James Heard the other Witness was out of this State and that said Deed could not be completed by said Witness
It was thereforge considered by court that said Deed be admitted to Registration.

Ordered by Court that the inhabitants of this Counth have liberty to teturn their taxeable polls of property at this Term.

James W. Lackey return of Taxeable 1 white pole & 261 acres.-

Robert Hannah)   Rule to show cause why t he party in this case should
    vs   )   not give security agreeable to an order of the Court.
John Russell)
Lowry Heirs.)

Love & Luttrell)
    vs   )
John Russell   )   On motion of plaintiffs atto. that Did Pot: issue to
              Georgia in August to take Deposition of James Heard
with giving 30 days to the Defts. Attorney

45.   Adam Peck   )
       vs   )
Richard Kirby)   On motion of Blantiffs ordered that Did Pot; issue to
              Bledsoe County to take the Deposition of Nicholas Spring
with giving 15 days notice to be taken at said Spring home.

Adam Peck   )
      vs   )
John Eddington)   On motion of Plaintiffs Atto. ordered that Did; Pot;
              issue to Bledsoe County to take the Deposition of
Nicholas Spring with giving 15 days notice to be taken at Said Spring Home.

A Bill of Sale from Alexandria Moore to James Montgomery was proven in open Court by Alexandria McCollom and Samuel Montgomery the witnesses thereto

David Dearmonds return of land Taxable remitted for the year 1808

Robert Young was admitted to administer on the estate of Andrew Young and entered into Bond with security as the Law directed.

The Court proceeded by Ballot to elect a Sheriff for the county of Blount when Samuel Cameron offered as a Candidate and was duly & Constitutionally elected.

The Court proceeded by ballot to elect a County Trustee when John Lowry Mercht. offered as a candidate and was duly & constitutionally elected.

46.   The Court proceeded by Ballot to Elect a Ranger for the County of Blount when John Gardiner, Esq. offered as a candidate and was duly & constitutionally elected.

Wm Maclin   )
    vs   )
Bolomon McCampbell) In the case Abraham Weir who was special Bail for
                             the Defendant came into Court and surrendered him
in discharge of himself and William Montgomery & Joseph Hart came into Court and confessed that he would pay the costs & Condemnation or surrender himself or they would pay the Costs & condemnation or surrender him in disaharge of themselves.

I. Trimble)
    vs   )
I. Ranken) Did Po Den bene issue to give Samuel Flannagan & Richard
                Kirby giving 5 Days notice to take Deposition of John
Dearmond in behalf of the Defendant.

Administration is granted to Daniel Durham on the Estate of James Williams Decd. he having given bond with approved Security.

An instrument of writing purported to be the last will & testament of Joshua Hannah was proven in open court by the oath of Saml George one of the witnesses thereto.

Court adjourned till tomorrow morning 9 Oclock

Wednesday 25th May Term, 1808

47.   Court met according to adjournment

          Present

      Samuel Hendly, William Lowry, John Waugh and Andrew Bogle, Esqrs. Justices &co.

Love & Co.)
    vs   )
Rebecka Reid) on Motion of E. Parsons it appears that the Plaintiff ob-
              tained a Judgment and Execution by the defendant for the
sum of Twenty Dollars & 90 cents Debt & Costs which execution was returned levied on a certain tract of Land whereon Rebecka Reid now living as the property of said Reid it is therefore considered by Court that said Land be exposed to sale agreably to law to satisfy said Debt & Costs.

Isac Little)
    vs   )
James Pearce) on motion of the Plaintiffs atto. ordered Did Pot; issue
               to take deposition of John Thurmon & Mary his wife in the
State of Kentucky with giving the Defendant 20 Days notice.

Ditto   )
    vs   )
Robert Pearce) on motion of plaintiffs atty. ordered that Did Pot is-
               sue to take the deposition of John Thurman and Mary his

wife in the State of Kentucky with giving the defendant 20 days notice

The petition of David Cusac overseer for a sledge & Crowbarr was granted.

48. A Deed of Conveyance from Joel Wallace to Jessee Wallace for land lying on Crooked Creek was proven in open Court by Charles Donahoo and Benjamin Alexander the witnesses thereto

4 It is therefore considered by Court that said Deed be admitted to Registration.

William Black)
    vs   )
Joseph Smith) This day came the parties by their Attorney and there-
               upon came a Jury "to wit."

1. Alexander Stuart	5. John Weldon	9. Saml. Weir
2. John B. Cusack	6. Sam'l McConnold	10. Alexander McCauley
3. Samuel Henery	7. John Bible	11. Joseph Walker
4. William Harris	8. James T. Steel	12. James Knight

who being elected tried and sworn do say the Defendant did assume up-on himself in manner and form as the plaintiff in his Decleration hath declared and that within three three years next before the swing out the writ in this case and they assessed the plaintiff damages to 18 $ 66 2/3 Cents for the ---------? damage thereof. Rule for new trial & granted.

I. Logan   )
    vs   )
S. McCampbell) In this case Robert Ferguson who was special Bail for
              the Defendant surrendered him in discharge of himself
& Burton Pride & John Hanna came into Court and confessed that the De-fendant would pay the Costs and condemnation or surrender himself or they would pay it or surrender him.

49. William Black)
    vs   )
Joseph Smith) In this case George Thomas was summoned as a witness on
            behalf of the Defendant and being solemnly called fail-
ing to appear.
         It is therefore considered by Court that the said Joseph Smith recover against the said George Thomas $125 agreable to the Statues in that case made & provided.

James Hall was fined fifty cents by order of the Court for Contempt shown to Court.

Present Saml. Hendley, James Gillespie & Jno. Reagan

Mathew Wallace)
    vs   ) This day came the parties by their attorney and there-
Robert Moore) upon came a Jury "to wit."

| 1. Archabald Frew | 5. John Reid | 9. John McConnald |
| 2. Joshua Parsons | 6. Abraham Philips | 10. John Wilson |

3. William Young	7. Saml. McGaughey	11. John Kenneday
4. William Logan	8. John Caldwell	12. David Thompson

who being elected tried and sworn the truth to speak do say the Deft is
Guilty of speaking the word &c. in manner and form as charged in the
plaintiffs Decleration & that within six months next before the swing
out the writ in this case and they assessthe plaintiffs Damages to
50. five Dollars & Costs and the Defendant by his attorney filed his record
for the arrest of the above Judgement which was tomorrow.

Court adjourned till tomorrow 9 Oclock.

Present

Thursday 26th May 1808

Court met according to adjournment

William Doneldson, John Reagen and John Waugh Esqrs, Justices &c.

State)
vs) Sci. Fac.
Morris Black) on motion of the Defendant in this Case the forfeiture
in this case is set aside on payment of costs.

Charles Donohoo was appointed Constable by Court and entered into bond
with John Lowry Mercht.

Ordered by Court that John Reagen & James T. Steele have liberty
to return their Saw gins containing 40 Saws & Steels 36 Reagen for his
the years 1805, 1806 & 1807 & Sixxix Steels for the years 1806 & 1807
It is ordered that they be released from double Tax.

Ordered by Court that John Reid be fined 50 cts. for contempt
shown to the Courts summons

51. Lowry & Waugh)
vs)
Robert J. Henery) This day came the parties by their Attornies and
thereupon came a Jury "to wit."

1. Walter Trimble	5. James Bailey	9. James Taylor
2. Morris Baker	6. John Bidle	10. James T. Steele
3. Reuben Charles	7. Alexander Tedford	11. Wm. Young
4. Joseph Henderson	8. John Reid	12. Alexander McCauley

The plaintiff not further prosecuting his suti It is ordered tat he be
non suited & pay the debts his costs by him expended in this behalf
Rule to set aside non suit & continued

Lowry & Waugh)
vs) Did: Pot: to issue to Baltimore with 30 days notice
Robert J. Henery) on behalf of both parties Notice on the Defts. atto
to be considered sufficient.

&

Henry Lendenbarger)
  vs   )
Lowry & Waugh   ) Did Pot to Issue to Baltimore with 30 Days notice
           on behalf of both parties notice on the Plfts atto
to be considered sufficient.

52. William Lackey)
    vs   )
Adam Kerr   ) This day came the parties by their attornies and there-
          upon came a Jury "to wit."

1. Joseph Tedford	5. James Baity	9. James Taylor
2. Morris Baker	6. John Bible	10. James T. Steel
3. Reuben Charles	7. Alexander Tedford	11. William Young
4. Joseph Henderson	8. John Reid	12. Alexander McCauley

who being sworn well & truly to enquire of damages in this case Do day
they assess the Plaintiffs Damages to $10. & costs.
   It is therefore considered by the Court that the Plaintiff
recover against the Defendant his damages aforesaid as by the Jury a-
foresaid axxhxxix assessed and also his costs by him in this behalf
expended amd the said Defendant is in mercy &c.

Gavin Black for Sarah Black)
    vs   ) Sci Fac.
William Lackey   ) In this case Charles Donahoo & Samuel
          Donahoo who was speckal Bail for the De-
fendant came into court and surrendered the Defendant in discharge of
themselves and the plaintiff by his attorney prays the Defend't in Custody of the Sheriff &c.

Edwd Lynch Assinee)
    vs   )
William Lackey   ) In this case Charles Donahoo who was special Bail
         for the Defendant came into open court & surrendered
the Defendant in discharge of himself.

   Ordered by Court that John McCalray be fined 50 cts. for contempt
shown to this court call.

Bardley McGhee   )
    vs   )
John Montgomery &)
John Lowry Exors of)
Thos. Berry   ) This day came the parties by their Attos. and
         thereupon came a Jury towit.

1. James McKamey	5. William Ranker	9. Joseph Walker
2. John Wilson	6. Warnor Martin	10. William Dines
3. John Ish	7. William McMahan	11. James Pearce
4. Saml Bogle	8. Thos. McClure, Senr.	12. James Knight

who being elected tried and sworn the truth to speak upon the issue
joined upon their oath do say that Thos Berry had not paid the Debt in
the declaration mentioned in his life time nor hath the Exors since his
decease and they assess the Plaintiffs Damages to $52.49½ by occasion

thereof and they further find that the Defendants hath fully administered all singular the Goods & Chattles Rights & Credits of the said
Thomas Berry Deceased in their hands to be Administered before the
swing out of the writ in this case as the said Defendant in pleading h
hath alledged.

Therefore It is considered by the Court that the plaintiff
recover against the Defendant their Debt & damages aforesaid as by the
Jury aforesaid assessed and also their costs by them in this behalf ex-
bended when assets sufficient shall come to their hands

Whereupon on motion of the plaintiffs A_tto. and on a suggestion that James Berry and Polly Berry, Betcy Berry, Patcy Berry Walker Berry & Tareza Berry infant children of Thomas & heirs of Thomas
Berry De,cd. are possessed of real Estate that descended from said Thos
Berry Decd.

54.   It is therefore ordered that a Scire Facias Issue directed
to John Montgomery Guardian to said Heirs requiring them to show
cause why said Judgment & Execution should not issue against the said
Heirs Estate for said Judgment & Costs.

An Assignment of a Plat and Certificate of Survey from Solomon
McCampbell to Jonathan Tipton was proven in open Court by John Gardiner
& John B. Cusack the witnesses thereto

Saml Hendley, Stephen Stafford & Robert Boyd Esqrs, Justices
present, &c.

Robert Gillespie)
    vs   ) case
John Lowry   ) This day came the partis by their attornies & there-
               upon came a Jury "to wit."

1. Joseph Tedford	5. John Bible	9. James T. Steel
2. Morris Baker	6. Alexander Tedford	10. Wm. Young
3. Joseph Henderson	7. Saml. Weir	11. Alexander McCauley
4. James Baity	8. James Taylor	12. Reuben Charles

who being elected tried and sworn the truth to speak upon the issue
joined upon their oath do say after retiring some time they cannot
agree and by and with the consent of the parties and assent of the
Court they make a Miss Trial

Isaac Little)
    vs   )
James Pearce) Did Pot. De bene epse to issue to Joseph Kirby & Saml
              Flannagan or either of them to take the Deposition of
Nicholas Bartlet in behalf of the Deft with goving 10 Days notice to
Reuben Tipton Atto in fact fof the plft.

55. Benjamin Bowman)
        vs   ) Certd.
Henery Parrott) This day came the parties by their attornies and
               thereupon came a Jury "to wit."

1. John Wilson Senr.	5. William McMahan	9. William Dines
2. John Ish	6. Thos. McClurkan	10. James Knight
3. William Rooker	7. Joseph Walker	11. Alexander McKee
4. Warmor Martin	8. James Pearce	12. John Gould

who being elected tried and sworn the truth to speak upon the matters of controversy the plaintiff not further prosecuting his suit
It is ordered that he be non suited Rule to set non suit aside & continued on that Rule

Saml Finley   )
     vs   )
Archabale Trimble) This day came the parties by their attornies & there-
                    upon Came a Jury "to wit"

1. John Wilson	5. Wm. McMahan	9. Wm Dines
2. John Ish	6. Thos McClurkin	10. James Knight
3. William Rooker	7. Joseph Walker	11. Alexander McGhee
4. Warnor Martin	8. James Pearce	12. John Gould

who being elected tried and sworn the truth to speak upon the matter of controversey Do say they find for the Defendant Rule for new Trial mad absolute.

56.   Ordered by court that Gideon Richey and orphan child now of the age of thirteen years be bound to Alexander McGhee until he arrives of at the age of twenty one years of age.

                Court adjourned till tomorrow morning 9 Oclock

                Friday Morning Court met according to adjournment

                        Present

        William Lowry, John Gardiner & James Gillespie, Esqrs.

State   )
   vs   )
Tibet Manuel) This day came the parties by their attornies and there-
               upon came a Jury "to wit."

1. John Bible	5. Saml Weir	9. Nicholas Airhart
2. Wm Logan	6. Alex McCauley	10. John Brickey
3. Alexander Tedford	7. John Reid	11. John Trimble
4. James Steel	8. James Taylor	12. Walter Trimble

who being sworn Do say do say the Defendant is not guilty of the Affray in manner & form as charged in the bill of Indictment
        Therefore it is considered by the court

State   )
   vs   )
James Roddy) This day came as well the Defendant by his attorney as E
               Parsons who prosecutes in behalf of the State and there-
upon came a Jury "to wit."

1. Adam Waffle	5.5. William Young	9. Alexander Harris
2. James Knight	6.7. Joseph Walker	10. Barcley McGhee
3. David Coldwell	7.8. William Harris	11. Allen Strain
4. John Hickland	8.9. Al Jesse Condron	12. John James

who being elected tried and sworn the truth to speak upon the Issue in traverse Do say the Defendant in manner & form as charged in the Bill of Indictment

It is therefore considered by Court

An Assignment of a plat and certificate of Survey from David Phillips to William Hess was proven in Open Court by James Houston & Enoch Parsons the Witnesses thereto.

A Bill of Sale from Joseph Irwin to Jacob Freshier for a tract of land was proven in open court by John Williams & George Freshier the witnesses thereto.

58. State   )
    vs   )
Jeremiah Brooks) This day comes as well the Deft by his attorney as
                E. Parsons who prosecutes in behalf of the State and
thereupon came a Jury "to wit."

1. John Kennedy	5. Alexander Tedford	9. John Reid
2. John Bentes	6. James Steel	10. James Taylor
3. John Bible	7. Saml. Weir	11. Nicholas Airhart
4. William Logan	8. Alexander McCauley	12. John Brickey

who being elected tried and sworn the truth to speak upon the issue in traverse upon their oaths do say the Deft is guilty of the Trespass Assaualt and Battery in manner & form as charged in the bill of Indictment.

It is therefore considered by the Court that the plaintiff

A Bill of Sale from Thomas Richey to Arch Lackey was proven in open Court by James Casley & John Lowry the witnesses thereto.

State   ) In this case the Deft being solomly called
    vs   ) came not   It is ordered that he. with Wm.
Nathl Norwell &   ) Harris his security forfeit their Recog-
Wm Harris his Securities)   nizance.

Ordered by Court that Saml Thammon be bound and at next court bf any Suitable person will apply to get him

59. State   )
    vs   ) This day came the parties by their attornies and
Ambros Bryant)   thereupon came a Jury to wit.

1. Samuel McCullock	5. John Hickland	9. Alexander Hartt
2. Adam Waffle	6. Jesse Condron	10. Barcley McGhee
3. David Caldwell	7. William Young	11. Allen Strain
4. James Knight	8. William Harris	12. John James.

who being elected tried and sworn the truth to speak upon the issue in

traverse upon their Oaths do say the Defendant is guilty of the Assault
in manner & form as charged in the bill of Indictment but not of the
Battery

It is therefore considered by court that

Henry Hampton)
    vs)
Samuel Findley)
& John Lowry &)
Jacob Niman)
his securities) On motion of P. H. Porter It appears that the plaintiff
obtained an Execution one Schrimsher for the sum of 18
Dollars & 50 cents Debt & costs which Execution said Defendant recovered
to Collect the money due thereon & failing to pay the money or return
the execution as the Law directs

It is therefore considered by court that the plaintiff recover against the Defendant & John Lowry & Jacob Niman his securities
as all costs by him in this behalf expended and the said Defendant is
in mercy.

Rule to set aside Judgment & Costs

60. Reuben Charles) Rule to show cause why the plaintiff in this case
    vs) should not give security for the prosecution of
James Mathews Heirs) the court.

Court adjourned till tomorrow morning 9 Oclock

Saturday Morning 28th May 1808

Court Met according to Adjournment

Present

William Lowry, James Gillespie, Henery Franks, Esqr, Justices &c.

Terrence Conner)
    vs) On motion of John Wilkinson Attor-
John Keys & Alexander Ford & John) ney for the plaintiff it appears
Sherrell his securities) that the plft obtained and execution
against one Kerr which Execution went
into the hands of said Keysand it appearing to the satisfaction of this
Court that he had collected the money & failing to pay but a part thereof and there being a balance yet due Viz Seven dollars

It is therefore considered by the Court that the Plaintiff
recover against the said Keys and Alexander Ford & John Sherrell his
securities his money which is yet due yet unpaid and the said Defendants
are in Mercy &co.

61. Ordered by Court that Benjamin Wallace be allowed eight dollars for
the Support of Nancy Hughes.

Nichols)
    vs)
Jno. Roney) On motion of E. Parsons It appears that an Execution issued against the Defendant for the Sum of fifteen Dollars
& twenty two and three fourth cents Debt & costs in behalf of the plaintiff which Execution was returned no goods Nor chattles to be found

levied on the land where he lives

It is therefore considered by Court that said be exposed to Sale Agreably to Law to satisfy said Execution.

White & Wilson)
vs) On motion of E. Parsons It appears that an execution
John Honey) Issued against the Defendant for the sum of thirty Dollars & forty three cents Debt & Costs in behalf of the plaintiff which Execution was returned no goods nor chattles to be found levied on the land where he lives

It is therefore considered by court that the said land be exposed to Sale agreable to Law to satisfy debt & costs.

Ordered by Court that William Lowry George Ewing & James Gillespie Esqrs be commissioners to settle with Nancy Scott Administratrix of William Scott Dec'd.

A Bill of sale from Saml. Cowan by A. Cowan his Deputy to John Brickey for a tract of land lying on N. Mile Creek was acknowledged in open court by A. Cowan.

62. Ordered by court that William Griffitt have liberty to return his saw gin which has 32 saws for the years 1806, 1807 & that he be released from Double Tax thereon.

Robert Gillespie)
vs) In this case ordered that Deps. Pot. issue to the
John Lowry) Mississippi Territory to take the Deposition of John Keys in behalf of the plaintiff with giving 30 days notice.

An Inventory of the personal Estate of James Williams Dec'd. filed and ordered by court that the same be exposed to sale agreably to Law.

Judge Advocates office)
vs) Fi Fa.
William Lowry Securities) In this case moved by James Trimble Attorney for the Defendant for Rule to show cause why the Executor allowed to issue should be quashed and other costs

Ordered by court that John Lowry have liberty to return his saw gin for the years 1806, 1807 which has 40 saws and that he be released from Double Tax.

Joseph Weir)
vs) Coveat
Barcley McGhee) Ordered by court that Robert Hamton make a survey of the land in dispute & return two plats to our next court.

Ordered by court that John Carroth return his saw gin for the years 1804,1805 which has 25 saws and that he be released from Double Tax.

62A. Miles & David Cunnihgham)
vs)
James W. Lackey)

On motion of E. Parsons It appears that an Execution Issued in behalf of the plaintiff against the Defendant for the sum of Fifty one Dollars & 43¾ cents Debt & costs which Execution was released "No property to be found levied on the land where he lives

      It is therefore considered by Court that said land or so much thereof as will satisfy said Debt & costs be exposed to Sale Agreably to Law.

Ditto)
  vs) On motion of E. Parsons Esqr it appears that an Execution issued
Ditto) in behalf of the plaintiffagainst the Defendant for the Sum of
      fifty one Dollars & 43¾ cents Debt & Costs which Execution was returned No property to be found levied on the land where he lives

      It is therefore considered by court that said land or so much thereof as will satisfy said Debt & Costs be exposed to sale agreably to Law

Ditto)
  vs) On motion of E. Parsons it appears that an Execution Issued on
Ditto) behalf of the plaintiff vs the Deft the Defendant for the sum of
      Twenth two Dollars & ninety three cents Debt & Costs which execution was returned "no property found levied on the land where he lives

    4   It is therefore considered by Court that said land or so much thereof as will satisfu said Debt & costs be exposed to sale agréably to law

62B.

King & Montgomery)
    vs   ) Sci Fac.
Andrew Miller) In this case It appears that the Defendant were Special Bail for Isaac Upton in a suit Kint & Montgomery vs Isaac Upton in which suit the plaintiff obtained Judgment for the sum of $171.52½ Debt & costs on which Judgment a ca. Sa Issued against the said Isaac & was returned not found & on which return a Sci. fac. issued & was returned not found

      It is therefore considered by Court that the Plaintiff recover agt. the said Miller & Chisholm his sum aforesaid & also his costs by him in this behalf expended &co.

    Ordered by court Josiah Danforth to be released from Paying Tax on all the land he returned but seven thousand acres of the return be made for Danforth Edwards &co.

William Black)
   vs   )
Joseph Smith) Ordered by court that Dep. Pot Issue to Kentucky to
      take the Deposition of George Thomas on behalf of the Defendant with giving 30 Days notice.

John Nichol   )
   vs   )
James W. Lackey) On motion of John Gardiner Esqr it appears that an
      Execution Issue in favour of the plaintiff vs said Lackey for the sum of thirty two Dollars & 43¾ cents Debt & costs which execution was returned to Court no property found levied on the land where he lives

      It is therefore considered by Court that said hand or so

much thereof as will satisfy said Debt & Costs be exposed to sale agreably to Law

Ordered by Court that when a Coveat is declared in this Court the party looking the pay for copy of the Verdict & Judgment

63. John Nicol)
    vs)   On motion of John Gardiner Esqr It appears that an Execu-
    James Lackey) tion issued in favour of the plaintiff against vs the De-
    fendant for the sum of Thirty Two Dollars three cents
    Debt & Costs which execution was returned no property found levied on
    the land where he lives

    It is therefore considered by court that the said land be exposed to sale or so much as will satisfy said Debt & costs agreably to Law.

Alexander Ford)
    vs)   On motion of the plft by J. Wilkinson his attorney he
    John Keys)   moved to obtain a Judgment an Execution against the De-
    fendant for the sum of $24.&10¼ Cents for money collec-
    ted of him as security for the said Keyw on an Execution John McColles-
    ter vs Keys Securities

    Therefore It is considered by Court that the plaintiff re-
    cover against the said John Keys his Money aforesaid & also his costs
    by him in this behalf expended and the said Defendant is in Mercy &co.

John Woods & John Waugh)
    vs)
    John Keys)   on motion of the Plft by E. Parsons their coun-
    sel moved to obtain a Judgment & Execution a-
    gainst the Defendant for the sum of $6&27½ Cents for Moneys collected of
    them as Securities for said Keys on an Execution the State vs Keys &
    Securities.

    Therefore It is considered by Court that the plaintiff re-
    cover against the Defendant aforesaid their Money aforesaid and their
    Costs by them expended in this behalf & the said Defendnat is in Mercy &c.

64. Alexander Ford)
    vs)
    John Keys)   On motion of the plft by J. Wilkinson his Counsel he
    moved to obtain a Judgment Execution against the De-
    fendant for the Sum of Nineteen Dollars & 28¾ Cents for Money Collected
    of him as Security for said Keys on An Execution Jacob Isen against
    said Keys & Securities

    Therefore It is considered by the Court that the plaintiff
    recover of the said Keys his Money aforesaid Also his costs by him in
    this behalf expended & the said Defendant is in Mercy &co.

    Ordered by Court that a Suppeona Issue to Samuel Finley & Charles
    Donahoo summoning them to appear as Constables to attend at our next
    Court

    A List of those who returned their taxable polls & property at
    May Term 1808

	Acres of land	W.P.	B.P.
James W. Lackey	261	2	
Samuel Ross	"	1	

	Acres of land	W.P.	B.P.
Thomas Shaddon	261	1	
Thomas Weir	143	1	
John Simons	206	1	
Martin Castator	160	1	
Stephen Stafford	216	1	
Elizabeth Moore	305		
Richard Bbdgell		1	2
William Wallace	347	1	1
Alexander Ford	338	1	

Court adjourned till Court in Course

65.　　Monday 22nd August Term 1808

At a Court of Pleas and Quarter Sessions began & held for the County of Blount at the Court House in Maryville on the fourth Monday of August 1808.

Present

William Lowry, James Houston & John Allison Esqrs & Justices &co.

Samuel Cowan Es qr, Sheriff of the County of Blount aforesaid returned our writ of Venire Executed on the following persons Viz, George Berry, James Beaty, James Gillespie, Senr. David Caldwell, John Russell William L. Taylor, Oliver Alexander, John B. Cusack, James Weir, Senr. Barcley McChee, Joseph Black, Senr, Joseph Bogle, Jr. James Kennard, Jonathan Trippett, John Houston, James McGinley, James Moore, Samuel Davidson, John Singleton, John Rankin Jr., Elias Debousk, Alexander Harris, John Minis, Samuel Gould, James McKamey, James Boyd, Samuel McCamron, William Armstrong, Hugh Cunningham, David Richey, Brice Blair, John Gould, Peter Bowerman, Morris Baker, Hugh Kelsoe, John Casteel, James Logan, David Wilson, & John Gibson

Out of which Venire the following persons were elected a grand Inquest for the County of Blount (Viz)

1. James McGinley
2. David Wilson
3. James Gillespie
4. John Russell
5. Elias Debousk
6. John Minis
7. Morris Baker
8. George Berry
9. James Moore
10. John Gibson
11. Sam. McCammon
12. James Beaty
13. David Richey
14. Joseph Bogle
15. Alex Harris

were sworn received their charge & retired to enquire of their presentments

66.　　The sale of the Estate of Hance Russell Decd. returned & filed.

The appraisment of the Estate of Andrew Young Decd returned & filed

William Mathews)
　　vs　　　　)　Rule to show cause why the plaintiff in this case
Micheal Nimon)　should not give Security

William Matthews)
    vs   )
Jacob Cupp   ) Rule to show cause why the plaintiff in this case
                 should not give Security

       A Power of attorney from Peter Bowerman & Catherine Bowerman to
George Mizer was acknowledged in open court by Peter Powerman & Cather-
ine Bowerman the subxcribers thereto

       A Deed of conveyance from Jacok Franks to Henry Bonds was proven
in open court by John Trimble & Aron Allen the subscribing witnesses there-
to
             It is therefore ordered that the same be registered.

       A Deed of conveyance from John Black to Joseph Stakes for a tract
of land on the waters of B. Creek was acknowkedged by said Black the
subscriber thereto
             It is therefore ordered that the same be registered.

Joseph Denton)
    vs   )
John F. Garnor) Rule to show cause why the plaintiff in this should
               not give Security.

John Trimble)
    vs   ) Ordered by court that Did: po Issue to the Mississippé
Andrew Miller) Territory to take the Deposition of John Lackey on be-
          half of the plaintiff with 20 Days notice.

67.   John Trimble   )
       vs   )
       Hance Russells Heirs) Ordered by Court that Did; pot. Issue to the Mis-
                     sissippi Territory to take the Diposition of John
Lackey on behalf of the plaintiff with giving 20 days notice.

J. Little)
   vs   )
Jas Pearce) Ordered by Court that Did pot Issue to the State of Kentucky
            to take the Deposition of John Therman & Mary Therman giv-
ing the Defendant 20 days notice.

Adam Peck   )
    vs   )
John Eddington) Ordered by court that Did Pot Issue to Bledsoe County
            to take the diposition of Nicholas Spring with giving
15 Days notice on behalf of the plaintiff to be taken at said Springs
House.

Isaac Little   )
    vs   )
Robert D. Pearce) Ordered by Court Did Pot Issue to the State of Ken-
            tucky to take the Deposition of John Tharman &
Mary Therman giving the Defendant 20 days notice .

Josiah Gamble)
    vs   )
Silas George) Ordered by Court that Did pot Issue to take the Deposition
              of John Jackson with giving 15 days notice on behalf of
the Defendant.

Silas George)
    vs   )
William Moore) Ordered by Court that Did; Pot; issue to take the Depo-
              sition of John Jackson in behalf of the plaintiff with
giving 15 days Notice.

68. Love & Co.)
        vs   )
    Nahhanl Fox.) On motion of E. Parsons Esqr It appears that an Execution
              in favour of the plaintiff vs the Defendant which was re-
turned no goods Nor chattles to be found Levied on Land lying on Crooked
Creek
          It is therefore considered by Court that the said lands be
exposed to sale to satisfy said Debt & Costs.

        Court adjourned till tomorrow morning 9 Oclock

        Court met according to adjournment Tuesday Morning 23, 1808

              Present

    Samuel Hendley, William Lowry, & William Davidson, Esqrs, Justices

John Trimble)
    vs   )
John Rankin) Ordered by Court that Did; pot. issue to take the Deposi-
              tion of John Dearmond to be taken this Evening at the
house of Andrew Thompson betwixt the hours of five & Eight to issue to
John Gardiner & Wm. Lowry Esqrs.

    Jacob peak produced a license authorising him to practice law in
the Several Courts of Law & Equity within this State & having taken the
necessary Oathes is admitted Accordingly to practice in this court.

    The Amount of the Sales of the Estate of James Williams Decd. re-
turned to Court & filed.

69. Isiah Bowman)
        vs   )
    John Ryder) on Motion of the plaintiffs Attorney It appears that Saml
              Hogg was summoned a witness in behalf of the plaintiff
and being solomenly called & failed to appear
          It is therefore considered by court that he forfeit and
pay unto the plaintiff the sum of one hundred & twenty five Dollars & his
Costs in this behalf expended &cO.

    A Bill of Sale from James W. Lackey & Andrew Lackey to William &
Woods Lackey for a tract of land on Holston River was proven in open
Court by Mathew Denny one of the witnesses thereto.

A power of Attorney from Elizabeth Hafley to George Mizer was acknowledged in open court by said Hafely the Subscriber thereto.

State   )
vs   )
George Sherrell) On motion of Enoch Parsons It appears .that John Coldwell was bound in Recobnizances to appear at this court & give Evidence in the above cause in behalf of the State & he altho solemnly called came not but made Default.

It is therefore considered by Court that he forfeit his recognizance unless he appear at our next court & Show sufficient reason for the same.

70. Adam Peck   )
vs   )
Richard Kirby) Ordered by Court that Did; pot. issue to take the Deposition of Robert D. Pearce in behalf of the plaintiff with giving 10 Days notice previous.

The Indentures binding Robert Tedford, Elias Gibson to Edward Eggins was brought into Court & he was rebound to John Licans.

State   )
vs   )
George Sherrell) On motion of E. Parsons Esqr It appearsthat William Sherrell was bound in Recognizance to appear and give evidence in behalf of the State vs. the Defendant and altho solomenly called came not but made default.

It is therefore considered by court that he forfeit his Ricognizance unless he appears at next court & show sufficient reasons to the contrary.

A Bill of sale from Anthkney Patton to Thomas Shaddon for certain Articles therein expressed was proven in open Court by Hugh Kelsoe, and John Eakin the Witnesses thereto.

A Power of Attorney from James Rhea & James Paul Decd. by Andrew Paul his Administrator.

Reuben Charles)
vs   )
Jessee Condron) The plaintiff is put under a Rule to Show cause why he should not give Security in this case

71. William Cox & Co.   )
vs   )
John Harris & Robert) On motion of E. Parsons Esqr It appears that
Strain his Securities) the plaintiff obtain an Execution against the Defendant for the sum of thirty Eight Dollars & Ten Cents Debt & $93\frac{3}{4}$ Cents Costs which Execution was returned levied on Land as the property of Robert Strain

It is therefore considered by court that said land or so much thereof as will satisfu said Debt & costs be exposed to sale agreeably to Law

72. Blank

73. Benjamin Rector for the use)
of John Toomey   ) This day came the plaintiff by his attorney
              vs   ) as well as the Defendant in his proper per-
James W. Lackey   ) son & they mutually agreed that If the De-
                         fendant would pay the costs of this suit
that the plft. would not further prosecute the same.

It is therefore considered by Court that the plaintiff recover against the defendant his Costs by him in this behalf expended and
the said Defendant is in Mercy &co.

Ordered by Court that Thursday next to set apart to do county
business & that this order be forthwith published on the Court House
Door.

Ordered by Court that Friday next next be set apart to do State business & this order be forthwith published on the court House Door.

Court adjourned till tomorrow Morning 9 Oclock

74. Wednesday 24th August Term 1808

Court met according to Adjournment

Present

Saml Hendley, Wm. Lowry, & Andrew Bogle, Esqrs &co.

William Cox & co.   )
              vs   ) On motion of E. Parson Esqr It appears that an
John B. Harris & Robert) Execution issued in favour of the plaintiff
Strain his Securities   ) vs the Defendant for the sum of $38 and 93¾
                        (Cents which was returned no goods nor chat-
tles to be found levied on the land the said Strain lives on As his property

It is therefore considered by Court that said land be exposed to sale agreably to Law to satisfy said Judgment & Costs.

Henry Hampton   )
              vs   )
Samuel Findley & John) On Motion of John Lowry Atto. on behalf of the
Lowry & Micheal Niman) Deft. it is ordered by the court that a rule
his Securities   ) should be given the Defendants to show cause
                          why the proceedings should be reversed & the
Execution quashed which was continued for argument until court.

Josiah Danforth)
              vs   ) Atta. Writ of Enquiry
John Garrison) This day came the plaintiff by his Attorney & there-
                  upon came a Jury (Viz)

1. John B. Cusack   5. Samuel Gould   9. Banjamin Wallace
2. David Coldwell   6. Burton pride   10. Robert Murrin
3. Samuel Eakin   7. William Armstrong   11. John Duncan
4. James Thompson   8. Joseph Black   12. Robert Pearce

75. who being elected tried and swoÐn well and truly to enquire of damages

in this case Do say they assess the plaintiffs damages to sixty seven Dollars & Costs

It is therefore considered by Court that the plaintiff recover the Defendant his damages aforesaid & Also his Costs by him in this behalf expended & the said Defendant is in mercy &c.

Andrew Bogle, James Wyley, James Gillespie Esqrs, Justices present &c.

Owen Hanna)
    vs   )
Ŧen Ghormley) The same Jury as in the Case Danforth vs Garrison who being elected & sworn Do say the Defendant is not guilty of the Tresspass as in pleading he hath alleged

It is therefore considered by our Court that the plaintiff take Nothing buŧ for his false clamour be in Mercy &c. & the Defendant go without day & recover against him his costs by him in his defence in this behalf expended & co.

Court adjourned till tomorrow Morning 9 Oclock

76.   Thursday 25th August Term 1808

Court met according to Adjournment

      Present

Samuel Hendley, Andrew Bogle & John Woods Esqrs, Justices &c.

Thomas Rugherford)
    vs   )
Peter Harris   ) Ordered by court that Did pot Issue to the States of North & South Carolina to take Deposition of Wm. Wallton & others with giving 30 days notice in behalf of the plaintiff.

William Black)
    vs   )
Joseph Smith) This day Came the parties by their Attornŧŧs and thereupon came a Jury to wit

1. John Gault	5. Wilson White	9. Samuel Gould
2. William L. Taylor	6. Oliver Alexaneer	10. James Kannard
3. David Coldwell	7. James McCamey	11. John Rankin
4. John Casteel	8. James Weir Senr	12. Joseph Black

Who being elected tried & sworn the truth to speak upon the issue Joined upontheir Oaths Do say the Defendant did assume upon himself in manner & form as the plaintiff in his declaration hath declared & within three years next before the swing out of the original Writ in this Case & by reason of the non performance of that assumpsit they assess the plaintiff Damages to thirty Dollars

It is therefore considered by court that the plaintiff recover agt. the Defendant aforesaid his damages aforesaid as by the Jury aforesaid assessed and also his costs by him in this behalf expended & the said Defendant is in mercy &c.

77.   Ordered by court that Mary Stephens be allowed a draft on the County

Treasury for Eight Shillings pr week until further orders and that she
have one Dollar pr week from February Term until May

Isaac Little   )
    vs   )
Robert D. Pearce) Ordered by Court that a commission issue to take the
                    Deposition of Nicholas Bartlet in behalf of the De-
fendant with giving 30 days notice & that commission issue to Samuel
Flanagan & Joseph Kirby Esqrs

Abraham Hackett)
    vs   )
James Houston) This day came the parties by their attornies and there-
               upon came a Jury (Viz)

1. James Logan	5. John Gould	9. William Anderson
2. Jonathan Trippett	6. William Armstrong	10. Benjamin Kilbourn
3. John B. Cusach	7. William Green	11. David Cupp
4. Hugh Cunniggham	8. William Campbell	12. Samuel D. Sanson

who being elected tried & sworn the truth to speak upon the Issue Joined
upon their Oaths Do say the Defendant is guilty of the Detention in manner and form as the plft in his declaration hath declared & that within
three years next before the swing out of the writ in this case & they
assess the plaintiffs Damages by occasion of the detention thereof to
$1.00 which may be discharged by the payment of the negro same Costs
        Therefore it is considered by court that the plaintiff re-
cover agt. the Defendant aforesaid his negro aforesaid if he can be had
if not his damages aforesaid as by the Jury aforesaid assessed & also
his costs by him in this behalf expended.

78.   A Bill of sale from Elijah Witt to James Houston for a negro man
named Lam was proven in open court by Henry Whitenbarger one of the subscribing witnesses thereto.

    A Bill of sale from William McMahan to Robert Sloan was proven in
open court by James Sloan & David Cook the witnesses thereto.

Barcley McGhee)
    vs   )
John McCullock) In this case James Turk & Robert Lowry who were Special bail for the Defendant came into court and surrendered him John
Woods & John Lowry Atto. came into court and agread that if the Defendant would pay the costs & condemnation or surrender himself in discharge of themselves.

               Grand Jury discharged

    A Bill of Sale from Henry Sprinkle to Charles Donahoo for a Negro
named Jacob was acknowledged in open Court by said sprinkle the subscribing thereto & admited to record let it be registered.

           Court adjourned till tomorrow Morning 9 Oclock

79. Friday 26 August Term, 1808

           Court met according to Adjournment

Present

Samuel Hendley James Houston & Stephen Stafford Esqrs &c.

Ordered by court that John Woods, William Gillespie & William Montgomery Esqrs. be commissioners to settle with John Hickland Administrator of William Davenport Decd.

Adam Saffley   )
    Vs   )
John Keys & Alexander Ford   )
& John Sherrell his securities)   on Motion of E. Parsons Esqr. It ap-
                        pears that an Execution issued in favour
of the plaintiff vs R. Charles for the Sum of $10.98¢ which Execution
was not returned as the Law directs not the money paid to the
            ᵗt is therefore considered by court & that the plft recover
against the Defendant his money aforesaid and also his Costs by him in
this behalf expended & the Defendants are in Mercy &c.

Ordered by court Archabald Jonston take Saml Tharman immediately
& that Indentures be executed at next court.
On motion of David Russell leave is granted him to Keep an ordinary in Maryville he having given bond & Security

Administration is granted on the Estate of John Hess Decd. to George
& John Snider & Mary Hess to whom of right the Administration belonged
came into court and relinquished her right to the same.

80.   State   )
      vs   )   T.A.B.
John Edington)   This day came as well the Deft. by His Attorney E. Par-
                 sons who prosecutes for the State & thereupon came a
Jury (to wit.)

1. John Gault   5. David Coldwell   9. James McKamey
2. James Logan   6. Hugh Cunningham   10. James Weir, Senr.
3. William L. Taylor 7. John Casteel   11. Saml Gould
4. John B. Cusack   8. Oliver Alexander   12. John Rankin

who being elected tried & sworn well & truly to try the Issue in Traverse upon their Oaths do say the Defendant is not guilty of the Trespass Assault & Batterh in manner & form as charged in the Bill of Indictment & the Defendant by his Attorney Came came into court & moved
to have a rule entered to tax the prosecutor with the costs of this
suit which when argued was ordered accordingly.

Ordered by Court that John Thornburry pay to those who have the
charge of a Base borne child who he is charged with being the father of
born of the body of Sarah Curtin fifty Shillings quarterly for one
year & that on failure of payment Execution Issue for the same

Henry Shields)
    vs   )
John Walker)   Ordered by Court that Did Po. issue to take the Deposi-
                 tion of John Walker senr. in behalf of the Defendant
with giving 10 days notice.

The appraisement of the Estate of John Hess Decd returned & filed & order of sale granted.

81. State   )
        vs   )
    John Edington) In this case the Defendant being called out on his re-
                    cognizances & not answering but appearing in court be-
    fore the forfeiture was entered.

    State   )
        vs   ) T.A.B.
    James Montgomery) This day came as well the Deft. by his Attorney as E.
                    Parsons who prosecutes in behalf of the State and
    thereupon came a Jury (to wit.)

    1. Jonathan Trippett   5. Henry Donahoo   9. Abraham Phillips
    2. James Kannard   6. Dnaiel Regin ✓   10. Jno. Kennedy
    3. William Armstrong   7. John Donahoo   11. Bennett James
    4. Joseph Black /   8. Robert Gray   12. James Ewing

    who being elected tried & xxx sworn well & truly to try the traverse up-
    on their Oaths Do say the Defendant is not guilty of the Trespass Assault
    & Batterh in Manner & form as charged in the bill of Indictment & the
    Deft by his Attorney unless a Rule to tax the prosecutor with the Costs
    of this suit when argued was made absolute.

82. Morgan Edwards   )
        vs   )
    Andrew Evens & Securities) On motion of John Gardner Esqr Attorney for
                              the plaintiff It appears that the plain-
    tiff obtained an Exec. for the sum of 25$ & 8¼ cents costs which Execu-
    tion went into the hands of said Evens to collect & he failing to pay
    the money & return the Execution as the law directs.
                    It is therefore considered by court that the plaintiff
    recover against the said Andrew Evins & George Evins his Securities his
    debt & Costs aforesaid and also his costs by him in this behalf expen-
    ded &c.

    State   )
        vs   ) Affray
    Nathenial Norwell) This day came as well the Defendant by his Attp.
                    as E. parsons who prosecutes for the State and
    thereuponcame a Jury (to wit.)

    1. John Weir   5. Jas. Black   9. Robert Gray
    2. Jonahtan Trippet   6. Henry Donahoo   10. Abraham Phillips
    3. James Kennard   7. David Reagen ✓   11. John Kennedy
    4. William Armstrong   8. John Donaho   12. Bennett James

    who being elected tried & sworn the truth to speak upon the Issue in
    traverse upon their Oaths do say the Defendant is not guilty of the af-
    fray in manner & form as charged in the bill of Indictment.

83.   Ordered by Court that Hugh Weir be allowed a draft on the Treasury
    of Ten Dollars for the use of Nancy McCollister until next Court or if
    she should not live until then to be drawn in proposition to that term.
    & sum.

State   )
  vs   )   Sci. Face
Nathanial Norwell) In this case there was a forfeiture taken at last
               court & a Sch. Fac rem to this Court which is set
aside on payment of costs.

State   )
  vs   )   Sci. Fac.
William Harris) In this case there was a forfeiture take n at last court
               & a Sci. Fac. rem to this court which is set aside on
payment of costs.

State   )
  vs   )   T.A.B.
Henry McGuire) This day came the parties by their attornies & there-
               upon came a Jury (to wit) the same Jury as was in No.
343 who being elected tried and sworn the truth to speak upon the issue in traverse upon their Oaths do say the Defendant is guilty of the
trespass Assault & Battery in manner & form as charged in the Bill of
Indictment
              It is therefore considered by court that for such his of-
fence he be fined two Dollars and may be taken &c.

85xx   Ordered by court that Hugh Weir be allowed
84. State   )
      vs   )   T.A.B.
Henry McGuire) This day came they as well the Deft by his Attorney as
               E. Parsons who prosecutes in behalf of the State and
thereupon came a Jury (to wit) the same Jury as in No. 343 who being
elected and sworn Do say the Defendant is Gulity of the Trespass Assault & Battery in Manner & form as charged in the Bill of Indictment
              It is therefore considered by Court that for such his of-
fence to be fined twenty five cents & May be taken &c.

             Courtadjourned till tomorrow morning 9 oclock

             Saturday Morning 27 of August 1808

             Court met according to Adjournment

                 Present

    Samuel Hendley William Lowry & John Tedford, Esqrs & Justices, &c.

State   )
  vs   )
Leon Perry) It appears that the Defendant was bound in Recognizances to
           appear at May T. 1808 & give evidence & prosecute Vaughns
and tho solomenly called came not but made default & a forfeiture was
taken & for sufficient reasons to the court now shown
           It is ordered that said forfeiture be set aside on payment
of Costs.

Montgomery for the use)
of Cowan)
     vs)
James Bradford) In this case it appears that an Execution issue
in favour of the Plaintiff against Doherty which
Execution was returned levied on a house & lot in Dandridge and an order
of Sale was granted.

Berrys Exors)
    vs) Fi Fa.
Barcley McGhee) On motion of the Defendant Thomas Dards Esqr a rule is
given him to show cause if any he can why the above
execution should be dismissed.

Ditto)
  vs) F. Fa.
Ditto) on Motion of the Defendant by Dardis his Attorney a rule is given
him to show cause why this Execution should be quashed.

Ditto)
  vs) Fi.Fa.
Ditto) On motion of the Defendant by Thomas Dardis Esqr his Attorney a
rule is given him to show cause why this Execution should be
quashed.

Jas. Denton)
    vs) Rule to show cause why the Deft in this case should not
Henerys Heirs) give Security

86. State)
    vs)
Vaughns) William Kendrick who was bound in one hundred dollars to appear at this & give Evidence vs the Defendant altho solomenly
called came not but made default.
        It is therefore considered by Court that he forfeit his
Recognizances unless he appears & show sufficient reasons to the contrary

Buck & Brander)
    vs)
Jacob Danforth) Order by Court that Did pot. issue to any two Justices
in the county to take the deposition of John Craige in
behalf of the plaintiff with giving 3 Days notice.

Buck & Brander)
    vs)
Jacob Danforth) Ordered by Court thatDid pot. issue to any two justices
of the peace for this county to take the Deposition of
John Craig with giving three Days notice to the Defendants Attorney to
be read in behalf of the Plaintiff

John Lowry Jr.)2
    vs)
D. White) Ordered by court that a commission issue to take the
deposition of William Black in behalf of the Defendant
with giving three Days Notice to the plfts Attorney

Robert Hanna)
   vs   )
Lowrys Heirs) Ordered by court that a commission issue to take the Depo-
              sition of the plft. with giving 3 Days notice to the Defts.
attorney.

87. Samuel King for the use of)
James Coulter   )
     vs   ) W. of Enquire
George Montgomery   ) this day came the Deft. by his Atto and there-
                      upon came a Jury (to wit.)

1. David Coldwell	5. James Kannard	9. John Brickey
2. Jonathan Trippitt	6. John B. Cusack	10. Alexander Moore
3. William L. Taylor	7. George Grigsby	11. John Coldwell
4. Joseph Black	8. John McGhee	12. David Campbell

who being elected tried and sworn well and truly to enquire of Damages
in this Cause do say they assess the plaintiffs Damages to Eighty three
Dollars & 71¾ cents & costs.
      It is therefore considered by court that the plaintiff re-
cover against the Defendants aforesaid his damages aforesaid by the Jury
aforesaid assessed and also his costs by him in this behalf expended &
the said Defendant is in Mercy &c.

M. Wallace)
   vs   )
R. Moore) In this case at last court there was a rule entered to ar-
            rest the Judgment and when solemnly argued on each side
and mature deliberation being had in court
      It was considered and adjudged by court that said Judgment
be arrested & that the plaintiff take nothing but for his false clamour be in mercy & co.
      From which Judgment the plaintiff prayed an appeal to our next
Superior Court of Law to be held for the district of Hamilton at the
Court House in Knoxville on the fourth Monday in September next& having filed his reasons & entered into bond with approved Security to him
it was granted.

88.   On motion of William Lackey it appears that in the Tax list of
1803 there were some men who were twice returned in said list & that he
was liable to and did pay the sum twice & having collected but for
one return.
      It is ordered by Court that he draw from the County Treasury
$18&40 cents the amount by him paid over & above what he collected.

State   )
  vs   )
William Fagg) Ordered by court that the fine in this case be continued
             until next for further consideration.

Lowry & Waugh)
   vs   )
Robert J. Henry) ordered by court that the non suit entered in this
              case at last court be set aside.

Ordered by court that the Indentures binding George Fox to Lambert Love be Null & Void

Lowry & Waugh)
vs)
Robert J. Henery) Ordered by court that Did pot issue to Baltimore to take the Deposition of Robert Henderson & others in behalf of both parties Notice served on the Defendants Attorney to be considered sufficient of thirty days.

Henry & Lindenbarger)
vs)
Lowry & Waugh) Ordered by court that a commission issue to Baltimore to take Deposition on behalf of both parties with 30 days notice served on the plfts atto. to be considered sufficient

89.   Samuel Law)
vs) Debt
Samuel Clarke) In this case the Deft being him solemnly called came not but made default.
It is therefore considered that Judgment go against him by default.

Jacob Derrick)
vs)
Jacob Wright) In this case the Defendant came into court and acknowledged the service of this writ in due time & confessed Judgment to the plaintiff for the sum of one hundred dollars.
It is therefore considered by court that the plaintiff recover against the defendant his money aforesaid & his costs by him in this behalf expended & the Defendant is in Mercy &c. the plaintiff stays Execution in this case Six months.

Ordered by court that William Lowry George Ewing & James Gillespie Esqrs be commissioners to Settle with Nancy Scott Administratrix of William Scott Decd.

Court adjourned till court in course.

90.   At a court of pleas & quarter Sessions began and held for the county of Blount at the court house in Maryville on the fourth Monday of November 1808.

Present

Samuel Hendley, William Lowry, & James Gillespie, Esqrs, Justices

Andrew Cowan Deputy Sheriff for the county aforesaid returned the Venire Facias Executed on the following persons to wit

1. Joseph Black   6. Stewart Montgomery   11. Richard Dearmond
2. Samuel McMurry   7. Robert McMurry   12. John Ewing
3. John Rhea   8. Fredrick Rush   13. James Regan
4. Alexander Patterson   9. Lewis Jones   14. John Beard
5. William Bowman   10. Richard Kirby   15. Samuel Henry

16. James Ewing	20. Ebenezar Jones	24. James Weir, Jr.
17. Thos Wallace	21. Moses Hughes	25. Oliver Alexander
18. David Thompson	22. Haron Allen	26. Robert Sterling
19. Saml. McCammron	23. John Brickey	27. Benj. Wallace
		28. William Long

Out of which Venire the following persons were elected a grand Jury to enquire for the body of the County to Wit

1. Benjamin Wallace	5. Robert Sterling	9. Moses Hughes
2. Lewis Jones	6. John Kennedy	1o. Saml. Henry
3. Alexander Patterson	7. Rich'd. Kirby	11. Robert McMurry
4. Thomas Wallace	8. James Weir	

91. John Ewing, Samuel Scott, Ebinezar Jones & Samuel McMurry who being sworn received their charges & retired to enquire of their presentments &c.

Jacob Tarwater)
  vs   ) Case
Charles Brunson) The plaintiff by Atto having filed his declaration the Defendant came into open court & confesses the plaintiffs Action for one hundred & one Dollars & fifty cents & costs of their suit

    Wherefore it is considered by Court that the plaintiff recover against the Defendant the Sum of one hundred & ene dollars & his Costs as aforesaid but the plaintiff orders a Stay of Exceution 3 months.

  A Deed of Conveyance from Hugh Cunningham to John Weir for 317 Acres of land was acknowledged in open Court by Hugh Cunningham the subscriber thereto.

Barney Holaway)
  vs   )
Colman Knight) In this case John McGhee who was special bail for the Defendant came into court & surrendered the Defendant in discharge of himself & Joseph Hollaway comes into bound & agrees that the Defendant will provide by & preform the Judgments of our court or he will for him or surrender him in discharge of himself.

  On motion of Martha Martin by her Atto John Wilkinson It is ordered that she have administration on the Estate of Marmor Martin Decd was Sworn & entered into bond with Wm Durham & John Singleton her Securities.

  An Additional Inventory of the Estate of William Davenport decd. returned & filed.

92. A Deed of conveyance from James Long & Sarah his wife to John Miller of Rickbridge County was acknowledged in open court by James Long & Sarah Long his wife the Subscribers thereto.

George Peary)
  vs   ) Covt.
James McCullock) In this case on affidavit of Thomas McCullock It is

ordered by court that a commission De bene epsee issue to take the Deposition of Samuel Glass at his own home with giving the Defendant five
days notice commissions issue to George Ewing or Samuel George.

A Bill of sale from Woods Lackey to William Lackey for Land lying
on Holston River was proven in open court by James W. Lackey the subscribing witnesses thereto

Pugh Heirs   )
    vs   )
Josiah Gamble) In this case there was a rule entered by the Defendants
               atto to dismiss the plaintiffs Coveat

A Bill of sale from Mary Lackey to William Lackey was proven in op-
en court by Archabald Cowan one of the Subscribing witnesses thereto.

A power of Attorney from Thomas Powel to Nicholass Stephenson was
acknowledged in Open court by said powel the Subscriber thereto.

Ordered by Court that John Waugh & John Woods & James Wyley
Esqrs Settle with the Guardian of John Tipton Decd.

93.   Court Adjourned till tomorrow 9 Oclock

Tuesday 29 Court Met according to adjournment

       Present

George Ewing, John Waugh & James Wyley Esqrs.

The last will & Testament of patrick Murry was produced in open
Court & was proven by Jeremiah Hammontree & John Boyd were qualified
Agreable to Law.

On Motion of Mary Murry relict of patrick Murry Decd. by her attorney John Lowry her protest is entered against the last will & Testament of Patrick Murry Decd.

94.   James S. Montgomery)
        vs   ) On Motion of
    James Hanna   ) John Gardiner Esqr. It appears that the plaintiff
                    obtained an Execution vs. the Deft which Execution
went into the hands of Charles Donahoo Constable & he collected a part
of the money & returned for the ballance yet unpaid on the same which
is $36.34 Cents levied on the land James Hanna lives on.
         It is therefore considered by Court that said land or so
much thereof as will be of value sufficient to satisfy the same be exposed to sale agreably to Law.

Samuel Donahoo)
    vs   )
John Pearce) On motion of the plaintiff by Enoch Parsons, Esq. his
              attorney It appears that the plaintiff Obtained an Ex-
ecution before John Waugh Esquire for the sum of Eight Dollars principal
$1¼ Cents which Execution Andrew Cowan D. Sheriff returned levied on a

tract of land lying on little River xxxx the land whereon Charles Doterty lives.

It is therefore considered by Court that said land or so much thereof as will be of value sufficient to satisfy the said Execution & costs be exposed to sale agreably to Law.

Henery Shields)
    vs   )   Ordered by court that commission De Bene issue to George
EwingWalker)   Ewing & Samuel George to take the Deposition of Saml.
John Walker)   Glass in favour of the plfts to be taken at his own
                house with four days Notice .

95.   A Deed of conveyance from LambertReid and Margaret Reid his wife from Henry Hogver & Zilpha his wife Robert Murrin & Catherine his wife & Adam ------? & Mary his wife to George Sullinger the acknowledgment of the Same by Robert Murrin his wife & Adam ------? & his wife was proven in open Court by John Gardiner & James Robertson the Subscribing Witnesses thereto.

Henry Shields)
    vs   )
Robert Walker)   Ordered by court that a commission De Bene issue to
              George Ewing & Samuel George to take the Deposition of
Samuel Glass at his own house with giving four Days notice.

Henery Shields)
    vs   )
Samuel Walker)   Ordered by Court that a commission De bene issue to George
              Ewing & Samuel George to take the Deposition of Samuel
Glass at his own house with giving four days notice.

A Relinquishment of land from Archbd. Lackey to William Lackey was proven in open Court by David Vaught the subscribing witness thereto

On motion of John Reagan administration was granted him on the Estate of James Young Dedd who entered into bond with Samuel Legg & James McNutt his Security.

A Morgage from George Grigsby to Samuel Low was proven in open Court by Enoch parsons & Charles Donahoe the Witnesses thereto.

96.   Court adjourned till tomorrow 9 Oclock.

Wednesday 30th

Court met according to Adjournment

      Present

Samuel Hendley, William Lowru, & William Gault Esquires Justices &c

Ordered by court that a summons Issue to Benjamin Irwin & Robert McCurdy to Summons them as constables to attend our next court.

49.

George Rutledge)
vs)
David Vance) On motion of the Defts Atto. the plaintiff is put under a Rule to show cause why he should not give Security

Ordered by court that Benjamin Kilbourn be fined in fifty cents for
Contempt shown to the court.

John Trimble)
vs)
John Rankin) Ordered by Court that a commission Issue to John Gardner
& John Waugh Esquires to take the Deposition of James W.
Lackey with giving five days notice.

A Bill of Sale from Moses Keywood to Michl. Robertson was proven
in open Court by Saml. Caywood & Edward Caywood the witnesses thereto
& It was ordered to be registered.

97. A Deed of conveyance from John Wilkinson & Margaret Wilkinson his
wife William Long & Mary Long his wife to John Gilbreath for a Lot of
Land lying in Rockbridge County & State of Virginia was produced &
Samuel Hendley & James Griffatts Esquires two of the Justices of said
County appointed by the court to take the privy examination of the said
Margaret & Mary Do certifu that the said Margaret & Mary truly and vol-
untarily and without any concive on the part of their respective hus-
bands have executed said Deed and that said John Wilkinson & William
Long & Mary Long respectively acknowledged in open Court that they
signed sealed & delivered said Deed of conveyance to the said John
Gilbreath.

Lowry & Waugh)
vs) Case
Robert J. Henery) This day came the parties by their attornies and
thereupon came a Jury to wit.

1. Alexander Stewart   5. Joseph Black   9. James Reagan
2. John Clark   6. William Bowman   10. John Brickey
3. William Montgomery   7. Oliver Alexander   11. William Long
4. Samuel Sanson   8. Frerick Rust Rush. 12. Stewart Montgomery

who being elected tried and sworn the truth to speak upon the issue
Joined upon their Oaths Do say the Defendant did not assume upon himself
in Manner & form as the Plaintiff against him hath Declared.
It is therefore considered by Court that the plaintiff
take nothing but for the false clamour be in Mercy &c. & that the
Deft. go without day and recover against the plft.

98. Rule for new trial and con. till next court.

Court adjourned till tomorrow Morning 9 Oclock
Thursday 1st December 1808
Court met according to adjournment

Present

Samuel Hendley James Gillespie & John Waugh Esqrs, Justices &c.

Ordered by court that James Boyd be allowed Ten Dollars for the use and Maintainance of George Fox until next court.

Samuel Hendley, James Wyley & James Wyley Gillespie Esquires Justices &c.

Hanna & Lindenbarger)
   vs   )
Lowry & Waugh   ) This day came the parties by their Attornies & thereupon came a Jury to wit

1. David Brown	5. James pearce	9. William Bowman
2. John Cox	6. William Findley	10. John Rhea
3. James T. Steel	7. Thomas McCullock	11. Aaron Allen
4. Washington Allen	8. James Weir Senr	12. James Reagin

who being elected tried & sworn the truth to speak upon the issue Joined upon their Oaths do say the Do say the Defendants did assume upon themselves in Manner as the plaintiff Against them have declared and they assess the plaintiffs damages by occasion of the non preformance of that assumpset to six hundred & seventy eight Dollars & six cents & costs.
Rule for new trial.

99.   The Grand Jurors discharged by Court

A Bill of sale from Woods Lackey to James W. Lackey for several negroes was proven in Open court by Niman Chamberlain & Polly Chamberlain two of the witnesses thereto.

An Assignment of the above mentioned bill of Sale from James W Lackey to John Brown was proven in open court by John Montgomery the witness thereto.

Joseph Brooks was appointed Guardian to William Gamble and he was released from entering into bond.

Court adjourned till tomorrow morning 9 Oclock

Friday 2nd December 1808

Court met according to adjournment

        Present

Samuel Hendley, William Davidson, John Reagen & James Gillespie Esqrs &c.

State   )
  vs   ) Sci. Fac.
John Coldwell) In this case there was a forfeiture taken at last court which is set aside on payt. of costs.

State   )
  vs   )
William Sherrell) Sci. Fac.
         In this case there was a forfeiture taken last court

which is set aside on payment of costs.

100.   Ordered by court that the following permiet be admitted to record to wit, Cherokee Agency

Nov. 17, 1808

Mr. Samuel Findley Officer of the peace of Blount County and State of Tennessee Complains that certain persons named Joel Wallace & Alexander Finley have in defiance of all order & in pretence of making the cherokee Nation an Asylum for their Neferious practices I do hereby permit any officer of officers of Blount County by order of the Honorable Court of said County to serve precept on any person or persons who have or may act contrary to the Law of the State of Tennessee.

W. L. Loveless   Agt.   Lovely
Agent for the Cherokees.

The Cherokees will be cautious in not interferring in matters between white people

Willo will be guided by this
W.L.W.

Ordered by court that the Officers of Blount County be guided Agreable to an act in Conformity to the above permit.

101.   Ordered by Court that the following majestrates take in & return agreable to Law.

Taxable poll & property in the following companies for the year 1808

Justices	Captains
John Waugh -0000-------------------	Cusack
George Ewing -----------------------	Caldwells
Henry Franks -----------------------	Dixons
Samuel Hendley ---------------------	Kelsoe
Mathew Wallace ---------------------	Thompson
William Gault ----------------------	Davidsons
William Davidson -------------------	Houstons
John Reagan ------------------------	Beards
William Murry ----------------------	Garnors
William Montgomery 00---------------	Foresters
William Gillespie ------------------	Wheelers
Robert Parks -----------------------	Allens
Joseph Alexander --------- -------	Buckhanas

Henry Shields)
   vs   )
John Walker) Ordered by court that commissioners Issue to James White & John McClelland ih Abingdon Virginia to take the Deposition of Jno. Davis giving 20 days notice to the Defendant

Henery Shields)
   vs   )
Robert Walker) Ordered by court that a commission Issue to James White & John McClelland ih Abingdon Virginia to take the Depo-

sition of John Davis giving 20 Days Notice to the defendant

Henery Shields)
    vs   )   The Same Rule
Samuel Walker)

102. Henery Shields)
          vs   )
      Robert Walker) Ordered by Court that commission Issue to take the Depo-
                    sition of John Walker Senr on behalf of the Plaintiff
to be taken in Maryville on Monday next & the plft acknowledged notice.

Henry Shields)
    vs   )
Samuel Walker) Ordered by Court that Commission Issue to take the Depo-
               sition of John Walker on behalf of the Defendant to be
taken in Maryville on Monday next the plaintiff acknowledged the services of this notice.

Andrew Scott)
    vs   )
Nancy Scott) Ordered by Court that a commission Issue to ———————?
              Virginia to take the Deposition of Joseph Cowan & James
Scott in the town of Fairfield in behalf of the plft giving 30 days
Notice.

    John Walker was by Court appointed constable & entered into bond
with William Davidson & John Reagan his Securities.

    Ordered by court that Mary Stephens be allowed Eleven Dollars for
her attentions to an orphan Child named Isoom Griffin from last Court
until his decease which was the 9 of October 1808.

    An Inventory of the Estate of Patrick Murry Decd. was returned to
Court & filed and it is ordered by court that the Execution of said
Estate proceed no further in the Execution of said will until Court

State   )
  vs   ) T.A.B.
William Fagg) In this case there was a fine assessed at last court
               to ten Dollars which was continued until this court
for a reconsideration & after mature reflection by our court said fine
was remitted to one Dollar.

State   )
  vs   )
Cornelius Goforth) In this case it Appears by the Record that John
                 Snider is bound as a witness on behalf of the Es-
tate
          It is therefore ordered by court that he be released un-
til the Defendant can be made to appear and Answer.

Robert McMurry)
    vs   )
James McClelland) In this case John Lowry who was special Bail for the

Deft came into open court & surrendered him in discharge of himself and
Fredrick Rush & Benjamin Kelbourn agred that the Defendant would pay the
costs & condemnation for him or surrender him in discharge of themselfes.

Preston Adams)
vs)
Archibald Trimble)   Ordered by Court that commission Issue to take the
                      Deposition of John Trimble on behalf of the plaintiff
with giving 10 days previous Notice

104. James Heard for the)
      use of John Keys   )
            vs   )
      John Russell   )   In this case the Defendant being Solemnly called
                             came not & failed to appear and defend his suit but
made default
            It is therefore considered by court that Judgment go for
the plaintiffs action by Default & that a writ of Enquiry be executed
at next court.

      James Heard for the use)
      of Samuel McReynolds   )
            vs   )
      John Russell   )   In this the Defendant being solomenly called
                                 came not but made default to appear and defend
his suit
            It is therefore considered by Court that Judgment go by
default for the plaintiffs course of action and the Defendant is in
Mercy &c.

      Isaac Upton)
         vs   )
      Robert Dial)   In this case the plaintiff being solomnly called came not
                     & failing to prosecute his suit
            It is therefore considered by Court that he be non prossed
and the Defendant go without a day and recover his costs &c.

      State   )
         vs   ) Sci. Fac.
      William Kendrick) Ordered by Court that the forfeiture taken at last
                         Term be set aside on payment of costs.

105. State   )
         vs   )
      Charles Rogers)   On Motion of John Lowry Atto a Nolli prosequi is or-
                        dered & John Lowry enters himself as security for
costs.

            Court adjourned till tomorrow morning 9 Oclock

            Saturday 3d of December 1808

            Court met according to adjournment

                  Present

      William Lowry, John Waugh & Henry Franks Esquires Justices &c.

On motion of George Dillard liberty is granted him to have his mark recorded which is Smoth crop & slit in the Right Ear & a Swallow fork & an under bit in the left ear.

Miles & David Cunningham)
vs)
William Stewart) Rule to show cause to Issue writs of Certiorari & Supersidias

It was ordered that the writs Issue accordingly.

106. James Benham)
vs)
Caleb Godrick William) On Motion of Enoch parsons Attorney for
Schrimsher James Schrimsher) the plaintiff It appeas xxxxxxxxxxxxx
that the plaintiff obtained an Execution
vs the Defendant for the sum of 4$ & 43 Cents Debt & Costs which Execution was returned by Benjamin Erwin Constable levied on a Tract of land the property of James Schrimsher on N. Mile Creek whereon he now lives.

It is therefore considered by Court thatsaid land or so much thereof as will be sufficient to satisfy said Debt & costs be exposed to Sale Agreably to Law to satisfy the same.

Francis Pain)
vs)
Salob Godrick, James Schrim-) On Motion of E. Parsons atto. for the
sher & William Schrimsher) plaintiff It appears that the plff. obtained an Execution before Robert Thompson Esquire for the sum of Seventeen Dollars & Seventy two & one third Cents which Execution was returned by Benjamin Erwin Consatble levied on a tract of land lying on nine Mile Creek the land whereon James Schrimsher now lives

It is therefore considered by Court that said land or so much as will satisfy said Ececution & Cost be exposed to sale agreably to Law to satisfy the same.

107. Love & Co.)
vs)
William Green) on Motion of John Gardiner Esquire It appears that the plaintiff obtained and Execution against the Defendant for the sum of Eighteen Dollars & Thirty Eight Cents on which Charles D Donahoo Constable for the county returned Levied on a tract of land adjoining Mary Lackey & others.

It is therefore considered by Court that said land or so much thereof as will satisfy said Judgment & Execution & costs be exposed to sale agreably to Law to satisfy the same.

Miles & David Cunningham)
vs)
William Stuard) on Motion of the plaintiff a rule was granted them (Viz)To set off so much of the money on the Execution obtained on the Judgment Robert Dial vs .Wm. Steward against the Judgment obtained by the plaintiff against said Stewart before John Waugh a Justice of the peace on which writ of certiorari is granted this term as will amount to the said Judgment of the said plfts. & that the said amount be ordered to be paid to the said Miles &

David Cunnintham.

A Bill of Sale from David Montgomery to Alexander Kebley was proven
in Open Court by James Logan the Witness thereto.

108. Samuel Love)
          vs   )
      Samuel Clarke) In this case It appearing to the court by the return of
                      the Sheriff on an Execution against the Goods & Chattles
lands & Tenements of Samuel Clarke that there was no property to satisfy
said Execution and also that the said Defendant hath removed out of the
County and whereas it also appears by the return of the said Sheriff that
Robert Hooks was agreably Summoned at the instance of the plaintiff or
Garnshee According to the act of the General Assembly in such cases
made & provided to declare upon oath what Sum or Sums of money he was indebted to the said Samuel Clarke on what property he had of the said
Clarke now live or not yet due or what money or property he knew of in
the hands of any other person and what person and the said Robert Hooks
being solomnly called on Thursday the fourth Day of the sessions & on
Saturday the last day of the Sission both of which times he the said
Robert failing or refusing to answer but made Default
4   It is therefore considered by Court that the plaintiff re-
coxer against the Said Robert Hooks the sum of

        Ordered by Court that Hugh Weir Jr. be allowed Eight Dollars for
maintaining Nancy McCallester & his attention to her & that the order
made at last court be void.

109.   Ordered by court that the Sheriff be exenerated for paying the following sums of money on the following machines (to wit)

$59150 cents on Thomas Berrys Machine
 23.25   on John Matsons machine
 14."   on John Carroths machine
 23125   on Robert Carroths machine
as they would not sell for the same as there was no other property to be
found.

        Ordered by Court that the commissioners appointed at last Term
to settle with the Admr's of William Scott be continued to next Term to
make said settlement.

Hanna   )
   vs   )
Lowries Heirs) Ordered by Court that Commission issue

110.   William Lackey Esquire late collectors of Taxes in Blount county
report to Court that the Taxes remain unpaid on the following tracts of
land & Free poles for the respectife years following & that he co'l'd
not find any goods & chattles of the owners thereof on which he could
distress for the year 1804.

Names	no. of acres	Situation	F.P.	Taxes	P.f	C.F.
George Allen	100		1	56	75	85
James Beard	640	L. River	1	1.79	75	85
William Black	320	C. Creek	1	90	75	85

Names	No. of acres	Situation	F.P.	Taxes	P;fee	C.F.
Samuel Cowan	100		1	56	75	85
Thomas Cochron	440		1	125	75	85
James Curry	300	Sinking Creek	1	1.12	75	85
Robert Donelson	175		1	77	85	85
Thos Davis	60		1	44	75	85
Adam Dunlap	100		1	56	75	85
Thomas Gamble	100		1	56	75	85
Marley Lineville	80		1	50	75	85
John Matson	150	Gallahar Creek	1	42	75	85
John Manuel	50	Little River	1	14	75	85
John Neel	50		1	42	75	85
Joseph Ranson	50		1	14	75	85
Joseph Smith	150		1	70	75	85
James Seaton	150			42	75	85
Isaac Tate	25	Little River	1	35	75	85
George Wallace	200		1	84	75	85
John Stevens	50		1	42	75	85

For the year 1805

Names	No. of acres	Situation	F.P.	Taxes	P;fee	C.F.
Adam Dunlap	100		1	62½	75	85
John Gibson	100		1	62½	75	85
Samuel McMurry	150		1	46¾	75	85
Wm Regal	25		1	38¼	75	85
Buckanan	50		1	46¾	75	85
Samuel Murry	25		1	07½	75	85
James Beates	60	Little River	1	50	75	85
Edley Murphy	10	Little River	1	03	75	85
John Tarwater	509	Little River	1	46½	75	85
John Likens	250		1	1.04½	75	85
John Waters, J.	20		1	39½	75	85
Benj. McDowell	200	Pistol Creek	1	93½	75	85
James Weir, J.	100		1	62½	75	85
Danl Bowers	50		1	46½	75	85
John Barlow	100		1	62½	75	85
Barnard Cochran	50		1	46½	75	85
John Holoway	60		1	50	75	85
William Hughes	100		1	62½	75	85
Patt Murry	100		1	31½	75	85
Henry Gamble	100		1	62½	75	85
James Anderson	100		1	62½	75	85

Therefore It is considered by Court that the Clerk make out a certificate of the said lands together with the amount of Taxes & charges due thereon and cause the same to be twice published in the Knoxville Gazelle giving notice that the said Tracts of land or so much there of of them respectively as will satisfy the taxes & costs due thereon will be sold as the State in that case made directs.

Court adjourned till court in course.

112.　　At a court of pleas & quarter Sessions began & held for the county of Blount at the court house in Maryville on the fourth Monday of February 1809, present William Davidson, John Tedford & James Houston.

Samuel Cowan Esquire for the   county aforesaid returned our Writ
of Venire to him directed Executed on the following persons (to wit)

1. John Weir Senr.
2. Miles Cunningham
3. James Eddington
4. Samuel McGaughey
5. William peary
6. Jonathan Lassiter
7. John Kennedy
8. James Gillespie
9. Josiah Patty
10. Henry Whitenbarger
11. Joseph Bogle
12. John Williams n
13. Samuel Bogle

14. Andrew Jackson
15. John Gould
16. George Tedford
17. Barcley McGhee
18. John Carson
19. Oliver Alexander
20. Josiah -Parks
21. Samuel Thompson
22. James Gillespie
23. James Beaty
24. Alexander Gamble
25. James Henery
26. William Williamson

27. Isaac Giddions Jr.
28. Step. Wise
29. Peter Hoyle
30 Jacob Frasher
31. Samuel Thompson
32. John Casteel
33. Bennett James
34. Henry Bond.
35. David Edmondson
36. Jonathan Weir
37. Richard Dearmond
38. Thomas Casteel
39. James McCullock
40. Samuel Dickey

113.   Our of whom the following persons were Elected a grand Inquest to
Enquire for the body of the County of Blount County (to wit)

1. Samuel Thompson
2. Alexander Gamble
3. Andrew Jackson
4. John Weir
5. John Casteel

6. Jonathan Weir
7. Bennett James
8. James Beaty
9. Jonathan Lassiter
10. Isaac Giddions

11. Saml. McGaughey
12. John Gault
13. Samuel Dickey
14. David Edmondson
15. James Gillespie

were sworn received their charge & retired to enquire of their presentments.

Traverse Jury.

1. Joseph Bogle
2. John Williams
3. Samuel Bogle
4. James Eddington
5. Richard Dearmond
6. James Henery

7. Thomas Caldwell
8. James McCullock
9. Jacob Trush
10. Joseph Parks
11. Josiah Patty
12. James Gillespie
19. Step. Wise.

13. John Kennedy
14. George Tedford
15. Henery Bond
16. Peter Hoyle
17. B. McGhee
18. Oliver Alexander
20. Samuel Thompson

Ordered by Court that Andrew Bogle & James Gillespie Esqrs be commissioners to settle with Admrs. of Nath. David Estate

114. Wm Walker   )
         vs   ) Ordered by Court that writs of Certiorari & supersidias Issue
Thomas Owens)   dias Issue

The Inventory of the Estate of Ephron Dunlap Decd. returned
to Court & filed and ordered by Court that the same be exposed to sale.

Ordered by court that Administration of the Estate of John B. Davis
be granted to George Colville & having given Bond with Security.

A morgage from Nathl Hewitt to Andrew Thompson was acknowledged in open court by Nathl Hewitt

Ordered by Court that Benj. Costner a Boy of thirteen years of age be bound to Samuel Tucker to learn the Blacksmith Trade.

The last will & Testament of Saml. Glass was proven by John Singleton & James Ewing

The last will & Testament of Robert Leatherdale was proven in open court by John James & James Kelkannon the witnesses to the same.

115. Mary Mountain who entered a protest agt. the will of patrick Murry at last court appeared by her attorney & has the same dismissed
It is therefore ordered that the Same Estate be exposed to Sale agreably to Law.

A Bill of Sale from William Malhattan to Isaac Woods for property therein named was proven in Open Court by William Matthews the witness thereto.

Samuel Blackbourn)
   vs   )
Alexander Moore) William Gray being summoned & sworn as Garnishee in this case deposeth & saigh that he owed Alexander Moore one hundred gallons of whiskey & that he paid seventy & that he also owes said Moore Fourty Gallons of whiskey by contract which he was bound to deliver to said Moore at Indian Creek some in the spring of 1809 & that he has no more of His Estate in possession nor does he Know of any other person that is indebted to said Moore.
Wherefore It is considered by court that the above quality of thirty gallons of whiskey the ballance of one hundred Galls. of whiskey now due be condemned and appropriated to the use of the said Saml Blackbourn and that an order of Sale issue for the same & that the residue of fourty gallons of whiskey due in the Spring be condemned and
116. appropriated to the use of the said Plaintiff and that on order of Sale from the same issue after the first day of May 1809.

Court adjourned till tomorrow Morning 9 Oclock

Tuesday 28th 1809

Court met according to adjournment

Present

Samuel Hendley, Henry Franks & John Waugh Esquires Justices &c.

Jas. Gamble)
  vs   ) Ordered by court that Did Potest De Benne issue to take
Silas George) the Deposition of William Condron in Maryville Thursday next with giving one days Notice to be read on behalf of the Deft. to be taken by John Gardner & Matt Wallace Esqrs

Silas George)
vs)
William Moore)   Ordered by Court that Did pot issue to take the Depo-
                 sition of William Condron in Maryville on thursday next
with giving on days Notice to the Defts to be made on behalf on the
plaintiff to be taken by John Gardiner & Mathew Wallace Esquires

117.   John Flanagan)
        vs)
    James Paul)   In this case it appears that the plaintiff for the sum
                 of fifteen Dollars & 43¾ Cents Debts & costs on which
Execution the plaintiff recover $10.85 cents and that Wm Fagg consta-
bles for the balance of said Execution retußned the same levied on the
land that James Paul now lives on
                 Therefore It is considered by Court that said land or so
much thereof as will satisfy said Debt & Costs be exposed to sale
agreably to Law.

John Wallace)
    vs)
James Paul)   In this case it appears that the plaintiff obtained an
                 Execution vs the Defendant for the sum of twenty one
Dollars & twenty Eight cents Debt & Costs which Execution was returned
by William Fagg Constable levied on the land Paul now lives on.
                 Therefore it is considered by Court that said land or so
much thereof as will satisfy said Debt & Costs be exposed to sale agreably to Law.

John Wallace)
    vs)
James Paul)   In this case it appears that the plaintiff obtained an
                 Execution vs the Defendant for the sum of twenty one Dol-
lars & twenty eight cents Debt & Cost which Execution was returned by
William Fagg Constable levied on the land paul now lives on.
          Wherefore It was considered by court that said land or so much there-
of as will satisfy said Debt & costs be exposed to Sale agreably to Law.

118.   James Fulkner)
        vs)
    William Hay)   In this case it appears that the plaintiff obtained an
                 Execution against the Defendant for the sum of seven
Dollars & Fourty three & three fourth cents Debt & Costs which Exors.
returned to court by William Fagg constable levied on land
                 Therefore It is considered by Court that said land or so
much thereof as will Satisfy said Debt & costs by exposed to sale agreably to Law.

John Trimble)
    vs)
John Rankin)   In this case it appears that Wm Greene was summoned a
                 Witness in this case on behalf of the plaintiff & being
Solemnly called came not but made default.
                 It is therefore considered by Court that he forfeit & pay
unto the said John Trimble the Sum of one hundred & Fourty five Dollars
& his Costs by him in this behalf expended.

119. Buck & Brander)
          vs   )
      John B. Cusack) Ordered by court that Did Pot. issue to any two Justices
                      for this county to take the Deposition of John Craige in
      behalf of the plaintiff withgiving 3 Days notice to the Defendants attor-
      ney.

          A Deed of conveyance from John Thornbury to John Lowby (Mercht.) for
      a lot of land lying in Maryville was acknowledged in open court by said
      Thornbury the subscriber thereto.

      William Cox & Co.)
            vs   )
      Reuben Charles   ) In this case Antin Ryder who was the plaintiffs Bail
                          by commit of parties was returned Andw Thompson
      came into open court and acknowledged himself bound in the final sum of
      Two hundred & fifty Dollars for the prosecutions of said sutt to be paid
      if he doth the Same into effect.

120.   An Assignment from John Benter to John Hess was proven in open
      Court by Mashed Tipton & Daniel Reuble the witnesses thereon.

          A Bill of Sale from Joseph Weir to John Weir for a Negro Boy
      named Tom was proven in open Court by John Montgomery a witness thereto.

          An Assignment from John Benter to Daniel Rinkle was proven in open
      Court by Mashec Tipton & George Snider the Witnesses to the same.

          An Assignment from John Benter to Masheck Tipton was proven in open
      court by Daniel Wrinkle & George Snider the Subscribing witnesses Wit-
      nesses thereto.

      Charles Henry)
            vs   )
      James Holaway) Ordered by Court that Did pot. issue to take the Depo-
      Barnes Hollaway)sition of Michal Cook & John Cook in behalf of the
                      plaintiff with giving 3 Days notice.

          Ordered by court that Andrew Bogle William Murray George Ewing
      Esquires be commissioners to settle with James Upton Executor of the
      Estate of Cornelius Hafley Decd.

          The Settlement of the Estate of Cornelious Hafley returned to
      court & filed.

121.   The last will & Testament of James Hogg was proven in open Court
      by William Edmondson & John Houston the witnesses thereto & Margaret
      Hogg was appointed Executor took an oath well & truly to Execute the
      same.

          Josiah Patty on his Motion is granted him to have his mark recorp
      ded which is a crop an under Bit in the Right Ear and a Slit in the
      left Ear.

          A Deed of conveyance from Thomas York to Isaac Wright was ac-
      knowledged in open court by Said York the Subscriber thereto.

Isaac Little)
   vs   )
James pearce)   Ordered by court that Did pot issue to Washington County
               in this State to take the Deposition of John Little &
James Little in behalf of the plaintiff with giving five days Notice to
be taken at James Littles House.

Isaac Little   )
   vs   )
Robert D. Pearce)   Ordered by court that Did pot issue to Washington
             County in this State to take the Deposition of James
Little & John Little in behalf of the plaintiff with giving five days
notice to be taken at James Littles House.

Court adjourned till tomorrow morning 9 Oclock

122.   Wednesday 1st March 1807

Court Met according to adjournment.

Present

Samuel Hendley, Andrew Bogle, Andrew Cowan, Henry Franks.
Esquires Justices &c.

State   )
   vs   )
Ellis Thomas)   In this case John Murphy was bound in recognizance to
           appear & prosecute the Defendant & being Solemnly called
came not but made default.
           It is therefore considered by court that he forfeit & pay
unto the State of Tennessee the Sum of one hundred Dollars & costs of
the Suit.

Adam Peck   )
  vs   )
John Eddington)   Ordered by Court that Did pot issue to Bledsoe County
           to take the Deposition of Nicholass Spring at his own
house with giving the Defendant fifteen Days Notice.

123. Henry Shields)
     vs   )
John Walker   )   Ordered by Court that Did pot issue to Abingdon in Vir-
           ginia to take the Deposition of John Davis & John Shut-
tle with giving fifteen Days Notice to be taken at James Whites house.

Henry Shields)
    vs   )
Samuel Walker)   Ordered by Court that Did pot issue to Abingdon in Vir-
           ginia to take the Deposition of John Davis & John Shuttle
with giving fifteen days notice to the Defendants atto. to be taken at
James Whites house in Abingdon.

A Deed of conveyance from Thomas pride to John Strain was duly
proven in open Court by James Strain & Robert Strain two of the witnesses
thereto.

124.   xxBxx
           George Rutledge)
                     vs   ) Covt.
           David Vance) In this case the plaintiff failing to give Security
                            Agreably to an order of Court
                    It is therefore ordered by court that the Same be dismissed.

           A Bill of Sale from Andrew Cowan Deputy Sheriff to Saml. Ross was ac-
           knowledged in open court by said Cowan the Subscriber thereto.

           A Bill of Sale from Andrew Cowan Deputy Sheriff to Gafin Black was
           acknowledged in open court land lying on Tennessee River by said Cowan
           the Subscriber thereto.

           The Administration of H. Russell)
                              vs   )
           Moses Keywood   ) In this case James Bell & Thomas Bell
                                 surrendered/who were Special Bail for the Deft.
           came into open court & surered the principal in discharge of themselved
           & Micheal Robertson & Edward Keywood appeared & agread that the Defy.
           would appear & Abide by the Costs & Condemnation or surrender him in dis-
           charge of themselves.

125.   Mary Maxwell)
                     vs   )
           Moses Keywood) In this case John Beaty & George Finley who were Special
                            Bail for the Deft. came into open court & surrendered the
           Deft. in discharge of themselves & Micheal Robertson & Edward Keywood
           & Smallmore Keywood Came agread that the Defendant would pay the costs &
           condemnation or Surrender him in discharge of themselves

                       Court adjourned till tomorrow 9 oclock

126.   Thursday 2nd of March 1809

                       Court Met according to Adjournment

                               Present

           Samuel Handley, Joseph Alexander, Henry Franks & John Waugh Esqrs &c

           George W. Allen)
                     vs   )
           James T. Steel) Ordered by Court that Did pot. issue to take the Depo-
                              sition of Isaac Brooks in behalf of the plft. with
           giving five days notice.

           Ichabot Taylor)
                     vs   )
           William Gay &) On Motion of John Gardiner Esquire Atto for the plft
           John Rogers   ) it appears that he obtained a Judgment of Exec. against
                              the Deft for the sum of twenty Dollars & Ninty three &
           three fourths Cents & Andrew Cowan Deputy Sheriff returned the same
           levied on a tract of land on Elijos Creek
                       It is therefore considered by Court that said Land or so
           much thereof when divided as will satisfy said Judgment & Costs be ex-

posed to sale agreably to Law to satisfy the same & the costs of this motion

McCullock & Poor)
  vs)
William Gay) on Motion of John Gardiner Esquire Atto. for the plft
        It appears that he obtained a Judgment & Exec. against the Defendant for the sum of fourty Six Dollars & 58 Cents Debt & costs except the buying fee & Andrew Cowan Depty Sheriff returned the same levied on the land that said Defendant now lives on.

     It is therefore considered by Court that said land or so much thereof as will satisfy said Execution with costs be exposed to sale agreably to Law to Satisfy the same.

127.

  A Deed of conveyance from Moses Caywood to Mathew Wallace was acknowledged in open Court by Moses Caywood the subscriber thereto wherefore it was ordered by Court that the same be admitted to Registration.

  A Bill of Sale from Andrew Ewing to James Ewing for sundrey articles therein mentioned was duly proven in open court by George Ewing & Jacob Kenney the witnesses thereto.

  The last will & Testament of Moses Caywood was proven in open Court by Richard Kirby one of the subscribing witnesses thereto.

  A Deed of conveyance from David Campbell yo Seml Law for two hundred & fifty five Acres of land was acknowledged in open court by said Campbell the subscriber thereto. Let it be Registered.

Samuel Love)
  vs) Sci. Facias
Robert Hooks) In this case Thomas Clark with the Defendant came into
      open Court & He confesses Judgment agreable to the plaintiffs Declaration & agrees to pay the costs of the original suit & the costs of the Sci. Facias.

128. John Black   )
    vs   ) On motion of Joel Wallace McCampbell Attorney for
Joel Wallace &   ) the plaintiff It appears that the plaintiff ob-
John Lowry Securities) tained a Judgment & Execon. vs. Attorney Pate
         for the sum of Thirty Dollars & Costs
     Leave is granted him to show cause to issue execution against the Deft. overruled & Appeal prayed & granted.

  Ordered by Court that Moses Gamble Junor be released from paying for a pole Tax.

John Balch   )
   vs   )
Joel Wallace & Securi-) Rule to issue Execution vs the Defendants on
ties, John Lowry) motion for an Execution as the law directs over-
         ruled & appeal prayed & granted

129. Alexander McGhee   )
   vs   )
George Sloan & his Securities as constable) In this case it appears on

motion of E. Parsons Attorney for the plft that an Execution issued agt.
George Stephens for the sum of Eight Dollars. which execution went into
the hands of Sloan Constable to collect the same & he failing to pay the
money or return the Execution as the Law directs.

It is therefore considered by Court that the plaintiff recover against the said George Sloan & his securities as Constable the
sum of Eight Dollars & the costs of this motion.

Bennett James)
    vs)
Holbert McClure & Securi-)
ties as Constable) Motion to issue Execution agt. the Defendant & Securities overruled.

130.   Grand Jurors to the Superior Court (to wit)

James Gillespie Senr. Henry McCulley James McNutt Hugh Kelsoe

A Bill of sale from John Woods to John McClelland for a Negro
man named David was proven in open Court by Barcley McGhee a subscribing witness thereto.

Court adjourned till tomorrow Morning 9 Oclock.

Friday Morning 3rd of March, 1809.

Court met according to Adjournment

Present

Saml Hendley, James Gillespie & James Houston Esquires

George W. Allen)
    vs) Ordered by Court that Did pot issue to John Gardiner
James T. Steele) Esquire & John Waugh Esquire to take the Deposition of
                   John Allison with giving one days notice to be taken
in Maryville to be read on behalf of the Defendant.

131.   Wm. Lackey)   )
       vs)   )
John Stephens)Barnard Cochran)
Jnol Waters, George Wallace)
John Gibson, Danl. Bowers,) On motion of John Wilkinson a Rule is
Jno. Neel, Patrick Murry, James) granted thereafter to show cause why
Seaton.) Judg. Should not be rendered agt. them.

Ordered by court that the following persons be admitted as delinquents in paying their Taxes for the year 1808 (to wit)

James Young, James Beard, Samuel Beal, John Murphy, John Keys, James
Mathews, John Mulholland, peter Bowerman Junr. Curtis G. Gray, John G.
Gray, William Robertson, ~~xxxxxxxxxxxxxxxx~~ William White, John Garnor,
Richard Canton, Gabriel Morgin, William Wright, Abraham York, Matthew
Denney, Patrick Fitzgerald, Alburry Wiss, Giles Latcher, George Moore,
Benjamin Steagall & David McClanahan & Richd Williams & that the Sher-
iff be released from payg. the Taxes due on their returns.

Ordered by Court that Susahah Matthews be allowed Forty Dollars

for keeping Sarah Holland Tanay & Mary Tanay until Febry Term 1809 & Ten
Dollars from Feby. to May T., 1809.

132.   Andrew Cowan Deputy Sheriff Collector of Taxes for the county aforesaid reports to court that the Taxes remain unpaid on the following
Tracts of land & Free poles for the year 1808 & that he could not find
any goods or chattles of the owner thereof on which he could destress.

Name	Acres	F. P.	Tax	C	P
Micheal Cook	88	1	83$\frac{3}{4}$	85	1.50
Absolom Little	74	1	76$\frac{1}{4}$	85	1.50
James Paul	281	1	1.66	85	1.50
John Thompson	41	1	52$\frac{1}{4}$	85	1.50
John Dunlap	120	1	95	85	1.50
William Gay	442	1	2.41	85	1.50
Josiah Danforth	60000	1	262.50	85	1.50

It is therefore considered by Court that the following lands or so
much thereof as may be sufficient to satisfy sd Tax & Charges shall be
exposed to Sale agreeable to law.

Ordered by Court that James McClanahan pay to Sally Johnston Twenty
Dollars for the mentainance of a child by the Said James Begotten on the
body of the said Sally & that Execution issue for the same.

133. State   )
      vs   )
Jno. pearce) Ordered by court that the State Witnesses in this case be
            released from attending as witnesses until the Debt be taken.

  State   )
   vs   )
Cornelius Goforth) In this case John Snider was bound Rule for forfeit-
            ure set aside.

  State)
   vs)
Vaughn) In this case Wm Kendrick & Leon Perry who were bound in Recog-
       nisance to appear & give evidence as the Deft. in this case
were Solomnly called came not but made default.
       It is therefore considered by Court that they forfeit their
Recognizance & that Scire Facias issue accordingly not to Issue to Next
Court

134.   Ordered by court that Andrew Thompson Esqr. Coroner be allowed
Four Dollars for an Inquest by him held over the body of Abalin
Burris out of the County Treasury

Ordered by court that Benjamin Erwin be allowed Two Dollars for
serving the Coroner preceipt.

       Court adjourned till tomorrow morning 9 Oclock

       Saturday 4th day of March 1809

Court met according to Adjournment

Present 4 Nov 1804

Samuel Handley John Regan & Robert Thompson Esqr.

Andrew Cowan, Deputy Sheriff for the county of Blount reported the following persons as not making a return of their taxable property agreable to Law.

It is therefore ordered that Samuel McAmmons pay a double tax on one white pole & 250 acres of land & that James Gilmore pay double tax on 1 white pole & one hundred & thirty acres of land & that Jacob Moore pay a double tax on 263 Acres of land.

135.   On motion Agnes Gamble was appointed Guardian to Wm Gamble a Minor orphan & entered into bond with James Houston & James Gillespie security as the law directs.

On motion of Agnes Scot guardian of the orphans of Wm Scott decd. It is ordered by court that the Sheriff summons a Jury of lawful men to xxxxk enquire of the damages the heirs of Wm Scott sustain by the passage of a road through their land lately laid out by the WidowRf Regans this order continued for argument to next court.

Andrew Scot)
     vs   )
Nancy Scot)   In this case the rule entered last court for commissions
                 for testimony was continued.

Robert Gillespie)
     vs   )
John Lowry   )   This day came the parties by their attorneys & thereupon came a Jury (to wit)

1. George McNutt	5. John Duncan	9. Samuel Mitchel
2. John Rankin	6. Steep. Wise	10. Henry Donaho
3. Adam Dinsmore	7. James Benham	11. John Cox
4. Thomas Clark	8. James Henry	12. George Cyle

who being elected tried & sworn the truth to speak on the issue Joined
136.   on their Oaths do say the Defendant did assume in manner & form as the plaintiff in his pleading against him hath alleged and by reason of the non preformance of sd assumpsit they do assess the plaintiffs damage to fifteen dollars besides his costs
     On motion of the Defendants Attorney a rule was entered for a new trial.

Ordered that the Jury tax be the same as last year.

On motion of David Cunningham for liberty to keep a public house in the town of Maryville, it was granted him & he entered into bond with Barcley McGhee & Charles Donaho Security agreeable to law.

Josiah & John Michol)
   vs   )
William Schrimsher) On motion of Enoch Parsons Esqr Attorney for the
         plaintiff It appears that they obtained a Judgment
& Execution against the Defendant for the sum of dollars & cents except
the buying fees.
    It is therefore ordered by Court that the sd land or so much
thereof as will satisfy sd Judgment with the costs be exposed to sale
agreeable to law to satisfy the same.

137.   On the petition of Thomas Hunter It is ordered that that John James
Hugh Weir Junr William Simons Robert Love & Archibald Frew view the road
past sd Hunters Spring & report the same to next court.

   On petition of James Benham ordered that the road that was opened
through his field be closed & that the road go round the same & that
James Irwin Wm Irwin James Duncan David Richey Robert Richey view & mark
the same on a petition of a number of the inhabitants of Blount County
it is ordered that David Dearmond Andrew Roddy John Wheeler Thomas
Coldwell John /Singleton Samuel McCullock Wm Ewing & James Beaty View
a road from the head of Barclets Mill pond where the Knox County Hits
the same until it intersects the Knoxville road in this county

   A power of attorney from John Craige to Barcley McGhee was acknowledged in open court by said Craige the subscriber thereto

    Court adjourned till court in course.

138.   Monday 22nd May Term 1809

   At a court of pleas and quarter Sessions began & held for the
county of Blount at the Court house in Maryville on the fourth Monday
of May 1809.

       Present,

   Samuel Cowan, Esquire Sheriff for the county aforesaid returned
our Writ of Venire to him directed Executed on the following persons
(to wit) Joseph Black Senr, Robert Finley, John F. Garnor, John Gillespie,
Alexander Stewart, Jessee James, John Hannah, Robert Hammel, Thomas Mc-
Clurkin, Mathew Timberman, Samuel Houston, Joseph Steele, Alexander Mc-
Collom, William McClung, Valentine Mayo, James Beaty, George Berry,
John McCauley, Isaac Tate, John McClure, John Stephenson, Andrew Thompson
Samuel Love, David Coldwell, George Dillard, Joseph Hartt, William Gray,
John Gibson, Samuel Dickey, Edward Casteel, Arch Jonston, Joseph Lam-
bert, John Weir, Saml Walker, William Kibble.
   Out of which Venire the following persons were elected a Grand In-
quest to inquire for the County of Blount

1. William McClung	6. Jesse James	11. Alexander McCollom
2. Wm. Gray	7. John Stephensen	12. Saml. Love
3. Oliver Alexander	8. Archer Jonston	13. Robert Hammell
4. James Beaty	9. Joseph Hartt	14. Thomas McClurken
5. Saml. Walker	10. Jno. McClure	15. Jno. Gillespie

22 May 1827

139.   Samuel Findley   )
            vs   )
       Archibald Trimble) This day came the plaintiff & agread to Dismiss
                          this case & Charles Donaho Assumed the clerks costs.
            It is therefore considered by court that the same stand dis-
       missed & that they pay the costs according to the above agreament.

140.   Blank.

141.   Were sworn received their charge & retired to enquire of their pre-
       sentments.

       4   Ordered by court that Jacob Thomas have liberty to Keep a publick
       House in Blount County he having given bond with approved Security.

            A Bill of sale from Charles T. Porter Marshal for East Tennessee
       to John Montgomery (John Lowry & David Lowry for Negroes was proven in
       open Court by James Trimble & John Wilkinson the subscribing witnesses
       thereto
            It was therefore ordered by court that the same be admit-
       ted to Registration.

            A Mortgage from William Walker to John Montgomery for Land & other
       property therein expressed was proven in open court by Saml Law & John
       Gardiner Jr. the witnesses thereto.

            Enoch parsons Esquire Solicitor for the county of Blount came into
       open court & resigned his appointment& John Wilkinson was duly & consti-
       tutionally elected to fill said vacancy.

            The last will & Testament of Nathanial Morrison Decd. was proven
       in open court by William Griffitts & Terrence Conner, the witnesses
       thereto & Thomas Jones & Wm. Griffitts the Exors. herein appointed Ap-
       pered & were qualified.

142.   An Additional Inventory of the Estate of Ephrium Dunlap & a sale
       of the property returned at last court was returned to court & filed.

            Samuel Houston & William Long were by the court appointed Guar-
       dians to Elisa Young, Jefferson Young & Rebecka Young minors & infants
       of Andrew Young Decd. who entered into bond with John Licans & John Wil-
       kinson his Securities.

            Ordered by court that Anne Wheeler daughter of Elizabeth Wheeler
       be allowed fife Dollars out of the poor Tax to be under the directionof
       Francis Jones.

            Ordered by court that Cornelius Alexander be released from paying
       for a Black poll returned in the name of Jean Alexander.

       Charles Henry   )
            vs   )
       James Holloway &) Ordered by court that Did pot issue to Alexander &
       Barnes Holloway) John Reagen Esquires to take the Deposition of Joseph

Holloway to be read in behalf of the Defendants with giving one days notice

Ordered by court that William Fagg Constable be allowed to make an alteration on an execution by him returned to court in the name of John Henderson vs James paul as to his own fees.

143. Josiah Bowman   )
            vs   )
      William Condron William   )   In this case on motion of John Gardiner
      Stuart John Trimble Reuben)   Esquire Attorney for the plaintiff obtained
      Charles & James Creswell   )   an Execution against the Defendants for
                                         the sum of Forty Nine Dollars Ninty eight
& three fourth cents on which Execution Benjamin Erwin constable returned received $6.05 & for the balance levyed on a tract of land on Nine Mile Creek whereon John Trimble now lives.
            It is therefore considered by Court that said land of so much thereof as will satisfy the balance of said Debt & costs be exposed to sale agreably to law.

Court adjourned till tomorrow morning 9 Oclock

Tuesday morning 23 May 1807

Court met according to adjournment

Present

Samuel Hendley, George Ewing & James Gillespie Esquires & c.

Ichabod Taylor)
        vs   )   Ven Exponas
William Gay   )   In this case on Motion of John Gardiner Esquire a
                      Rule is granted the Defendant to show cause to quash
the Execution which when argued was quashed.

A Mortgage from Samuel McGaughey to Samuel Law for the land said McGaughey now lives on was proven in open court by Polaskey Wallace & John Gardiner Junior the witnesses thereto

144.   Ordered by court that William Gaylt William Lowry, John Waugh & John Gardiner Esquires be commissioners to settle with Robert young Admor of Andrew Young Decd.

A plat & certificate of survey from John McKnight to John Montgomery for a tract of land lying on the waters of L. River was acknowledged in open Court by said McKnight the subscriber thereto.

Ordered by court that the personal Estate of Andrew Young Decd. be exposed to sale agreably to law.

Henry Shields)
        vs   )
John Walker)   In this case it appears Thomas Snoddy & James Ewing were
                     summoned witnesses in behalf of the plaintiff & they
being solemnly called came not but made default.

It is therefore considered by court that they forfeit according to an act of assembly in this case made & provided but they now appearing in time for the plft to be advantaged of their testimony It was ordered by court that forfeiture be set aside on payment of costs.

Court adjourned for one hour

Court met according to adjournment

Present

John Tedford, William Murry, & Stephen Stafford Esquires.

Ordered by court that Mxhxx Mashac Tipton have liberty to return his taxable polls & property for tye year 1809, which is one white pole & 207 acres of land.

145.   A Deed of conveyance to James Martin to James Henery for 291 acres of land was acknowledged in open court by said Martin Wherefore It is ordered by court that the same be entitled to Registration.

The last will & Testament of Moses Gamble was produced in open court & proven by Wilson White John White & Thomas Hood the witnesses thereto & John Gamble & Samuel Henry their Executors therein named appeared & were qualified well & truly to execute the same.

Court adjourned till tomorrow morning 9 Oclock.

Court met according to Adjournment

Present   24 May 1809

John Tedford William Murry & Stephen Stafford Esquires Justices &c.

The Inventory of the Estate of George B. Davis returned to court & filed.

A power of Attorney from Josiah Bowerman to James Houston was proven in open court by John Montgomery & John Gardiner the witnesses thereto.

Reuben Charles)
  vs)
Jno. Wallace) Ordered by court that if the plft does not give se-
      curity agreable to the rules of this court that his
coveat be dismissed.

Ditto)
 vs) Ditto
William Wallace)

Ditto)
 vs } Ditto
Wm. Condron)

146. Reuben Charles)
         vs   )
     Mathews Heirs)   Ordered by court that if the plft. does not give securi-
                         ty agreably to an order of this court that his coveat
     be dismissed,

         Ordered by court John McCampbell Esquire be fined five dollars for
     a contempt shown to court yesterday.

     James Heard for the use of)
     John Keys   )
               vs   )   This day came the parties by their attor-
     John Russell   )   nies and thereupon came a Jury (to wit)

     1. George Berry   5. Robert McGill   9. Samuel Henry
     2. Isaac Tate   6. John McCartney   10. Nicholass Earhartt
     3. John Weir   7. John Wilson   11. Jesse Ray
     4. David Coldwell   8. Alexander Harris   12. Samuel McConnald

     who being elected tried & sworn well & truly to enquire of damages in
     this case Do say they assess the plaintiff damages to Forty Six Dol-
     lars & Twenty Six cents besides costs.
                 It is therefore considered by Court that the plaintiff re-
     cover of the Defendant his damages aforesaid as by the Jury aforesaid
     assessed & also his costs by him in this behalf expended & the said
     Defendant is in Mercy & c.

     Adam Peck   )
          vs   )
     John Eddington)   Ordered by court that Did pot. issue to take the
                         Deposition of Nicholass Spring in Bledsow County
     at his own house with giving the Defendant fifteen days notice,

147. Adam Peck   )
          vs   )
     Richd. Kirby)   Ordered by court that Did pot. issue to take the Depot. of
                         Nicholas Spring at his own house in Bledsoe Cty. with
     giving the Defendant fifteen days notice.

     Samuel Blackbourn)
          vs   )
     Alexander Moore)   James Montgomery being summoned a Garnashee in this
                            case & being duly sworn Deposeth & said he does not
     owe the Defendant any thing neither did he at the time of being summoned
     nor hath he neither had he at the time of being summoned any of the Ef-
     fects of the said Defendant in his possession but he further states
     that the Defendant gave him an order to Burtin pride for two Dollars &
     sayd he understood pride assumed to pay the same in trade but further
     he knoweth not.

     Love & Luttrell)
          vs   )
     John Russell   )   The same Jury that delivered a verdict in the case
                          Heard for Keys against John Russell After being sworn
     & the plfts not being ready for trial it is ordered by court that a
     non suit be entered.

Rule to set aside the non suit

148. Love & Luttrell)
          vs   )
John Russell   ) The same Jury that that served in the last case After
being sworn Do say the Defendant was not an Infant under the age of twenty one years at the time of signing & sealing the Instrument of writing declared on as the Defendant in pleading hath alledged & they assess the plaintiff damages by occasion of the detention of that debt. to Seventeen Dollars 49¾ cents besides costs.

      It is therefore considered by court that the plaintiff recover against the Defendant aforesaid his debt in the Declaration mentioned also his damages aforesaid as by the Jury aforesaid Assessed also his costs by him by him in his behalf expended.

      Court adjourned till tomorrow morning 9 Oclock

      Thursday 23 May 1807

      Court met according to Adjournment

          Present

    William Davidson, Andrew Bogle, James Houston & Stephen Stafford Esquires Justices &c.

    Ordered by court that the Sheriff be allowed 70$ for his exoficia services for the year 1808.

    Ordered by court that the Clerk be allowed $60 for his exoficia service for the year 1808.

    Ordered by court that the County Solicitor be allowed $12.50 Each Session until this court make another in this case

4   A Bill of Sale from John Lowry & John Waugh to Andrew Cowan was acknowledged in open court by said Lowry & Waugh the subscribers thereto

149. John McCartney)
          vs   ) T. A. B.
Greenbury Edwards) This day came the parties by Attornies and thereupon came a Jury (to wit.)

1. David Cook	5. David Coldwell	9. Danl. Rinkle
2. Saml. McConnald	6. Alexander Stewart	10. Isaac Tate
3. Thomas Henderson	7. John Weir	11. John Hanna
4. Jonathan Tipton	8. John McCulley	12. Samuel Houston

who being elected tried & sworn the truth to speak upon the issue Joined upon their Oaths Do say the Defendant is guilty of the Trespass Assault & Batterh in manner & form as charged in the plaintiffs Declaration & not Justifiable in any manner as in pleading he hath alleged & they assess the plaintiff by occasion thereof to Two dollars Costs.

      It is therefore considered by court that the plaintiff recover against the Defendant his damages aforesaid as by the Jury assessed also his Costs by him in this behalf expended & the said Defendant is in Mercy & c.

Ordered by court thatAndrew Bogle, William Gault & Samuel Love be Judges at our next Election for State offices &c.

150.   Ordered by court that William Fagg & Robert Murrin be constables to attend our next court of pleas & c on thefourth Monday of August next

Justices Present

William Davidson, William Gault, & James Gillespie, Esquires &c.

Robert Cammron)
    vs
John Keys   ) This day came the parties by their Attos. & thereupon came a Jury (to wit)

1. Thomas Wallace	5. Patrick Culton	9. Edward Sharp
2. Robert McGill	6. James Logan	10. David Thompson
3. Charles Kirkpatrick	7. John Kennedy	11. Daniel Bowers
4. Isom Blankenship	8. JohnWilson	12. George Berry

who being elected & sworn Do say the Defendant hath not Kept & preformed his covenant but hath broken the same in manner & form as the plaintiff against him hath declared & they assess the plaintiffs damages by occasion of the non preformance of that covenant to one hundred & thirty seven Dollars & 40 Cents besides costs.
      It is therefore considered by Court that the plaintiff recover against the Defendant aforesaid his damages aforesaid as by the Jury aforesaid assessed also his costs by him in this behalf expended & the Defendant may be taken &c.

Grand Jury dismissed

151. Robert Bailey   )
          vs   ) -
Martha Martin Admr &) This day came the parties by their attor. &
Warner Martin Dect.   ) thereupon came the same Jury that delivered in
                        the case McCampbell to Greenberry Edwards being sworn &c. do say after having retired some time that they cannot agree
      It is therefore ordered by court with the consent of the counsil on each side that they make a miss trial.

Ditto)
  vs)
Ditto) In this case Leon perry having been summoned a Witness on behalf of the plaintiff & being solemnly called came not but made default.
      It is therefore ordered by court that he forfeit accordingly to the act of assembly in this case made & provided & that Scire Facias issue accordingly.

Court adjourned till tomorrow morning 9 Oclock

Friday Morning court met according to adjournment

Present

William Lowry, John Waugh, William Gault, Esquires, &c

Ordered by court that Danel Best have liberty to erect a Mill on his own land on Nine Mile creek.

152. Ordered by court that the personal Estate of George B. Davis be exposed to sale agreably to Law.

Court adjourned till 1 Oclock P.M.

Court met according to adjournment

Present

William Lowry, James Houston & Robert Boyd, Esqr.

State
  vs
Andrew Ferguson)   In this case the Defendant together with Micheal Cook, his security for his appearance at this court to answer to a charge of the State for committing Basterdy being solomnly called came not but made default.

It is therefore considered by court that they forfeit their Recognizance Aforesaid & that Scire Facias issue accordingly.

Ordered by court that James Giddions of Tuckalecha have liberty to make return of his Taxable polls & property for the present year which is one white poll and Sixty acres of lane.

It appears by a commission forwarded by Robert Houston Secretary of State that John Walker has been commissioned a Justice of the peace for the county of Blount & the said Walker took an oath well & truly to execute said commission in open court.

153. The Sale of the Estate of John Hess Decd. returned to Court & filed.

Samuel Gould)
  vs
Peter Hoyle) Ordered by Court that Did pot. issue to take the Deposition of John Jackson with giving five days notice to the Defendant.

154. It appears that Jacob Moore has not made a return of his land for the year 1808 & the Sheriff made a return thereof and of course was liable to a double Tax
It is therefore ordered by court that said double taxibls be remitted with the payment of costs.

Court adjourned till tomorrow morning 9 oclock

154. Saturday 27th May Term, 1809

Saturday Morning court met according to adjournment.

Present

William Lowry, James Gillespie, John Waugh, Esquires.

John Jackson)
    vs)
William Steward)   On motion of Gardiner Atto. for the plaintiff It appears
                that the plaintiff obtained an Execution before John
Waugh Esquire for the sum of $38.34½ which Execution was returned No goods
nor chattles to be found levied on land on land on Nine Mile Creek whereon John Trimble now lives .
            It is therefore considered by Court that said land or so
much thereof as will satisfy said Execution & costs & the costs of this
motion be exposed to sale agreably to Law.

State   )
    vs   )   Basterdy
William Walker)   On motion of the Solicitor of this county in this case
                It is ordered by court that William Walker pay into
the hands of Peter Bowerman for the use of a Bastard child bond of the
body of Mary Bowerman Six Dollars every quarter of year for the time of
two years next ensuing.

       A Bill of sale from Samuel Cowan Sheriff of Blount County to David
Russell for a tract of land was acknowledged in open Court by said Cowan
the Subscriber

155.   A Deed of conveyance from Joseph Colville high Sheriff to Samuel &
Robert Walker Jr. the witnesses thereto

Andrew Scott)
    vs   )
Nancy Scott)   Ordered by court that Did pot. issue to Virginia to take
                the deposition of Joseph Cowan & James Nelson with giving
20 days notice to the Defendant.

RobertHanna)
    vs   )
Lowrys Heirs)   Ordered by court that Did Pot issue to Virginia to take
                the Deposition of Reuben Bradley & George Woods with
giving 10 days notice to the plaintiffs attorney to be read in behalf
of the Defendant.

       Ordered by court that David Coldwell be released from paying for
a black poll as this appears to Law been one more on the last ~~shdxxdxxx~~
than he returned.

Elizabeth Steele)
    vs   )
Andrew James   )   In this case the Defendant being solemnly called came
                not but made default
           It is therefore considered by court that Judgment by default
go against him.

       William Wallace return of Taxables for the present year one white
poll one Black & two hundred & Seventy Acres of land.

156.   Ordered by court that Josiah Danforth have liberty to Keep an or-

dinary at his own house in Maryville he having given bond with approved security as the law directs.

Ordered by court that the following places be exposed to sale a-greanly to Law to satisfy the Taxes & costs due for the year 1804-1805, James Beards place, Samuel Cowans, Thomas Coker, James Curry, Robert Donelson, Thomas Davis, Adam Dunlap, Thomas Gamble, John Neel, Joseph Smith, James Seaton, George Wallace, Jno. Stephens, Adam Dunlap, John Gibson, Samuel McMurry, William Riggill, ------- Richardson, Samuel Murry, James Beates, Eddy Murphy, John Tarwater, John Likins, Benjamin McDowell, James Weir, Jr. John Barlow, William Hughs, Henery Yandle & J James Anderson.

Daniel McCallister)
      vs   )   Debt.
James W. Lackey)   This day came the plaintiff by Attorney & filed
                        their Declaration & the Defendant being solomnly
called came not but made default

      It is therefore considered by Court that Judgment by default go against the Defendant & he is in Mercy &c. The plaintiff stays Execution 3 months.

David Robertson)
      vs   )   Debt
James W. Lackey)   This day came the plaintiff by his attorney & filed
                        his declaration & the Defendant being solomnly called
came not but made default.

      It is therefore ordered by court that Judgment by default go against the Defendant the plaintiff stays Execution 3 months

157.   At a court of pleas & quarter Sessions begun & held for the County of Blount at the Court house in Maryville on the fourth Monday of August, 1809.

Present

William Lowry, John Tedford, James Houston, Samuel George Esquires Justices &c.

Samuel Cowan Esquire Sheriff of the County Aforesaid returned our writ of Venire to him directed Executed on the following persons (to wit)

1. Oliver Alexander	13. William L. Taylor	25. James McNutt
2. Henry Snider	14. Wm. Peary	26. John Coldwell
3. John Woods	15. Jonathan Lassiter	27. Robert Sterling
4. John Carson	16. Arthur Greene	28. Jonathan Weir
5. William Morrison	17. David Eagleton	29. John Duncan
6. Robert Ferguson	18. James Adams	30. Joseph Bogle
7. Robert Wilson	19. Samuel Thompson	31. Robert McClure
8. Henry Dunlap	20. Mathew Samples	32. Samuel Henry
9. Joseph Henderson	21. Moses Hughes	33. James Reagan
10. George Mizer	22. Thomas Cartwright	34. William Wallace
11. John Gault	23. John Washam	35. John Walker
12. David Vance	24. James Gillespie	36. Thos. Wallace

158.   Monday 28th August Term, 1809

The Sale of the Estate of George B. David returned to Court & filed

Out of wich venire the following persons were elected a Grand Inquest to enquire for the county of Blouht aforesaid to wit

1. David Eagleton	6. Joseph Bogle	11. Wm. L. Taylor
2. Thomas Campbell	7. Moses Hughs	12. Joseph Henderson
3. Robert Ferguson	8. Thos. Wallace	13. Oliver Alexander
4. Henery Sanders	9. John Gault	14. Henry Dunlap
5. James Reagan	10. Henery Creswell	15. George Mizer

who being sworn & charged retired to enquire of their presentments

Andrew Cowan Deputy Sheriff returned our summons for constables executed on William Fagg & Robert Murrin to Attend on this Court.

Traverse Jury

John Washam	Jonathan Weir
Robert McTeer	Wm. Peary
James McNutt	Samuel Thompson
Thomas Cartright	Jonathan Lassiter
John Duncan	David Vance
John Woods	James Gillespie
Robert Wilson	Mathew Samples
John Wallace	Saml Henry
Jno. Coldwell	Richard Ramsey
Arthur Greene	

A Bill of sale from Samuel Cowan Sheriff of the County of Blount to James Wilson & John Nicol was acknowledged in open court by said Cowan the subscriber thereto
Wherefore It is ordered by Court that the same be admitted to Registration & the clerks protest

A Bill of sale from Samuel Cowan Sheriff of the County of Blount to David Walker was acknowledged in open court by said Cowan the subscriber thereto wherefore
It is ordered that the same be admitted to the protest of Registration.

Samuel Love   )
vs   )
Samuel McCullock)   Ordered by court that procedendo issue to the Justice
in the case to proceed to the Execution of his Judg.

Samuel Love   )
vs   )
Saml. McCullock)   Ordered by court that a procedendo Issue to the Justice who rendered the Judgment in this case to proceed to the Execution of his Judgment.

~~Samuel Dix Cowan~~

Samuel D. Cowan)
     vs   )
David Campbell)   Ordered by court that a proceedendo issue to the Justice who rendered the Judgment in this case to proceed in the Execution of his Judgment.

160.   A Deed of conveyance from David Love to John Cox was acknowledged in open court by said Love the subscriber thereto wherefore
        It is ordered by court that the same be entitled to the Clerks probet & Registration

    A Bill of Sale from Samuel McCullock to Thomas McCullock & Alexander McCullock for land & other property was proven in open court by John Wilkinson & John Lowry the witnesses thereto.
        It is therefore to be registered.

Isaac Brooks)
     vs   )
William Baker)   Ordered by court that writs of certiorari & supersedias issue in this case

    A Power of Attorney from Elizabeth Stock to Henery Toops was acknowledged in open Court by said Stock the subscriber thereto wherefore
        It is ordered by court that the same be admitted to Registration.

    A Power of Attorney from Elizabeth Hafely to Henry Toops was acknowledged in open court by said Hafley the subscriber thereto.
        It is therefore ordered by court that the same be admitted to Registration.

161.   A Bill of sale from John Byrd to John Rankin for a tract of land on Holston River was proven in open court by William Gillespie a witness thereto.
        It is therefore ordered by court that the same be admitted to Registration & Wm Gillespy being further Sworn to make true answer to such questions as the court may ask him in the matter before them, Saith that Joseph Young who is the other witness to said Instrument of writing resides out of the limits of this State so that the same cannot be entitled to his probate.

    A bill of Sale from Joseph Black David Craige & Alexander Kelly commissioners was to Jacob Danforth
        Wherefore It is ordered by Court that the same be admitted to Registration.

    Joseph Hartt was by court appointed Guardian to Jane L. Warren & others Minors & Infants of Mich Warrin & he entered into Bond with David Eagleton & Saml. McGaughey his Securities.

162.   A Bill of Sale from John Craige to Jacob Danforth for the land Joining Maryville was proven in open court by John Wilkinson & Josiah Danforth the Witnesses thereto

Danforth the witnesses thereto
        Wherefore It is ordered by court that the same be admitted
to Registration.

        A Deed of conveyance from Abner Vaugh & Theodocia Vaughn his wife
to William Hodge was proven in open court by John Eddington & Harrison
Brady the Subscribing witness thereto for a tract of land in Holison
County Virginia
        Wherefore It is therefore ordered by court that the same
be admitted to Registration.

        Ordered by court that Jerimiah Brook he allowed Eight Dollars in
Addition to what he has here tofore received for Keeping George Fox.

        Ordered by Court that Wm. Blackbourn be allowed five Dollars for
Keeping an orphan child until next court of the name of Elizabeth Clem-
ants.

        A Deed of Conveyance from Mary & Jenny Chamberlain to Hanna & Ni-
man Chamberlain for land in Granger County was acknowledged in open
Court by said Mary & Jenny the Subscribing witnesses thereto
        It is therefore ordered by Court that the same be admit-
ted to Registration.

163.   A Deed of conveyance from John Hackett to John Wilson for a Tract
of land of Two hundred & fifty Acres was proven in open court by John
Wilson & James Gardiner the witnesses thereto
        Wherefore It is ordered by court that the same be admitted
to Registration.

Archibald Trimble)
        vs   ) Fi. Fa.
Samuel Findley   ) on motion of John Lowry Atto. for the Defendant a
                        Rule is granted him to shew cause why the Execu-
tion Should be quashed.

        A Bill of Sale from John Jackson to Peter Hoyle for land on the
waters of Nine Mila Creek was proven in open court by Samuel Norwood the
witness thereto thxx to the same It is ordered to be Registered.

        Wm. Floyd, having given bond with approved Security leave is
granted him to keep an ordinary in Maryville.

164.   Josiah Danforth)
          vs   ) Atto.
        John Craige   ) In this Samuel Cowan Sheriff of the County of Blount
                        Returned no property to be found summoned Samuel
Findley vs Garnishee & the said Findley appearing in open court & after
being duly Sworn deposeth & Saith that he is indebted to the John Craige
the sum of Two hundred & Ninety Eight Dollars 98 cents to be paid in the
fall September 18010 Horses & 200$ in horses to be paid in September
18011 which sum remain due & the Said John Craige after making a deduc-
tion for Seventy Acres of land as there wanted that quantity to make up
the amount sold by the said John to the Said Samuel & 16$ of an account
owed by the said John to the said Samuel and he further saith that George

Coope is indebted to him Sixty Gallons of whiskey to be paid in March next besides some the quantity he does not Know which he believes now due & further Saith that It is therefore ordered by court that the property due the aforesaid Jno. Craigs remain in the hands it now is in subject to the plaintiffs demand when established According to law and it is further ordered that all proceedings in this case be Staid according to act of Assembly for Six Months.

165.   Tuesday 28th August Term 1809

            Court Met according to Adjournment

                    Present

    William Lowry Mathew Wallace & John Waugh Esquires Justices &c.

    A Bill of Sale from William Bones to John Montgomery was proven in open court by John Drew & James Berry for a tract of land on the waters of Pistol Creek
            Wherefore It is ordered by court that the same be admitted to Registration.

    A Deed of conveyance from Joseph Date to Samuel Saffle for land lying on Lackeys Creek was proven in open court by Henry Whitenbarger & William K. Roginson the witnesses thereto
            It is therefore ordered by Court that the same be admitted to Registration.

xxxx   William Cox &c.)
              vs   )
       James Hall   )   The Defendant acknowledged the plaintiffs action &
                           confesses Judgment for two hundred & Twenty Dollars
       & the plaintiff Stays Execution three months.

166.   John Grine   )
              vs   )
       William Wallace)   This day came the parties by their attornies and
                          thereupon came a Jury (to wit)

    1. John Washam   5. Robert Wilson   9. Jonathan Weir
    2. Robert McTear   6. John Walker   10. David Vance
    3. John Duncan   7. John Coldwell   11. William Peary
    4. John Woods   8. Arthur Greene   12. Mathew Samples

who being elected tried & sworn well & truly to try this matter of controversy upon their Oaths do say they find for the plaintiff and assess his damages his damages to Twenty one Dollars 58 2/3 cents & the Defendant by atte comes & files his reasons in arrest of Judgment which after being solemnly argued by the Council on both sides and Mature deliberation being had by the court
            It is ordered by the Court that Judgment be arrested in this Case from the Verdict aforesaid & that the Defendant go without day and recover against the plaintiff aforesaid his costs by him in this behalf expended &c.

William Walker was by Court appointed constable having given bond with Security & taken the Oath of office.

167. Josiah & John Nichol)
           vs   )
     Thomas McGuire   )   In this case on motion of E. Parsons Esquire It
                              appears the plaintiff obtained Execution before
John Gardiner Esquire for the sum of Twenty Eight Dollars six three
fourth Cents on which Execution Charles Donahoo constable Returned
received $5. & no more goods no chattles to be found leveyed on the land
whereon McGuire lives
               It is therefore considered by court that said land or so
much thereof as will Satisfy the Same be exposed to Sale agreably to Law

               A Bill of Sale from James Carr & Henry Airhart to Andrew Miller for
land was proven in open court by Hugh Kelsoe & the said Hugh being further Sworn to make true answers to such questions as the Court may now
ask him relative to the other Wientsses to this Instrument & Saith
that Patrick -------? who is the other witness is out of the State so
that the same cannot be entitled to his probet wherefore
               It is ordered by court that the Same be entitled to Regis-
tration.

168. Armistead Blevins)
           vs   ) Certr.
     John Keys   ) This day came the parties by their Attornies &
                            thereupon came a Jury to wit

1. George McNutt   5. Samuel Henery   9. Hugh Weir
2. Micheal Bowerman   6. Richard Ramsey   10. Josiah Patty
3. James McNutt   7. James Hall   11. John Eddington
4. James Gillespie   8. Thomas McCullock   12. John B. Cusack

who being elected tried & sworn to try the matter of controversy Do
say they find for the Defendant
               It is therefore considered by Court that the Defendant go
without day and recover against the plaintiff his costs by him in
this behalf expended in his defence &c.

               The last will & Testament of Joseph Weir was proven in open court
by John Montgomery & John Weir the subscribing witnesses thereto.

               Samuel Hendley Esquire presiding Justice of this Court came into
open Court & resigned his appointment
               Whereupon It is ordered by Court that there be an elec-
tion on Friday the 1st day of September 1809 to fillsaid vacancy.

169. Baker & Russell   )
           vs   )
     Josiah Gamble &   ) Debt
     William Donnelson) This day came the Deft. Josiah Gamble & Confesses
                              Judgment for fifty eight Dollars & Ninty two cents.
               It is therefore considered by court that the plaintiff re-
cover against the Defendant aforesaid his costs by him in this behalf
expended as well as the sum aforesaid as by the Defendant aforesaid con-

fessed.

Justices present, Wm Lowry, Andrew Bogle & Wm. Gillespie

Robert Baily)
vs)
Martha Martin, Admr) Case
of Warner Martin) This day came the parties by their attornies &
thereupon came a Jury (to wit) the same Jury that
Served in the case Greene vs Wallace except Alexander Harris in lieu of
Robert McTear who being elected tried & sworn Do say they But the Jury
aforesaid from rendering their verdict and retired until tomorrow.
respited

170.   A Deed of conveyance from SamuelLove to John Montgomery for Five
Hundred & Fifty five Acres of land on the waters of pistol creek was
acknowledged in open court by said Love the subscriber thereto Let it
be registered.

Isaac Wright)
vs)
Nathanial Hewett) This day came the parties & the Defendant confesses
Judgment for Sixty Dollars & costs & the plaintiff
agrees to stay Execution for the principal until further orders.
It is therefore considered by Court that the plaintiff recover against the Deft. his sum of Sixty Dollars as by the Defendant
confessed also his costs by him in this behalf expended & the Said defendant is in Mercy &c.

171.   Wednesday 30th August T. 1809

Wednesday Morning Court met according to Adjournment

Present

William Davidson, Andrew Bogle & William Gillespie

Samuel Love)
vs)
Samuel McCullock) On motion of E. Parsons Attorney for the plft it
appears the plft obtained an Execution against the
Defendant for the sum of Eleven Dollars & Twenty Seven & one fourth
cents which Execution was returned to Court Leveyed on the land whereon Samuel McCullock lives.
It is therefore considered by court that the said land or
se much thereof as will be of value sufficient to satisfy said Debt &
costs be exposed to sale agreably to Law togather with the costs of
his order.

Love & Luttrell)
vs)
John Russell) In this case at last court there was a non suit entered It is therefore ordered by court that the same
be set aside.

William Bryant)
vs)
James McClanahan) Ordered by court that commission de bene ipse issue

to Wm. Davidson & John Walker Esquires to take the Deposition of Stephen Stafford in behalf of the plft with giving him five days notice.

172.   Samuel Love   )
              vs   )
       Samuel McCullock)   On motion of E. Parsons Esquire Attorney for the
                            plaintiff recovered a Judg. and Execution against
the Defendant for the sum of Fifty Two dollars thirty five and one fourth cents Debt & costs which Execution was returned by Charles Donahol to court Leveyed on the land where Samuel McCullock lives
            It is therefore considered by Court that said land or so much thereof as will satisfy the said Debt & costs together with the costs of this order be exposed to sale agreably to Law.

            Ordered by Court that Samuel Thurman be bound to Henry Snider.

            A Bill of Sale from Ebinezer Jones to Joseph Duncan for a Tract of land on McCulleys Creek of Two hundred & Seventeen Acres was acknowldeged in open court by Said Jones the Subscriber
            It is therefore ordered that the same be admitted to Registration.

       Bailey)
           vs)
       Martin)   The Jury aforesaid who were respited untill this day do say
                  they have not time to mature this case properly on this day they therefore pray a respute untill tomorrow and with the assent of the Counsil on both sides to them It was granted.

173.   Court adjourned till tomorrow 9 Oclock

              Thursday Morning 31st August 1809

              Court met according to Adjournment

                    Present

            An Inventory of the Estate of Moses Gamble Decd. returned to Court & Filed & an order of Sale was granted.

       R. Bailey)
            vs   )
       Martin   )   The Jury aforesaid as reputed aforesaid from rendering
                     their verdict until this day appeared & Say that Warnor Martin the former defendant did assume upon himself in Manner & form as charged in the plaintiffs declaration & they assess the plaintiffs damages by occasion of the non preformance of that Assumpsit to $150.98 Cents & costs the Defendant by Atto. enters a Rule for a new trial.

174.   Solomon McCampbell)
              vs   ) Case
       John McCartney   ) Assumpset This day came the parties by their At-
                           tornies & thereuponcame a Jury (to wit.)

       1. James McNutt   5. Benja. Harbet   9. Saml. Montgomery
       2. William Davis   6. William Scott   10. Abraham Phillips

3. Robert McTear	7. Richard Ramsey	11. John Brickey
4. James Gillespie	8. Robert McGill	12. James Smith

who being elected tried & Sworn Do say the Defendant did assume upon himself in Manner & form as charged in the plaintiffs Declaration & they further find the Defendant made no accord as in pleading he hath alledged & they assess the plaintiff damages by occasion of the non performance of that Assumpsit to $161.73 cents & Costs Rule for new trial.

175.
　　　Edward Lynch)
　　　　　vs　　　)
　　　Barcley McGhee) This day came the parties by their attornies & thereupon came a Jury (to wit)

1. John Warshaw	5. Robert Wilson	9. Jonathan Weir
2. Samuel Henry	6. John Walker	10. David Vance
3. John Duncan	7. John Coldwell	11. William Peary
4. John Woods	8. Arthur Greer	12. Mathew Samples

who being sworn & tried do say the Defendant did assume in manner & form as charged in the plaintiffs Declaration and they assess the plaintiffs Damages by occasion of the non preformance of that assumption to $187.8½ Cents & costs.
　　　　　Therefore It is considered by court that the plaintiff recover against the Defendant aforesaid his damages aforesaid as by the Jury aforesaid assessed also his costs by him in this behalf expended &c. & the Defendant prays an appeal to the Superior Court of Hamilton District & to him it was granted.

176.
　　　A Bill of Sale from Rebecka Reed & James C. Reed for land on Little River was acknowledged in open Court by Rebecka Reed a Subscriber thereto.
　　　　　It is therefore ordered to be Registered.

　　　A Bill of Sale from William Maclin to John Montgomery for a Negro Boy named Lewis was acknowledged in open Court by said Macklin the Subscriber.
　　　　　Wherefore It is ordered to be admitted to registration.

Samuel Love)
　　　vs　　)　Debt.
John Sherrell) This day came the attornies & thereupon came a Jury
　　　　　　(to wit)

1. James McNutt	5. John Brickey	9. Edward Sharp
2. Robert McTear	6. Benja Harbet	10. James Gilmore
3. James Gillespie	7. David Coldwell	11. William Martin
4. Richard Ramsey	8. John Findley	12. John Nichol

who being elected & sworn Do say the Defendant hath not paid the Debt in the Declaration mentioned except the sum of five Dollars as in pleading he hath alledged & they assess the plaintiff damages by occasion of the detention thereof to $75.70 Cents & Costs.

177. Samuel Love)
     vs   )   Debt
John Sharp)   This day came the parties by their attornies & there-
                upon came a Jury to wit

      The same Jury as in the case Love vs Sherrell Do say the Defendant hath not paid the Debt in the Declaration as in pleading he hath De- clared and they assess the plaintiffs damages by occasion of the de- tention of that Debt to $10.23½ cents & the Defendant by Atto. entered a Rule for a new trial
      Rule dismissed by plaintiff
          It is therefore considered by court that the plaintiff re- cover against the Defendant aforesaid his Debt & damages aforesaid & the Defendant is in Mercy &c.

      Ordered by court that the Sheriff be released from paying into the Treasury the Tax due on Seven Thousand Acres of land returned by Josiah Danforth for the year 1808 as it would not sell for the same nor any part thereof.

           Court adjourned till tomorrow morning 9 Oclock

178.   Friday 1st Day of September 1809

          Court met according to Adjournment

              Present

    John Tedford, Mathew Wallace & James Gillespie Esquires Justices

Samuel Love, Assinee)
     vs   )   Debt
Reuben Charles   )   This day came the plaintiff by his Attorney & filed his declaration and the Defendant being Solmnely called came not but made default.
          It is therefore considered by court that the plaintiff recover against the Defendant Aforesaid his Debt in the Declaration Mentioned also his costs by him in this behalf expended & the Defen- dant is in mercy &co.

      John Montgomery who was appointed an Executor in the Last will & Testament of Joseph Weir appeared in Open Court & Made a relinquish- ment of the same & Jonathan Weir who was the other Executor was in open court duly qualified to execute the same.

179.   Ordered by court that Samuel George, John Tedford, & William Gillespie Esquires be commissioners to Settle with Lowry & Montgomery Exor of Thos Berry Decd.

Nathan Aldridge)
     vs   )
John Drew   )   This day came the plaintiff by Attorney & filed his Declaration & the Defendant being Solmnly called came not but made default.

It is therefore considered by Court that the plaintiff recover agt. the

The last will & Testament of John Hackney Decd. was proven in open court by James Holden & Rebecka Hackney the withesses thereto & Hugh Hackney & Rebecka Hackney the Executors appointed in Said will appeared & were solemnly Affirmed to execute the same Agreably to Law.

180.   A Bill of from Samuel Cowan Sheriff of the County of Blount for a tract of land lying on waters of Little River to Robert Houston was acknowledged in Open court by said Cowan the Subscriber thereto
                    It is therefore ordered by court that the Same be Admitted to Registration

A Settlement of the Estate of Thomas Berry Decd. returned to Court appraised & filed.

Ordered by Court that Mathew Samples be allowed a draft on the County Treasury of 3¾ Cents which was collected as Tax of the said Mathew through a mistake.

Agreable to an order of court there was an Election held this day for presiding Justice when James Gillespie Esquire was duly & constitutionally elected.

The court agreable to law have appointed John Reagen, George Ewing, Robert Thompson, Mathew Wallace & Joseph Alexander Esquires Justices to hold our next comeat court on the third Monday of Nov. next.

181.   Ordered by court that a commission issue to Robert McCurdy Constable to Attend on our next Coveat Court & William Walker & Robert Murrin constables to Attend our next court of pleas & c.

Ordered by court that Susannah Matthews be allowed Twenty Dollars out of the poore tax for Keeping two orphan children now in her care Six months next ensuing.

Ordered by court that John Thornbury pay to Sarah Curtain Eight Dollars thirty three & a third cents quarterly for the term of one year next ensuing for the maintainance of an elligitimate child by him begotten on the body of the said Sarah Curtain single woman & that on failure of payment Execution issue for the same in her name.

182.   Ordered by Court that the Indentures binding lending Robert Tedford to John Likens be null & void & that Said Robert Tedford be bound unto Robert Henderson he having entered into Indentures.

State   )
   vs   )   Basterdy
George Coldwell)   In this case the Defendant being bound to appear
                     at this Court & answer to a charge of Basterdy &
the Defendant appearing & the Council on both sides and after argument & Mature deliberation being had thereon

It is ordered by court that the same proceedings be dismissed

Court adjourned till tomorrow morning 9 Oclock

183.

Saturday 1st day of Sept. 1809

Court met according to adjournment

Present

James Gillespie, John Waugh & William Lowry Esquires Justices &c.

Ordered by court that Charlotte Anderson be bound unto Elias Debusk.

A Bill of Sale from Josiah Danforth to John Wilkinson & John B. Cusack was proven in open court by David Cusack & Margaret Keys the witnesses thereto
Wherefore it is ordered that the same be admitted to registration istration .

A Deed of conveyance from Josiah Danforth to John McNeely for a tract of land on pistol Creek was proven by John Wilkinson & Margaret Wilkinson the witnesses thereto
It is ordered by court that the same be admitted to registration.

184.

A Power of Attorney from John Lyle to John Gardiner Esquire was proven in open court by Robert Houston the witness to the same
It is ordered by court that the same be Admitted to Registration.

Two deeds of Conveyance from John Gardner Esquire Attorney in fact for John Lyle to James Houston for two lots of land in Maryville was acknowledged in open court by said Gardiner the Subscriber thereto
Wherefore It is ordered by court that they be admitted to Registration.

The report of the Guardianship of William Gamble returned to Court by Nancy Gamble Guardian & filed.

State   )
  vs   ) Rule to show cause to dismiss the proceedings in
Ambrose Bryantt) this case

The sales of the Estate of Andrew Young Decd. returned to court & filed.

John Gilespie appeared in Open court & made oath that James Chandler was Justly indebted to him $38.1¼ Cents

185. Joseph Smith   )
        vs   )   Sire Facias
      Wm. Black & Joseph Lackey)   This day came the plft by Attorney & it
                              appearing that two nikels was returned
and the defendant being Sollam Calld came not.
            It is therefore considered by Court that the plaintiff
recover against the deft the costs in the Sire facas mentioned with
his costs about his suit in this behalf expended & sd Daft in mercy
&c.

                    Court adjourned till Court in course
                          Saml. Hendly
                            presiding Justice

186.   At a court of pleas & quarter session began & held for the County of Blount at the court house in Maryville on the fourth Monday of
November 1809.

                        Present

        Andrew Bogle, Robert parks & John Waugh Esqrs. Justices & co.

        Andrew Cowan Esquire Deputy Sheriff of the County aforesaid re-
turned our writ of Venire to him directed
        Executed on the following persons (to wit)

1. John Simpson	14. John Thornbury	27. George Hogg
2. Morrice Mitchel	15. William Houston	28. Samuel Montgomery
3. Adam Caldwell	16. David Eagleby	29. Thomas Wallace
4. Charles Henry	17. John McNabb	30. Alexander Henderson
5. David Coldwell	18. Edward Casteel	31. George Moore
6. John Ewing Senr	19. John Ewing	32. Nathan Lea
7. James Weir Jr.	20. Robert Finley	33. Abraham Utter
8. Edwin Allan	21. William McClerge	34. Hugh Kelsoe
9. Robert McCulley	22. William Maxwell	35. Jonathan Lassiter
10. David Walker	23. David Dearmond	36. Banner Shields
11. William Armstrong	24. Joseph Walker	37. Mathew Timberman
12. Andrew Rogers	25. Robert McMurrey	38. James McGinley
13. John Carson	26. William James	39. Abraham Wallace

187.   Out of which Venire the following persons were elected a Grand Inquest for the County of Blount (to wit)

1. David Caldwell	6. George Moore	11. John Ewing
2. Morrice Mitchell	7. William Maxwell	12. William Houston
3. Andrew Rogers	8. William James	13. James McGinley
4. John Cowan	9. Edward Casteel	14. William McClarge
5. Jonathan Lassiter	10. David Eagleby	15. Hobert McMurry

were sworn received their charge & retired to enquire of their presentments.

A Bill of Sale from Mathew Pate to Henry Whitenbarger for a Negro boy was proven in open court by Stephen Pate the subscriber thereto
It is ordered that the same be registered.

A Bill of Sale from Mathew Pate to Henry Whitenbarger for a Negro Girl was proven in open court by John Edmonds one of the witnesses to the same
It is ordered that the same be Registered.

An Instrument of writing purporting to be the last will & Testament of John Williams Decd. was produced in open court & proven by Andrew Bogle & Joseph Bogle Jr. & John Williams & John Gamble the Exors herein named appeared in Ct. and were qualified

188.
An Instrument of writing purporting to be the last will & Testament of Allison Washam was produced in open court & proven by Jeremiah Washam & John Simpson the witnesses thereto

A Bill of Sale from James Insk to John Woods for an Island in Tennessee River was proven in open court by John Lowry the witness to the same Registration of the same is ordered accordingly.

Administration of the Estate of James Halliday Decd. is granted to David Russell he having given bond with approved Security and having filed an Inventory of said Estate an order of Sale of the same is granted.

Andrew Ferguson)
    vs   )
Thomas Thompson) Ordered by Court that Writs of Certiorarie & Supersideas issue to to the office & co.

David Durham relishing to Emancipate his negro Slave Peter & having given bond to indemnify the county the same is Ordered accordingly.

An Instrument of writing from Stockley Donelson to Hugh Dunlap was proven in open court by Abner Witt & Solomon Reid the witnesses to the same wherefore It is ordered by court that the same be admitted to Record Registration.

189.
Court adjourned till tomorrow morning 9 Oclock

Tuesday Morning 28th November 1809

Court met according to Adjournment

Present

William Gillespie, William Garrett & John Waugh, Esquires Justices. & c.

A Deed of Conveyance from George Worley to John Lowry Mercht for twenty

twenty six acres & one quarter acres of land was proven in open court by James Houston & Alexander Tedford two of the witnesses to the same.

Wherefore It is ordered by court that the same be admitted to Record & Registration.

190.

Love & Luttrell)
vs) Case
John Russell) This day came the parties by their attornies and thereupon came a Jury (to wit)

1. George Hogg
2. John Thornbury
3. William Armstrong
4. Mr John Ewing
5.&. Nathan Lea
6. James Weir
7. Andrew Gamble
8. Silas George
9. Joseph Sloss
10. Edward Hartt
11. Abraham Wallace
12. Joseph Walker

who being elected tried and sworn the truth to speak upon the Issue Joined upon their oaths do say the Defendant did assume upon himself in Manner & form as the plaintiff against him hath declared and they assess the plaintiff damages by occasion of the non performance of that assumpset to ninty Dollars eighty Six and one fourth Cents.

Therefore It is considered by Court that the plaintiff recover against the Defendant aforesaid their damages as by the Jury aforesaid assessed likewise their costs by them about their suit in this behalf expended & the said Defendant is in mercy. &c.

191.

On motion of William Fagg & he having given bond with Adam Sofley & Andrew Cowan his security he is appointed a constable for the county & was qualified accordingly.

Same court as before

Thomas Mc Clark)
vs) Detinee
John Millon) This day came the parties by their attornies and thereupon came a Jury (to wit)

1. Charles Henery
2. David Walker
3. Martin Rorax
4. William Henery
5. James Moore
6. James Carruthers
7. Jeremiah Hammontree
8. Alexander Craig
9. Samuel Weir
10. John McCalroy
11. John Holloway
12. Samuel Dickey

who being elected tried and sworn the truth to speak upon the issue joined upon their oaths do say the Defendant doth detain the Stud horse in manner & form as the plff against him hath complained & say that said Horse is of the Value of one thousand Dollars & they assess the plaintiff damages by occasion of the detention thereof to $300 and costs.

193.

Therefore It is considered by court that the plaintiff recover of the Defendant aforesaid his horse aforesaid if to be had if not his value aforesaid as by the Jury aforesaid assessed together with his damages which he hath sustained by occasion of the detention aforesaid likewise his costs by him about his suit in this behalf expended & the said Defendant is in Mercy from which verdict and

Judgment the Defendant prayed an appeal to the Honorable Superior Court of Hamilton District and now claim the Defendant by his Attorney & dismissed his former Rule and entered a Rule for a new trial

An Assignment of a plat & certificate of Survey from Edward Murphy to peter Bowerman was acknowledged in open court by said Murphy the subscriber thereto.

On motion of William Kelly Esquire & he having taken an Oath of an Attorney he is admitted to practice according in this Court.

An assignment of a plat & certificate of Survey from Mathew Kelly to Thomas York was acknowledged in open court by said Kelly the subscriber thereto.

193.   A power of Attorney from Margaret Weir to John Weir was acknowledged in open court by said Margaret Weir the subscriber thereto.

A Deed of conveyance from John Gillespy to Greenfield Taylor was proven in open court by William Gillespie & James Weir the witnesses to the same.

Thomas M. Clarke)
   vs   )
John Miller   )   In this case Andrew Miller who was Special Bail for the Defendant appeared in open court & surrendered him & on Motion of the plaintiff by his Attorney, the Deft. is prayed in Custody &c.

A Bill of Sale from Edward Eggins to Robert Eaken for a tract of land on Nine mile creek was proven in open court by RobertMcCulley a witness to the same wherefore It is ordered by court that the same be admitted to Record & Registration.

194.   On Motion of John Wilkinson Esquire ordered by court that John Shafer be bound to Keep the peace & he togather with John Gardner & Andrew Cowan entered into bond for his will & true observation & safe Keeping of the same one year.

Thomas Ruthford)
   vs   )
Peter Harris)   This cause having been by the parties submitted to arbitration which was returned in favour of the Defendant.

In confirmation whereof it is considered by court that the plaintiff cause of action be dismissed & that he pay the costs of this suit.

Court adjourned till tomorrow morning 9 Oclock

Wednesday 29th November 1809

Court met according to Adjournment

Present

George Ewing, James Wyley & John Waugh Esquires Justices &c.

Andrew Miller)
vs)
Edward Teele) Ordered by court that Did pot. issue to take the Deposition of James P. Chisholm to be read in behalf of the
Defendant with giving the Defendant 20 days notice.

195. John Wilkinson Assinee)
vs) Covt.
John Montgomery & John Lowry) This day came the parties by their Attornies & thereupon came a Jury to wit.

1. Benja Harbert	5. James Richey	9. David Walker
2. Edward Hartt	6. Alexander Patterson	10. John Thornbyry
3. Joseph Hartt	7. Henry Donahoo	11. James Weir
4. James McClanahan	8. Nathan Lea	12. William Armstong

who being elected tried and Sworn the truth to speak upon the issue
Jointd upon their oaths do say the Testator in his lifetime hath not
kept & preformed his covenant but hath broken the same in Manner &
form as the plaintiff against him hath complained & they assess the
plaintiff Damages by occasion thereof to Seventy three Dollars &
Seventy five Cents & they say the Deced. did not pay as in pleading
alledged & they further find and say the Defts have fully administrated all and singular the Goods & Chattles, rights & credits of the said
Decident to be administrated.

Therefore It is considered by court that the plaintiff recover against Defendants aforesaid their damages aforesaid as by the
Jury aforesaid assessed to be leveyed on the proper goods & chattles
of the said Decendant when assetts sufficient shall come to their
hands likewise his costs by him about his suit in this behalf expended
and the said Defendant are in mercy &c.

196.

A Bill of Sale from Charles Donahoo constable to John Montgomery
for a negro Girl was acknowledged in open court by said Donahoo the
subscriber thereto.

Thomas M. Clarke)
vs)
John Miller) This day came Hugh Kelsoe & Andrew Miller and undertook for the Defendant that in case he is cast in
this suit he will pay and satisfy the costs & Condemnation or surrender himself in Execution of the same or that they will pay the
same or surrender him in discharge of themselfes.

A Bill of Sale from Andrew Cowan Duputy Sheriff for a tract of
land on the waters of McCulleys Creek was acknowledged in open court
by said Cowan
Wherefore It is ordered by Court that the same be admitted to Record & Registration.

197.   George W. Allen)
        vs   )   Certiorarea
   James T. Steele)   This day came the parties by their Attornies & thereupon came a Jury to wit

1. William Sloan	5. John Weir	9. John Ewing
2. Benjamin Erwin	6. Robert Wilson	10. Joseph Walker
3. Thomas Wallace	7. James Weir	11. Alexander Wallace
4. John Finley	8. Charles Henery	12. Thomas Gamble

who being elected tried and sworn the truth to speak upon the Matter of controversy upon their Oaths do say they find for the plaintiff & assess his damages to Thirteen Dollars & Sixty Nine Cents and thereupon came the Defendant by attorney & entered a Rule for new trial.

A Bill of Sale from Samuel Cowan Sheriff to John Montgomery fxx for a negro boy named Moses was acknowledged in open court by said Cowan.

198.   William Floyd   )
        vs   )
   Benjamin Kelbourn)   This day came the parties by their Attornies & thereupon came a Jury (to wit)

1. Benj. Harbert	5. Alexander Patterson	9. John Thornbury
2. Joseph Hartt	6. Henery Donahoo	10. James Weir
3. James McClanahan	7. Nathan Lea	11. William Armstrong
4. James Richey	8. David Walker	12. James Hall

who being elected tried and sworn the truth to speak upon the matter of controversy upon their Oaths do say they find for the Defendant & thereupon came the plaintiff by Attorney and entered a Rule for a New trial.

Administration of the Estate of Cornelias Bagartt Decd. is granted to John Rankin Senr. he having given bond with approved decurity.

199.   Alexander Ford)
        vs   )
   George Sloan   )   Washington Allen who was special bail for the Deft. appeared in open court & surrendered him in discharge of himself & David Cook & Isaac Brooks appeared in open court & undertook for the Defendant that in case he will cast in this suit that he will pay the costs & condemnation or render himself into prison in Execution of the same or they will do it for him.

Barclay McGhee)
       vs   )   Sci. Fac.
John Montgomery)   This day came the parties by their attornies &
Guardian of Ber-)   the Defendants plea of null ----? Record being sub-
ries Heirs   )   mitted to the court and the matters arising there-
               upon.
             It seems to the court here there is no such Record as the Defendant in pleading hath alleged the plf. not further prosecuting It

is ord. that his suit be dismissed

Barcley McGhee)
　　　　vs　　) Sci. Fac.
Ditto　　　　) This day came the parties by their attor & the Defendants
　　　　　　　 plea of Nul ----? Record being argued
4　　　　　　　It is ordered by court that the same be overruled.

200.　　　　A Draft on the Treasury of this County in favour of Susannah Matthew for Twenty Dollars was returned to court & It is ordered by court
that order be Null & Void on which said Draft is founded.

~~Elihu Embra~~)
　　　　vs　　)
~~Isaac Wright) Assinee for the use of~~

Elihu Embra Assinee for the use of Francis Willitt)
　　　　vs　　　　　　　　　　　　　　　　　　　　　)
Isaac Wright　　　　　　　　　　　　　　　　　　　) This day came
　　　　　　　　　　　　　　　　　　　　　　　　　　 the Defendant in his
proper person and confessed Judgment for Three hundred & Twenty four
Dollars and Costs.
　　　　　Therefore with the Assent of the plaintiff it is considered by the Court that the plaintiff recover against the Deft. the
Sum aforesaid together with his costs by him in this behalf expended
the Deft. in mercy &c.

　　　　　Court adjourned till tomorrow morning 9 Oclock

　　　　　Thursday Morning Court Met according to adjournment.

　　　　　　　　Present

　　　William Davidson, James Wyley & John Tedford Esquires Justices &c.

Barcley McGhee)
　　　　vs　　)
John Montgomery) This day came the parties & the first plea of the
Guardian to　) Deft. to with the plea of Null ----? Record being sub-
Berryes heirs) mitted to the court & the circumstances arising there-
　　　　　　　　 upon
　　　　　It seems to the court here there is no such Record from
which Judgment the plft prayed an appeal Dismissed & the plft. not
further prosecuting It is ordered that the same be dismissed.

201.　Barcley McGhee)
　　　　　vs　　　)
　　John Montgomery) Sci. Fac.
　　Guardian to　) This day came the parties by their attornies &
　　Berries Heirs) thereupon came a Jury to wit

1. William Armstrong　　5. Charles Henery　　　9. Robert Cooper
2. Abraham Wallace　　　6. David Walker　　　　10. Archer Johston
3. Joseph Wallace　　　　7. Samuel Davidson　　11. William Sims
4. Nathan Lea　　　　　　8. John Gould　　　　　12. Thos. D. Oconnor

who being elected tried and sworn the truth to speak upon the issue
Joined who after having retired some time ago to make up a verdict in
this case returned into court & say the cannot agree

Therefore by an with the consent of the parties and the
assent of the court it is agreed they make a miss trial & this suit is
continued until the next court.

202.   A Deed of Conveyance from Jereimah Caywood Smallwodd, Caywood & Edward Caywood to James Anderson for one hundred & twenty acres of land
was proven in open court by Burtin pride & William pride the witnesses
to the same wherefore

It is ordered by court that the same be admitted to Record
& Registration.

Ordered by court that David Russell have the liberty & that Li-
cence issue to keep public House at his own Farm in Maryville he having
given bond with appraised Security for the same.

Ordered by court that Andrew Bogle James Gillespie & John Walker
Esquires be commissioners to settle with the Admors of William Reagan
Decd. & do report to our next court

Court Adjourned till tomorrow morning 9 Oclock

203.   Friday Morning 1st December 1809

Friday Morning Court met according to their Adjournment

Present

William Davidson, George Ewing & James Houston Esquires Justices

Samuel Love & Co.)
        vs   )
Samuel McCullock)   on motion of Enoch Parsons Esquire Attorney for the
                      plaintiff It appears the plaintiff obtained a Judg-
ment & Execution before John Gardiner Esqr against the said Defendant
which Execution was returned to this court Leveyed on the tract of land
said McCullock lives on.

It is therefore considered by court that the said land be
exposed to Sale Agreably to Law to satisfy the Aforesaid Execution together with the costs of this order.

Ditto)
 vs)
Ditto) On motion of Enoch parsons Esquire Attorney for the plaintiff
        obtained Execution agt. the said Defendant for the sum of
which Execution was returned to this court Leveyed on the tract of land
which said Defendant lives on

It is therefore considered by court that said land or so
much thereof as will be sufficient to satisfy the said Execution together with the costs of this Motion be exposed to Sale agreably to Law

204.   A Deed of conveyance from James Bayles to Charles H. Warren for one hundred & Sixty Seven Acres & three Rods of land was proven in open Court by patrick Beard & William Young Junior two of the witnesses to the same

     Wherefore it is ordered by court that the same be admitted to Record & Registration.

     Ordered by Court that William Blackbourn be allowed twenty Dollars for Keeping an orphan child named Betcy Clements one year from the Date hereof & that he be allowed drafts quarterly in proportion to the whole sum.

     An Inventory of the Estate of Cornelius Bogart returned to court by John Rankin the Admor. and an order of Sale of the same is granted

     A Deed of conveyance from Josiah Danforth to Jonathan Weir for Four hundred Acres of land more or less was proven in open court by Hugh Weir one of the witnesses to the same wherefore

     It is ordered by court that the same be admitted to Record & Registration.

     Administration of the Estate of James Greenaway Decd. is granted to Nancy Greenway & Samuel ~~they having given bond with~~ Douthett and they having given bond with approved Security.

     Ordered by court that David Coldwell & David Russell be appointed Guardians to the Minors and orphans of James Greenway they having given bond with approved Security as the law directs.

205.   State   )
       vs   ) Riot
    William Wallace) This day came the parties by their Attornies and
                 thereupon came a Jury (to wit.)

1. John Thornbury	5. Joseph Walker	9. David Walker
2. William Armstrong	6. Nathan Lea	10. Robert McTear
3. John Ewing	7. John Gamble	11. William Blackbourn
4. James Weir	8. Charles Henry	12. George Harris

who being Elected and sworn the truth to speak upon the issue in Traverse upon their Oaths do say the Defendant is guilty in manner & form as charged in the Bill of Indictment.

     It is therefore considered by court that for such his Riot aforesaid he be fined in the sum of one Dollar & that he pay the costs of this suit and the said Defendant is in mercy &c.

    State   )
      vs   )
    Ellis Thomas) The Defendant pleads guilty and is find Twenty five cents

206.   State   )
       vs   ) John Waugh Henry Franks & Andrew Cowan
    Cornelious Miller Esquire)

This day came the parties by their attornies and thereupon came a Jury (to wit.)

1. John Gould	5. Samuel Weir	9. Joshua Parsons
2. Abraham Wallace	6. John Gould	10. John Reagan
3. John Glass	7. William Walboe	11. James Hammell
4. David Cupp	8. Micheal Smith	12. William Henery

who being elected tried and sworn the truth to speak upon the issue in Traverse upon their Oaths do say the Deft. is not guilty in manner & form as charged in the Bill of Indictment.

It is therefore considered by court that the Defendant be requitted and released

On motion of Benjamin Erwin and he having big given bond with approved Security he is appointed a constable for this County.

207.   A Deed of conveyance from John Wilkinson & Margarett his wife & William Long & Mary Long his wife to John Jordon for one half of a Lot in the town of Lexington was produced in open court and John Gardiner & Andrew Bogle Esquires two of the Acting Justices of said county appointed by the court to take the privy Examination of said Margaret and Mary have freely volintarily and without any concion on the part of their respective husbands have Executed the said Deed and the said John Wilkinson & William Long & Mary Long respectively acknowledged they signed the same for the purpose therein expressed wherefore

It is ordered that the same be admitted to Record and Registration.

A Deed of conveyance from John Wilkinson & Margaritt Wilkinson his wife and William Long & Mary Long his wife to Jacob Fuller for one lot of land in the town of Lexington was produced in open court by John Gardiner & Andrew Bogle Esquires for said county appointed by the Court to take the privy examination of said Margarett & Mary Do certify that said Margaret & Mary freely and volintorily and without any cancion on the part of the respective husbands have Executed the said Deed and the said John Wilkinson & Margarett Wilkinson & William Long & Mary Long respectively acknowledged they signed the same for the purposes therein expressed

Whreefore it is ordered by court that the same be admitted to Record & Registration.

208.   A Deed of conveyance from William Long & Mary Long his wife & John Wilkinson & Margarett Wilkinson his wife to William Carruthers for land in Rockbridge County was produced in open court & John Gardiner & Andrew Bogle Esquires two of the Acting Justices for said county & to take the privy Examination of said Margarett & Mary do certify that they freely & volintarily and without any coercion on the part of the part of their respective husbands have Executed the said Deed and the said William Long & Mary Long his wife & John Wilkinson & Margarett Wilkinson his wife respectively acknowledged they signed the same for the purpose therein expressed wherefore

It is considered by Court that the same be admitted to Record and Registration

A Deed of conveyance from William Long & Mary Long his wife & John Wilkinson & Margarett Wilkinson his wife to Hugh Elliott and John Long for a tract of land in Rockbridge County was produced in open court and John Gardiner & Andrew Bogle Esquire two of the Acting Justices for said County to take the privy Examination of said Mary & Margarett Do certify that they freely & volintarily and without any cercion on the part of their respective husbands have executed the said Deed & the said William Long & Mary Long & John Wilkinson & Margaret Wilkinson respectively acknowledged they issued the same for the purposes therein expressed wherefore

It is ordered by court that the same be admitted to Record & Registration.

Robert Boyd Esquire this day handed into court his resignation as a Justice of the peace for this county

Court adjourned untill tomorrow morning 9 Oclock

209.

Saturday 2nd Dec. 1809

Court met according to Adjournment

Present

James Houston, Andrew Cowan & John Waugh, Esqrs

A Deed of conveyance from one moity of Several lots of land from James S. Montgomery to John Thornbury was proven in open court by Samuel Donahoo & William Tool wherefore

It is ordered by court that the same be admitted to Record & Registration.

State
vs
John Farr & Thomas Wright) On motion of the Defendants by attorney
Nolle presequi is ordered

John Caldwell)
vs
Robert McFear) The plaintiff comes into court and voluntary dismisses his suit & the Deft agrees to pay the costs
It is therefore ordered by court that Judgment be confirmed accordingly.

A Deed of conveyance from James S. Montgomery to Henry Thornbury for a lot in Maryville to wit Lot 55 was acknowledged in open court by said Montgomery the subscriber thereto
Wherefore It is ordered by court that it be admitted to Record & Registration.

A Deed of conveyance from James S. Montgomery to John Thorbury for lots was acknowledged in open court by said Montgomery the subscriber thereto
Wherefore it is ordered by court that the same be admitted

to Record & Registration

210.   Ordered by court that the majistrate take in the List of Taxable property in the captains companies opposite their names

James Wyley Esqr.	Capt.	Dixons Company
Andrew Cowan	"	Hendersons Company
Andrew Boyd	"	Garmors Company
William Davidson	"	Davidsons Company
Mathew Wallace	"	Thompsons Company
James Gillespy	"	Coldwells Company
John Waugh	"	Cusacks Company
James Houston	"	Buckhanans Company
Joseph Alexander	"	Houstons Company
Parks	"	Allens Company
Samuel George	"	Wheelers Company

and make return of the same at our next court

Ordered by court that the Executor of Joseph Weir Decd. make sale of a mare as allowed of the will

On motion of Samuel Findley & he having given bond with approved Security to preform duties of said office he is appointed a constable in the bounds of Capt. Thompsons Company and was qualified accordingly

Ordered by court that summons issue to Benjamin Erwin & William Walker Constables to attend our next court.

211.   State)
        vs) T.B.
Samuel Donahoo)   This day came as well John Wilkinson who prosecutes in behalf of the State as the Defendant by his Attorney and thereupon came a Jury (to wit)

1. Jacob Cupp   5. Joseph Walker   9. John Duncan
2. John Ewing   6. Nathan Lea   10. Washington Allen
3. James Weir   7. David Walker   11. John McGhee
4. Abraham Wallace   8. William Glass   12. Moses Caywood

who being elected tried and Sworn the truth to speak upon the issue in Traverse upon their Oaths do say the Defendant is guilty in manner & form as charged in the Bill of Indictment
        It is therefore considered by Court that for such his Trespass Assault & Battery as charged in the Bill of Indictment be find twenty five cents & pay the costs of this Indictment & he is in Merch &c.

212.   State)
        vs)
Miles Cunningham)
~~axJohnxWaughxxxx~~   This day came as well John Wilkinson Esquire who pro-
~~Esquires~~   secutes in behalf of the State as the Defendant by his Attornies & the reupon came a Jury (to wit.)

1. Samuel Henry	5. William Harris	9. Alexander Malcum
2. Robert Cooper	6. Richard Chandler	10. William Moore
3. Thomas Gardiner	7. Alexander Ford	11. Charles Kenery
4. James Dunlap	8. Thomas Cooper	12. William Armstrong

who being elected tried and sworn the truth to speak upon the issue in traverse who after retiring some time returned here into court and say they cannot agra

      wherefore It is agreed by the parties & with the assent of the court that they make a miss Trial & this cause is continued until next Ct.

State   )
  vs   )
John Findley, John Wallace &)
Gavin Black.   ) In this case It appears to us the State recovered an Execution against the said Finley & John Wallace his Security for Eight Dollars & four cents & they availing themselves as an act of assembly relative to the stay of Execution entered into bond together with said Black their Security agreably to said Statute and failing to comply with requestions of the same.

      It is therefore considered by court that the State recover against the said John Findley, John Wallace & Gavin Black the amount of the Execution aforesaid together with the costs of this Motion & the said Defendants are in Mercy &c.

213. Isiah Bowman   )
      vs   )
William Steward, William Condron)
John Trimble, Reuben Charles,   )
James Cresswell & Thomas Henderson) In this case It appears to us on motion of E. Parsons Esquire the plaintiff obtained an execution before a Majestrate which was returned to Court Leved on a tract of land for which an order of sale granted & the said William Wishing to avoid himself of an act of assembly relative to his stay of executions entered into bond together with Thomas Henderson his Security agreable to said Law & failing to comply with the requestions thereof

      It is therefore considered by Court that the plaintiff recover against the Defendants aforesaid & Thomas Henderson Security as aforesaid Fifty four Dollars thirteen & three fourth cents the amount of the Aforesaid Execution together with his costs in prosecuting this motion & the said Defendants are in Mercy &c.

John Montgomery, Assinee)
      vs   )
James Paul, William Taylor) In this case it appears to us on motion of
& Crawfield Taylor   ) E. parsons Esqr. the plaintiff obtained an Execution before a Majestrate which was returned to court Levyed on the land said Paul lives on & for which an order of Sale was granted & the said James wishing to avail himself of an act of Assembly relative to the stay of Executin entered into Bond together with the said William & Taylor & Crawfield Taylor & they failing to comply with the conditions by court that the plaintiff recover

214. Against the said James Paul William L. Taylor & Crasfield Taylor Eight
      Dollars Sixty three and three fourth Cents the amount of said said exe-
      cution together with the costs of this Motion & they are in Mercy &c.

      John Montgomery Assinee   )
      of John Wallace Assinee &c.   )
             vs   )   In this case on Motion of Enoch parsons
      James Paul William L. Taylor)   esquire It appears to us that the plain-
      & Crawfield Taylor   )   tiff obrained an Execution against the
                                         said Paul before a Majistrate which was
      returned to Court Levyed on the Land said paul lives on & he wishing to
      avail himself of an act of Assembly relative to the stay of Execution
      entered into bond together with said William & Crawfield and they fail-
      ing to comply with the conditions thereof.
             It is therefore consideredby court that the plaintiff re-
      cover against the James Paul William L. Taylor & Crawfield Taylor twenty
      five Dollars Eighty three & three fourth Cents the amount of said order
      together with the costs of this motion & the said Defendants are in
      Mercy &c.

      Barcley McGhee)
            vs   )
      Berries Heirs)

215. State   )
            vs   )   Basterdy
      John Glass)   By consent of the parties this case is continued until next
                       Court

      State)
        vs)   Ditto
      Ditto)

      Barcley McGhee   )
            vs   )
      John Montgomery & John Lowry)   This day came the plaintiff by his Attor-
      Exors of Thomas Berry Decd.)   ney and dismissed his rule for a new trial
                                         & moved for Judgment on the verdict for-
      merly rendered in this case.
             Therefore It is considered by court that the plaintiff re-
      cover against the Defendant aforesaid $90&80 cents his damages afore-
      said as by the Jury in this case formerly assessed together with his
      costs by him in this behalf expanded.
             To be levyed of the proper Goods & chattles of the said Tes-
      tator when assetts sufficient shall come to their hands to be administra-
      ted whereupon on motion of the plaintiff of the plaintiffs Attorney and
      on a suggestion that the said Testator decd. seized and possessed of
      Real Estate which Decended to James Berry polly Berry Betcy Berry Patch
216. Berry Walker Berry & Tareza Berry Infants, children & Heirs of the said
      Thomas Berry
             It is therefore ordered that a Sci Facias issue to John
      Montgomery their Guardian for them by him to show cause why Judgment
      should not be entered against their real Estate held by descent as
      aforesaid & Execution issue for the same

afaresaid & Execution issue for the same

Barcley McGhee)
    vs   )
John Montgomery) Whereupon on Motion of E. parsons the plaintiff
& John Lowry   / and on a suggestion that the said Testator decd.
Exors of Thomas) seized and possessed of real Estate which decended
Berry Decd.   ) to James Berry, polly Berry, Betcy Berry, Patcy Ber-
                  ry. Walker Berry and Tareza Berry Infants, children
& Heirs of the said Thomas Berry
          It is therefore ordered that a Scb, Facias Issue to John
Montgomery their Guardian for them by him to show cause why Execution
for this Debt and damages should not issue against their real Estate
held by descent as aforesaid.

Jacob Danforth)
    vs   ) Serifacis
Wm. Sherrell) In this case no plea being entered& the aforesaid Wm.
               Sherrellbeing called & came not
          It is therefore ordered that Judgment issue agreable to
sire facis

          Court adjourned until court in course

217.   At a court of pleas and quarter Sessions began & held for the County
of Blount at the court house in Maryville on the fourth Monday of March
1810.
              Present

    James Gillespy, Andrew Bogle, & Samuel George Esquires

    Andrew Cowan Deputy Sheriff of the County aforesaid returned ouS
writ of Venire to him directedexecuted on the following persons to wit.

1. Joseph Stukes	9. James Tipton	17. George Berry
2. Valentine Mayo	10. Saml. Love	18. James McNutt
3. Henery Whitenbarger	11. Hugh Weir	19. John Ewing
4. William Barnes	12. George Dillard	20. Robert Henderson
5. George Tedford	13. Jonathan Trippett	21. Robert Straine
6. Thomas Morrison	14. Joseph Tedford	22. Patrick Culton
7. John McNally	15. Alexander McCullock	23. Thomas Wallace
8. Stephen Graves	16. John Coldwell	24. Thomas Gamble

    A Deed of conveyance from James Kendrick to Martin Bonham for one
hundred & Sixty Eight of land was proven in open court by John Cox &
Nehimiah Bonham
          It is therefore ordered bhat the same be admitted to
Record Let it be registered.

218.   Clement C. Clay & George B. Balch took the oath of Attornbes and
were admitted to practice in this court accordingly.

    James Turk having entered into Indentures as the Law directs for
the binding of John Jones to him as an apprintice to the Saddler trade
          It is ordered that he be bound unto the said Turk until

he arrives at the age of twenty one years.

A Bill of Sale from William Montgomery to John -------? was proven in open court by Alexander Patterson & William Gray wherefore
It is ordered that the same be admitted to Record Let it be registered.

A Deed of conveyance from William Kendrick to Josiah Patty for one hundred & Sixty Eight Acres of land was proven in open court by Nath Hood & Zarabable Patty the witnesses thereto Wherefore
It is admitted to Record let it be registered.

Jessee Wallace & Robert Mc^Cully appeared in open court took an oath to support the constitution of the United States an oath to support the constitution of the State of Tennessee and the oath prescribed by Law for Justices of the peace and are recognized as such by this court there commissioners having been forwarded by the Governor

219.   Ordered by court that the Sheriff by a Jury of twelve freeholders enquire into the State of ^Wm. Carger as mind respects his Idiocy or lunacy and make return of the same to our next court.

Ordered by court that friday & Saturday be days on which Arguments shall be taken up in this Court.

Ordered by Court that Thomas Moore be Guardian for John Washam Jeremiah Washam Isabella Washam & Polly Washam he having given bond as the Law directs.

John Lowry Esqr. County Trustee came into open court and resigned his appointment as such

Samuel Cowan Esquire Sheriff of the County of Blount came into open court and resigned his commission as such.

Ordered that an Election be opened and held tomorrow to commence at twelve Oclock to elect a Sheriff Coroner & County Trustee for the county of Blount.

Ordered by court that Andrew Cowan Esqr act as Coroner for the county of Blount until tomorrow 12 Oclock

220.   Joseph Hartt Guardian of the orphens of Micheal Warren Decd. returned an account of said Estate in his hands

John Hickland)
    vs   )
Isaac Brooks) This day came the plaintiff by Enoch parsons Esquire
                his Attorney and suggests to this court that an Execution Issue in favour of him from William Lowry Esqr for Eighty Seven Dollars & Eighty Cents for Debt & costs which was returned to Court by Charles Donahoo Constable D_ecd. Fifty one Dollars and for the ballance Levied on the tract of Land Said Brooks now lives on

It is therefore considered by Court that said Land or so much thereof as will satisfy the ballance of the aforesaid Debt be exposed to Sale
agreably to Law to Satisfy the Same.

Enoch Parsons for the use of)
James Perry   )
           vs   )
Isaac Brooks   )   This day came the plaintiff by John Gar-
                                 diner Esquire his A.to. and suggests to
this Court that an Execution issued in favour of him for Eleven Dollars
& thirteen cents from John Gardiner Esquire which Exec. went into the
hands of Andrew Cowan Deputy Sheriff for collection and was by him returned to Court No goods nor chattles to be found levied on the Land
that said Brooks now lives on
            It is therefore considered by court that said land or so
much thereof as will satisfy the ballance of the aforesaid Debt be ex-
221.   posed to Sale agreably to Law to Satisfy the same

            Court Adjourned till tomorrow morning 9 Oclock

            Tuesday 27th March 1810

            Court met according to Adjournment

                    Present

        George Ewing, Robert McCulley & Henry Franks Esquire

        An Instrument of writing purporting to be the last will & Testament
of Henry Cox was produced in open court and proven by George & Mathew
Whitenbarger two of the witnesses thereto & John Cox & Samuel Saffle
the executors therein named were qualified as the Law directs.

        A Bill of Sale from Alexander Hale to James Montgomery for two ne-
groes was acknowledged in open court by said Hale the Subscriber thereto
            It is therefore ordered that the same be admitted to Record
Let it be registered.

222.   Joel Wallace)
           vs   )
        Andrew Cowan)   This day came the parties by their attornies & thereupon
                       came a Jury to wit.

1. Henery Whitenbarger   5. James McKenney   9. Stephen Graves
2. William Barnes   6. Andrew Jackson   10. Jonathan Trippett
3. James Tipton   7. Saml. Gould   11. Alex. McCullock
4. Thomas Morrison   8. Morrice Mitcheal   12. George Tedford

who being elected tried and sworn the truth to speak upon the issue
Joined But the plaintiff not being ready for trial
            It is ordered that he be non suited and that he pay the
costs of this suit.

        A Deed of conveyance from Henry Thomas to Margaret Nimon for two hundred & forty acres of land was proven in open court by John Gardiner & Saml. Love witnesses thereto

A power of Attorney from James Anderson to Morrice Mitcheal was proven in open court by Alexander Kelly one of the witnesses thereto
It is therefore ordered by court that the same be admitted to Record Let it be registered.

223. Barcley McGhee)
           vs   ) Sci. Fac.
      Berries Heirs) This day came the parties by their attornies and there-
                      upon came a Jury (to wit)

1. Henery Whitenbarger	5. James McKenny	9. Stephen Graves
2. William Barnes	6. Andrew Jackson	10. Jonathan Trippett
3. James Tipton	7. Samuel Gould	11. Alexander McCullock
4. Thomas Morrison	8. Morrice Mitcheal	12. George Tedford

who being elected tried and Sworn the truth to speak upon the issue Joined from rendering their Verdict and respited untill tomorrow.

Samuel Bogle Senr. & William McKeggs having entered into bond with approved Security for the faithful discharge of their Duty as constables
It is ordered that they Act in confirmation thereto.

Henery Franks Esquire returned into the office four Dollars & Fif-ty Cents as fines by him Collected of Eli Casteel Benjamin Bogard & William Washam.

A Deed of conveyance from Enoch Parsons to Wm. Fagg for a lot of land in Maryville was acknowledged in open court
It is thereforeordered that the same be admitted to Record Let it be registered.

223.   Ordered by Court that the Sheriff summons John Sloan, John McGhee, Carolinis Miller, William Harris, Robert Wilson, Saml. Gould, Nicholas Airhart, James Boyd, James Henry, Micheal Higgans, Josiah Hutton & Joseph Posey to view the vacant land near Cooks Iron Works & report to our next Ct. whether the farm be fit for Cultivation or not agreably to the Act of Assembly in this Case made & provided.

A Bill of Sale from Saml. Cowan to John Gamble was acknowledged in open court by said Cowan the subscriber thereto.
WhereforeIt is ordered by Court that it be admitted to Record, let it be registered.

Agreable to an order of yesterday the court proceeded to elect a Sheriff when Samuel Cowan offered as a candidate and was duly and con-stitutionally elected and thereupon entered into bond as the Law directs.

The Court then proceeded to appoint a county Trustee when John Lowry Mercht offered as a Candidate and was duly and constitutionally elected.

The Court then proceeded to appoint a Coroner for the county of Blount when Andrew Thompson was duly and constitutionally elected

Court adjourned till tomorrow 9 Oclock.

Wednesday 28th March 1810

Court met according to Adjournment

Present

William Davidson, William Gillespy, & Henry Franks

223.
225.

Barcley Mc^Ghee)
vs)
Thomas Berries Heirs) This day came the parties by their Attornies & the Jury who from rendering a Verdict yesterday in this case were respited upon their Oath do say that lands & Tenements which were of the said Thomas Berry At the time of his Decease did decend to James Berry & others his Heirs Mentioned in the said Sci Facias
It is therefore considered by Court that the plaintiffs Execution May issue against the Land descended as aforesaid Accordingly to the form and effect of the Acts of Assembly in this case made & provided.
From which Judgment the Defendant prayed an appeal to the Honorable the Cerciut Court to be held for Blount County on the first Monday in August Next.

Two deeds of Conveyance from James Houston to Josiah Smith for Two lots of land in Maryville was acknowledged in open court by said Houston the subscriber thereto wherefore
It is admitted to Record Let it be registered.

226.
Joseph Colville)
vs)
John Hanna)
This day came the plaintiff by his Attorney and dismissed his suit
It is therefore considered by court that the same be dismissed & that the plaintiff pay the costs of this suit.

William Walker)
vs)
Thomas Owens)
This day came the Defendant and dismissed his writs of certioraria & Supersidias & agrees to pay the costs of the same
It is therefor considered by court that Judgment go accordingly & that a procedendo issue in this case to the Justice.

Jesse Wallace)
vs)
Barcley McGhee)
& Andrew Thompson)
This day came the plaintiff & dismissed his suit
It is therefore considered by court that the same be dismissed & that the plaintiff pay the costs of this suit.

A Bill of Sale from John McBride to Joseph Houston was acknowledged in open court by said McBride the subscriber thereto

Wherefore It is ordered by court that It be admitted to record Let it be registered.

227.   Samuel Cowan appeared in open court & took the Oaths prescribed by Law for a Sheriff Samuel Cowan produced in open court a Deputation from Samuel Cowan high Sheriff of the County aforesaid and took the necessary oaths of office

Archibald Davis an orphan boy was this day bound to Hugh Kelsoe by Indentures executed.

228.   Thursday 29th Marcy Term 1810

                    Court met according to Adjournment

                              Present

James Gillespie John Waugh & Henry Franks

Ordered by court that the Sheriff bring George Fox an orphan into court tomorrow morning

Barcley McGhee)
      vs   ) Sci. Facias
Berrys Heirs) This day came the plaintiff by his attorney and dismissed his writ
        It is therefore considered by court that the same be dis-
missed & that the plft. py the costs of this suit.

Ditto)
  vs) Sci. Fac.
Ditto) This day came the plaintiff by his attorney & dismissed his suit
        It is therefore considered by Court that the same be dis-
missed and that the plaintiff pay the costs of this suit.

Ordered that William Fagg attend as constable at our next Court

Ordered vy court that Samuel Bogle & Charles Donahoo be summoned as Constables to attend our next circiut Court.

229. King & Montgomery)
          vs   )
Isaac Upton   ) This day came James Upton Saml. Blackbourn & Robert
                         Houston who were summoned as Garnishees in this Case
the said Upton being sworn deposeth and saith that he owes the Defendant nothing nor does he know of any other person that owes him any and
further Saith not & Robert Houston & Samuel Blackbourn were sworn deposeth & saith that they as partners in trade owe the Defendant Seven
Dollars & no more & that they know of no other person owing him anything.
        It is therefore considered by court that the plft. recover
of the said Samuel Blackbourn & Robert Houston the Aforesaid Seven Dollars

& no more & that they Know of no other person owing him anything.

It is therefore considered by Court that the plft recover of the said Samuel Blackbourn & Robert Houston the aforesaid Seven Dollars.

Andrew Cowan & Robert Thompson Esqrs. Justices of the peace came into Court and resigned their commissions as such.

Ordered by court that Robert McCully Esqr take in and return to our next ct. the amount of Taxable polls & property in the bounds of Capt. Forresters Company

230.

Administrators of)
George Preston   )
      vs   ) Covenant
Archibald Trimble) This day came the parties by their Attornies and
              thereupon came a Jury (to wit)

1. Joseph Stukes	5. Thomas Morrison	9. Jonathan Trippet
2. Henery Whitenbarger	6. Stephen Graves	10. Joseph Tedford
3. William Barnes	7. George Tedford	11. James McNutt
4. James Tipton	8. Samuel Love	12. Patrick Culton

who being elected tried and sworn the truth to speak upon their Oaths do say the Defendant hath not kept & preformed his covenant with the plaintiff in the Declaration mentioned but hath broken the same in manner & form as the plaintiff against him hath complained Neither hath he paid the negro girl in Satisfaction thereof as the plaintiff by replying hath alleged and they assess the plaintiff damages by occasion thereof considered by Court that the plaintiff recover against the Defendant his damages aforesaid in form aforesaid assessed & his costs by him about his suit in this behalf expended and the said Defendant in Mercy &c.

231

Josiah & John Nichol)
      vs   ) Appeal
Archabald Lackey   ) This day came the parties by their attornies and
              thereupon came a Jury (to wit)

1. Thomas Gamble	5. Josiah Pearce	9. John Scott
2. Alexander McCullock	6. William Henery	10. Benjah Harbert
3. John McAnally	7. John McGhee	11. John McMahan
4. Josiah Payne	8. Joseph Wilson	12. Andrew Gamble

who being elected and sworn the truth to speak upon the matter in controversie upon their Oaths do Say they find for the plaintiff & they assess his damages to Twenty Nine dollars & Twenty three cents besides his costs.

It is therefore considered by Court that the plaintiff recover against the said Archabald Lackey & John Lowry his Security his damages aforesaid as by the Jury aforesaid assessed & his costs by him in this behalf expended & the said Defendant in mercy.

The sale of the Estate of Cornelius Bogard returned & filed.

232.   Samuel Steele)
            vs   ) Appl.
        Joshua Parsons) This day came the parties by their attornies and there-
                         upon came a Jury, the same Jury as in No. 1018 Do say
they find for the Defendant
                It is therefore considered by court that the plaintiff take
nothing but for his false clamour be in mercy and that the Defendant go
without day and recover against the plaintiff his costs by him in this
behalf expended.

        Matthew Gilmore)
            vs   ) This day came the parties by their attornies and
        Thomas Maxwell) on motion of the Defendt. the Judgment by default
in this case is set aside and thereupon came a Jury to wit, the Same
Jury as in no. 1083 Do say the Deft. hath not paid the Debt in the
Decl. mentioned as the plaintiff against him hath complained but hath
paid one hundred Dollars part of the Debt aforesaid and they assess
the plaintiffs damages by occasion of the detention of that debt to
fifty Eight dollars & forty cents besides costs
                Therefore It is considered by court that the plaintiff
recover against the Defendant the residue of his debt aforesaid after
deducting the $100 together with his damages aforesaid as by the jury
aforesaid assessed & his costs by him about his suit in this behalf
233.   expended and the said Defendant in mercy &c.

        Jesse Wallace)
            vs   )
        Lowry & Waugh) This day came the Defendant and relinquished their
                        pleas by them pleaded in this behalf and Say they can-
                        not gainsay the plaintiffs action
                It is therefore considered by court that the plaintiff re-
cover against the Defendant the Debt in the Declaration Mentioned together with Interest &c and his costs by him in this behalf expended
and the Said Deft. in Mercy &c.

        David Cooke)
            vs   )
        David Grass) This day came the plaintiff by John Wilkinson Esquire
                      his Attorney and Suggests to this court that an attach-
ment issued in favour of him against the Defendant for the sum of Thirty one Dollars & Sixty Cents Debt & costs which was returned to Court
by John McMahan a Deputy Constable Levied on a tract of land as the
property of the Defendant whereon the Defendants family now lives.
                It is therefore considered by court that said land or so
much thereof as will be sufficient to Satisfy the aforesaid Debt &
Costs together with the costs of the motion be exposed to Sale agreable
234.   to law.

        William Cox)
            vs   )
        William Cook &) This day came the parties by their attornies and there-
        Matheas Cooke) upon came a Jury to wit the same Jury as in No. 1081
                         Do say the Defendant hath not paid the Debt in the
Declaration mentioned nor any part thereof as the plaintiff agt. him
hath complained and they assess the plaintiffs damages by occasion of

the detention of that Debt to Eleven Dollars & Twenty one cents besides costs.

It is therefore considered by court that the plaintiff recover against the Deft. his Debt in the Declaration Mentioned together with his damages aforesaid as by the Jury aforesaid assessed & his costs by him about his suit in this behalf expended and the Said Debt in Mercy

Charles Donahoo Constable having entered into bond for the faithful discharge of his duty as such

It is ordered that he act in conformity thereto

235. David Edmondson & Wil-)
liam Paxton, Exors of)
John Paxton Decd.) Debt.
vs) This day came the parties by their Attornies
James Alexander) and thereupon came a Jury to wit the same Jury
as in No. 1081 hath paid the Debt in the
Declaration mentioned.

It is therefore considered by court that the defendant take nothing by his bill but for his false clamour be in Mercy &c. and that the Defendant go without day and recover against the plaintiff his costs by him about him about his suit in this behalf expended.

Ordered by Court that Thomas Robertson be allowed Six Dollars for a Maintinance to next Court.

John Thornburg)
vs) on Motion of John Wilkinson the plaintiffs Attorney,
James T. Steele) It appears that an Execution issued in favour of the
plaintiff against the Defendant for ths sum of Twenty
nine Thirty Seven and a half cents Debt & Costs which was returned to
Court by Andrew Bowan Deputy Sheriff no goods nor chattles to be found
levied on a tract of land the place whereon William Walker xxxxxxxx
erected a Cotton Machine also one tract of Land whereon Samuel Steele
& James Mosre now lives.

It is therefore considered by court that said Land or so
236. much thereof as will be sufficient to Satisfy the aforesaid Debt & costs together with the costs of this motion be exposed to Sale agreably to Law.

Barcley McGhee)
vs)
John Waugh) This day came the parties and agrees to transfer this
cause to the Circuit Court of Blount County to be held
on the first Monday in August Next
It is therefore ordered by Court that the Clerk Certify a complete transcript of the same to said Circuit Court.

Court adjourned till tomorrow morning 9 Oclock

233. Friday 30 March 1810

Court Met according to Adjournment

Present

George Ewing, John Waugh & John Tedford Esquires

William Sloan)
    vs)
William Schrimsher)   This day came the plaintiff by John Lowry Esquire
                        his Attorney and Suggests to this court that an
Execution issued in favour of him against the Defendant for the Sum of
Twenty one Dollars $25.60 Debt & Costs which was returned to court by
Samuel Findley Constable Levied on the land whereon William Schrimsher
formerly lived
            It is therefore considered by Court that said Land or so
much thereof as will be sufficient to satisfy the aforesaid Debt & Costs
together with the costs of this Motion be exposed to Sale Agreably to
Law.

        A Bill of Sale from John Gamble to Jesse Dold was proven in open
court by Samuel Cowan & Alexander Tedford the witnesses thereto wherefore
        It is admitted to Record Let it be registered.

238.   A Bill of Sale from John Johnson to Robert Gray was proven in open
court by Robert Harrison & John Grayham the witnesses thereto and admitted to Record Let it be registered

        Ordered by court that James Gillispy, John Gardiner, & John Waugh
Esquires Settle with David Russell Administrator of the Estate of James
Holliday Decd.

        The Settlement of the Commissions with the Administrators of
William Reagan Decd. returned & filed.

        A Bill of Sale from William Macklin to Joseph Green for four ne-
groes was proven in open court by James McKenney and & John Means two of
the Witnesses thereto
                Wherefore It is admitted to Record Let it be registered .

        On the affidavit of James Reagan ordered that the Clerk issue him
a ticket for his Attendance as a Juror at August Term 1809

        James Houston Esqr. resigned his commission as a Justice of the
peace.

239.   Barclay McGhee)
            vs Thomas Ber-) Sci. Fac.
        ries Heirs   ) This day came the Defendant by his Attorney and en-
                            tered their reasons from an Appeal by them prayed
in this case by Jno. Montgomery their Guardian & entered into bond for
the performance of the same with David Coldwell & David Russell his
Security & to them it was granted.

        A Deed of Mortgage from Mark Moore to James Houston was proven in
open court by Enoch parsons & John Lowry the witnesses thereto And ad-

mitted to Record Let it be registered.

A Power of Attorney from Neal to Gideon Blackbourn and Andrew Thompson was admitted to Record on the Mayor of Baltimore Certification of its probet Let it be registered.

State   )
   vs   )   Basterdy
James Singleton)   This day came as well who appears for the State
                     in this behalf as John Lowry the Defendants Attorney
and Solemn Argrement of Council being held and Mature deliberation by
the Court.
          It is considered & adjudged by the court that the said
James Singleton is the reputed father of a Bastard child named Jane by
him begotten on the body of Polly Eddington which was born in the
county of Blount and it is further considered by Court that the said
James pay into the hands of John Eddington Junier Sixty Dollars for
the use and Mantainance of the said Illigitimate child named Jane &

240.   that Execution issue for the same.

Lowry & Waugh)
     vs   )
Robert J. Henry)   In this case there was a Rule for a new trial which
                     was argued and mature deliberation being had by the
court was made absolute.

Henery & Lindenbarger)
       vs   )
Lowry & Waugh   )   In this case there was a Rule entered for a
                           new trial which wneh argued was made absolute

Benjamin Bowerman)
      vs   )   In this case the plaintiff having been non suited
~~RatahyxfagrattarsgxxxBxkxxixxatxthsxsamsxxxtdsxndxnswxtxthixxday~~
Henery Parrott   )   and having entered a Rule to set the same aside
                       and now at this day came the parties by their
attornies and Solemn argement being had

241.   It is considered by the court that the Rule be discharged

Robert Gillespy)
     vs   )
John Lowry   )   In this case there was a rule entered for a new trial
                     which when argued was discharged
          It is therefore considered by court that the plaintiff re-
cover agt. the Defendant his damages as by the Jury in this case formerly assessed & his costs by him about his suit in this behalf expended.

Thomas N. Clark)
     vs   )
John Miller   )   In this case there was a rule entered for a new trial
                     which wnen argued was confessed.

Steele)
vs)
Joshua Parsons) This day came the plaintiff by Atto and moved to have
a rule entered for a New trial which Motion when argued
was overruled

John McCartney)
vs)
Greenbury Edwards & Solloman McCampble) In this case on motion it appearing to court that an Execution issued from this court in favour of the plaintiff against the Defendant for 41.12 cents & he wishing to avail himself of the benefit of the Oath of Assembly in that case made & provided entered into bond with Solloman McCampble his security & this failing to comply with the conditions thereof

It is therefore ordered that the plaintiff recover of Greenbury Edwards or Solomon McCampble his security forty one dollars & One & a half cents besides the costs of this motion & the sd Defts. in mercy & c.

Court adjourned till tomorrow 9 Oclock.

242.   Saturday 31st March 1810

Court met according to Adjournment

Present

James Gillespie, Matthew Wallace & John Waugh, Esqrs.

Charles Donahoo)
vs)
Andrew Egnew) on motion of Charles Donahoo by John Lowry his attorney it appearing to the court here that Charles Donahoo & Andrew Egnew were Special Bail for John Keys in a suit brought by Robert Cannon Assinee against sd Keys & it also appearing to our sd. Court that sd, charles Donahoo has paid the amount of sd. Judgment & costs amounting to $149.77 Cents

It is therefore considered & adjudged by our sd Court that the sd. Charles Donahoo recover of the sd Andrew Egnew half the amount of the aforesaid Judgment & costs amounting to 74.88¾ cents agreable to the act of Assembly in that case made & provided & the sd. Andrew in Mercy.

The Settlement of the Estate of James Holaway Decd. returned & fild

A Bill of Sale from Wm. Cowan for a claim of land on Crooked Creek was proven in open court by James Gillespie & John Ewing the witnesses thereto & admitted to Record let it be registered.

243.   Samuel Dickey)
vs) an attachment
James T. Steele) This day came the plft. by Attorney & fild his Declaration & the Deft. being sollemnly called came not

31 Mar 1810

It is therefore considered by Court that the Plaintiff recover against the Deft. the debt in the Declaration Mentioned & his
Costs about his suit in this behalf expended & the sd. Deft. in Mercy &c

Robert Bailey)
    vs)
Warnor Martin) This day Came the parties & dismissed their suit for
               New trial & the Plaintiff releases seventy Dollars of
the Judgment

Josiah Danforth)
    vs) Sire Fac.
Wm. Sherell) In this case the defendant came not tho Sollemly cal-
             led & having no plea in Court Ordered that Judgment be
returned agreable to sire facias

Wm Walker Assinee)
of Saml Eakin)
    vs)
James Steele) This day came the plaintiff by John Wilkinson his
             Atrorney & suggests to this court that an attach-
ment issued in favour of him against the Defendant for the sum of
$43.33 1/3 Cents.

    Benjamin Irwin Constable returned no goods & chattles found levyed
on a lot of land on Walkers Mill Creek.

244.   It is therefore ordered by Court that the land or so much
thereof as is of value sufficient to satisfy the aforesaid Debt & costs
together with the costs of this Motion be exposed to sale Agreeable to
Law

    On Motion of Wm. Regan & John Regan they were admitted as guar-
dians of Henery Regan Joseph L. Regan Barbara Regan peggy Regan & Jef-
ferson Regan heirs & orphans of Wm Regan Decd.& entered into bond with
Gavin Black & Ahimas Regan security in the sum of two thousand Dollars
as the Law directs.

    A Bill of Sale from Margaret Thomas to Jacob Thomas was proven
in open court by Margaret Warfel & John Gardiner the subscribing witnesses thereto & admitted to record let it be registered.

245. State)
    vs) Basterdy
John Glass) This day came the Defendant by his Attorney and moved to
           have the Recognizance discharged which when argued was over-
ruled and the court adjudged the said Glass to be the father of said
Elligitimate child begotten on the body of Eleven Caldwell and the said
John Glass entered into bond for the Maintainance of the said child.
                          Elenor

William Snider)
    vs) Certr.
Joseph Eldon) This day came the plaintiff by John Gardiner his Attor-
           ney and the Defendant being Solemnly called came not
        It is therefore considered by court that Judgment be en-

246.   tered against the Deft. for the costs the plaintiff relinquishing any
further claim onthe Deft. and the said Defendant in Mercy &c.

John Gillespy took the Oath prescribed by Law for a Justice of
the peace and is recobnized as such by this court.

James Gillespy one of the orphans of John Kelly Decd. returned
an inventory of the Situation of Sd. Estate & It was fild.

Ordered that George Ewing Andrew Bogle & John Walker be commissioners to settle with John Regan Adms. of the Estate of James Young Dec.
& report the same to Next Court.

George W. Allen)
      vs   )   In this case there was a rule entered for a new trial
James Steele   )   & now at this time the rule was dismissed.

247.   Judge Advocates Office)
              vs   )
Wm. Lackey   )   Sire Facias
                              This case staying on a motion to quash & the
prties appearing by their Atternies when Solemnly argued & on due deliberation of the court the sd. Rule is discharged

Andrew Gamble)
      vs   )   In this case an Execution Issued for the plaintiff
Andrew Ewins)   against John Drew for the sum of ten Dollars & seventy
                  five Cents debt & costs & sd Evins failed to return sd.
Execution orp pay the money agreable to Law.
              It is therefore considered by Court that the plaintiff re-
cover against the Deft. the sum of on dollars & seventy five cents besides his Costs for this motion.

Josiah Danforth)
      vs   )   Attachment
Amos Edwards   )   In the above case ordered by Court that all proceedings
                    be stayed for six months according to the act of As-
sembly in that case made & provided for Defts living out of the State.

248.   Solloman McCamble)
              vs   )
John McCartney   )   In this case there was a Ruel entered for a new trial
                            and when argued was made ix absolute.

George W. Campble)
      vs   )   Debt.
John Minis   )   This day came the plaintiff by Wm. Kelley his Attorney
                     & the Defendant being Solemnly called came not but
made default.
              It is therefore considered by court that the plft recover
against the Defendant the Debt in the Declaration mentioned with Interest
& c. & his costs by him in this behalf expended and the Said Deft. in
mercy. &c.

Thomas Elliott)
      vs   )
William Floyd)   This day came the Defendant by his Attorney and the plain

being Solemnly called came not

It is therefore considered by Court that the plaintiff be nonsuited & that he pay thecosts of this suit.

Courtadjourned till court in course

James Gillespie
presiding Justice

249.   At a court of pleas and quarterSessions began and held for the county of Blount at the court House in Maryville on the fourth Monday of June 1810

Present

James Gillespy, George Ewing, William Gault, Wm. Gillespie, Jesse Wallace, & Robert McCulley Esquires Justices &c.

Samuel Cowan Esquire Sheriff of the county aforesaid returned our writ of Venire to him directed executed on the following persons to wit

1. Thomas Blackbourn   5. George Coldwell   9. Hugh Weir
2. Thomas McCullock   6. Peter Snider   10. Henry Bond
3. George Love   7. Robert McCampbell   11. Robert Gray
4. Masheck Tipton   8. James Turk   12. John McGhee
          13. Nathanl Ewing   14. John Miniss

Isoom Blankenship)
       vs   )
Burtin Pride   ) On motion of the plaintiff and for reasons appearing in his affidavid

It is ordered that a commission Issue to any two Justices of Maddison County Mississippi Terretory to take the Deposition of Henry Ferguson, David Linsey, James Deaton & Thomas Lindsay to be read as evidence in his behalf at the trial of this case

250.   Monday June 25y 1810

With giving the Defendants thirty days previous notice of the time & place of taking the same

An Instrument of writing purporting to be the last will & Testament of David Williams Decd. was produced in Open court by Thomas Jones & Jonathan Band the witnesses thereto & Azariah Williamson one of the Executors was qualified as such.

Ordered by court that George Ewing, Andrew Bogle & John Reagan Esquires settle with Martha Martin Administratrix of Warner Martin Decd.

On motion Martha Martin is appointed Guardian of Henry Martin, peter Martin, & Joshua Martin Minors & orphans of Warner Martin Decd. and entered into bond with Micheal Wyman, George Coldwell & John Lowry, Atto. her Securities in the Sum of Three thousand Dollars.

Martha Martin Administratrix of Warmor Martin Decd. returned an additional Inventory of the Estate of Said Warnor

251.   James Gillespy, George Ewing & Jesse Wallace Esqrs.

Lowry & Waugh)
        vs   )   Case
Robert L. Henry)   This day came the parties by their Attornies & there-
                   upon came a Jury (to wit)

1. Abraham Bogard	5. James Clerk	9. Robert Gray
2. Samuel McGaughey	6. Peter Snider	10. Alexander Hartt
3. Micheal Nyman	7. Robert Campbell	11. David Coldwell
4. Robert Young	8. Hugh Weir	13. William L. Taylor

who being elected tried and Sworn the truth to Speak upon the issue
Joined upon their Oaths Do say the Defendant did assume upon himself
in manner & form as the plaintiff against him hath complained & that
the plaintiffs were not deted to the Deft. as in pleading he hath alleged & they assess the plaintiff Damages by occasion of the Non preformance of that Assumption to one hundred & thirty one Dollars & Seventy five cents besides his costs.
        It is therefore considered by court that the plft . re-
cover against the Deft. the Damages aforesaid as by the Jury aforesaid assessed & their costs by them about their Suit in this behalf
expended and the said Deft. in Mercy &c. Rule for new trial.

252.   A Deed of conveyance from David Love to Josiah patty for fifty
five acres of Land on Lackeys Creek was acknowledged in open court by
said Love the Subscriber thereto and admitted to Record Let it be
registered.

                Court adjourned till tomorrow morning 9 Oclock

                Tuesday 26th June 1810

                Court met according to Adjournment

                        Present

        James Gillespy, Jessee Wallace & Wm. Gault, Esqrs

        A Bill of Sale from David Russell to David Grass for land was
acknowledged in open court by said Russell the subscriber thereto where
fore it is admitted to Record let it be registered

253.   Four Instruments of writing perporting to be relinquishments of a
tract of land in Davidson County by Thomas McGuire one of the witnesses
thereto wherefore they were admitted to Record Let it be registered.
        Which relinquishments were from Isan Bridwell, Joshua Bridwell,
James Bridwell, Mary Bridwell to Mary Bridwell & George Bridwell.

Henery X Lindenbarger)
        vs   )
Lowry & Waugh   )   On motion of the plaintiff & for reasons appear-

ing in their Affidavit

It is ordered that a Commission issue to Robert Henderson & Thomas Doneland to take the Deposition of Thomas Bailey & John Henry of Baltimore to be read at the trail of this Case in behalf of the plaintiff with giving the Defendant 30 days previous Notice of the time & place of taking the same.

Abnor Underwood appeared here in open court and Satisfyed the Court he has a License Authorising him to practice as an attorney in the Several Courts of Law & Equity within the State and thereupon took the Oath of an Attorney and is admitted to practise in this court Accordingly

Sollomon McCampbell)	
vs)	Case
John McCartney)	This day came the parties by their Attornies and thereupon came a Jury (to wit.)

John Norwood	Josiah Payne	Robert Cooper
Thomas Wooden	Samuel Campbell	Thomas Blair
Peter Snider	Jonathan Lassites	John McMahan
John McGhee	Robert Gray m	Benjamin Harbert

who being elected tried and sworn the truth to speak upon the issue Joined upon their Oaths do say the Defendant did assume upon himself in Manner & form as the plaintiff against him hath complained & they further find that the Defendants made no accord or Satisfaction as the plaintiff in pleading hath alleged & they assess the plaintiff Damages by occasion of the Non preformance of that Assumption to one hundred & thirty one Dollars & Seventy five cents besides his Costs

It is therefore considered by Court that the plaintiff recover against the Defendant his damages aforesaid as by the Jury aforesaid assessed & his costs by him about his suit in this behalf expended and the said Defendant in Mercy &c.

255. A Bill of Sale from John Shaffer to Joseph Cresswell for sixty one acres of Land lying on Millstone Creek was acknowledged in open court by John Shaffer the Subscriber thereto and admitted to Record Let it be registered.

John Green)	
vs)	Fi.Fa.
Wm Wallace)	It is ordered that a writ of Error be granted in this case

and that the clerk make out a complete Transcript of this cause and certify the same to the next court to be held for the county of Blount on the First Monday of August next.

A Disolution of the partnership of Samuel Love & Co was proven in open court by James Berry one of the Subscribing witnesses thereto and Admitted to Record Let it be Registered

Court adjourned till tomorrow Morning 9 Oclock

256. Wednesday 27th June 1810

Wednesday Morning

Present

James Gillespy Esquire

There not being Majistrates Sufficient to make a court
It is ordered that the business Stand Adjourned untill to-morrow morning 9 Oclock

Thursday Morning the 28th of June 1810

Court met according to Adjournment

Present

George Ewing, Joseph Alexander & John Walker Esqrs.

Ordered by Court that Robert Gauld be Guardian to Edward Gault to defend a Suit brought by Hugh Weir against the Said Robert & Edward
Ordered by court that John Walker be guardian to Mary Hess he having entered into bond with approved Security as the law directs.

Ordered by court that Thomas Stewart be Guardian to John Wood who together with John Walker & Andrew Gamble acknowledged their bond in the Sum of One Thousand Dollars as the Law directs.

257.   A Bill of Sale from Jesse Wallace to Lowry & Waugh was proven in Open court by Barcley McGhee the Subscribing witness thereto and admit-ted to Record Let it be registered

A Bill of Sale from Andrew Cowan Deputy Sheriff to John purris was acknowledged in Open Court for land lying on Gallahers Creek by Said Andrew the subscriber thereto Wherefore
It is ordered that the same be admitted to Record Let it be registered.

Samuel Lane for the use of) *LOVE*
John Montgomery   )
                vs   )   Debt.
Robert Rhea   )   This day came the plaintiff by his Attorney
                               and filed his Declaration and the Defendant
being Solemnly called came not but made default.
It is therefore considered by Court that the plaintiff re-cover against the Defendant 185.6 cents with lawfull intrust the Debt in the Declaration Mentioned and his costs by him about his suit in this behalf expended and the said Defendant in Mercy.

258.   Lowry & Waugh)
             vs   )   Casement
       Jesse Wallace)   This day came the parties by their Attornies and there-
                         upon came a Jury (to wit.)

1. Samuel Henry	5. Alexander Harris	9. Josiah Paine
2. Benja. Harbert	6. Samuel Harris	10. James Douglass
3. Joseph McFadeon	7. Peter Snider	11. James Gillespy
4. William Harris	8. Robert Gray	12. Wilson White

who being elected tried and Sworn the truth to speak upon the issue
Joined upon their Oaths do say the Defendant hath not Kept & preformed
his covenant with the plaintiff but hath broken the same in Manner &
form as the plaintiff against him hath complained & they assess the
plaintiffs damages by occasion thereof to twenty five Dollars besides
Costs

    It is therefore considered by Court that the plaintiff
recover against the Defendant his damages aforesaid as by the Jury a-
fore asaid assessed & their costs by them about their suit in this behalf expended and the said Defendant is in mercy &c.

    Court adjourned till tomorrow Morning 9 Oclock

259.   Friday 29th June Term 1810

            Court metaccording to Adjournment

                 Present

    James Gillspy, George Ewing & Robert McCulley Esqurs

    A Bill of Sale from Andrew Cowan Deputy Sheriff to John Hickland
for Land was acknowledged in open court by said cowan the Subscriber
thereto
    Wherefore It is admitted admitted to Record Let it be registered.

    A Bill of Sale from William Maclin to Miles & David Cunningham was
proven in open court by John Wilkinson a witness thereto for a Negro boy
named Jess
    Wherefore It is admitted to Record Let it be registered

    Ordered by court that the commissioners appointed to attend to
fixing the Court houseattend as expeditionally as possible to finishing
the Same

    A Power of Attorney from Samuel Rowan to James Wilson was acknow-
ledged in open court by said Rowan the Subscriber thereto
    Wherefore It is admitted to Record Let it be registered

260.   A power of Attorney from James Hammell to James Willson was acknowledged in open court by Said James Hammell the Subscriber thereto
and Admitted to Record Let it be registered

    A Bill of Sale from William Baker to James Moore was proven in
open court by Samuel Steele & Jacob Baker two of the the Witnesses
thereto and admitted to Record Let it be registered.

State   )
  vs   ) On Motion of John Wilkinson Esqr. who prosecutes for
Miles Cunningham) the State & it appearing the Defendant has been bound
                    in Recognizance to appear here and answer the charge
of the State & he not appearing tho Solemnly called
    It is therefore considered by court that the Defendant for-
feit & pay Two hundredDollars the amount of his Recognizance aforesaid
According to the form & Effect of his Recognizance aforesaid unless
he appear at next term & show sufficient reasons to the contrary

261.   John Sharp)
        vs   )   Enquiry
   Nancy Scott)   This day came the parties by their Atto. and thereupon
                      came a Jury (to wit.)

1. Micheal Smith	5. Francis Henderson	9. Hugh Weir
2. John Finley	6. Wm. L. Taylor	10. John McGhee
3. George Grigsby	7. George Coldwell	11. Robert Gray
4. Thomas Harris	8. Peter Snider	12. Alexander McNutt

who being elected tried and sworn well & truly to enquire of Damages in this cause do say they assess the plaintiffs Damages to one hundred & fifteen Dollars & forty four cents.

It is therefore considered by court that the plaintiff recover against the Defendant his damages aforesaid as by the Jury aforesaid assessed & his costs by him in this behalf expended & the Said Deft. in Mercy &c.

262:   John Coldwell Guardian)
   of Kellies Heirs   )
           vs   )   Attachment
   Andrew Woods   )   This day came the plaintiff by his Atto. & filed
                      his Declaration & the Defendant being Solemnly
called came not but made default

It is therefore considered by Court that the plaintiff recover against the Defendant two hundred & Sixty Six Dollars & Sixty Six Cents the Debt in the Declaration mentioned & their costs by them in this behalf expended & the said Defendant in Mercy &c.

Josiah Danforth)
      vs   )   Atto.
John Craige   )   This day came the plaintiff by Attorney & filed his
                    declaration & the Defendant being Solemnly called came
not but made default

It is therefore considered by court that the plaintiff recover against the Defendant three hundred & thirty three dollars & 33 1/3 cents his Debt in the Declaration mentioned and his costs by him in his suit in this behalf expended & the Said Deft. in Mercy &c.

263.   Steele & Love)
        vs   )   Sci. Fac.
Andrew Miller)   This day came the plaintiff by Atto & it appearing by
                  the Sci. Facias returned by the Sheriff that there has
been two nichols returned in this cause and the Defendant being Solemnly called came not but made default

It is therefore considered by court that the plaintiff recover against the Deft. Seventy Eighty one Dollars the amount mentioned in Said Sci. Facias together with the further Sum of the costs by them in this behalf expended & the Said Defendant is Mercy &c.

Robert Dyal   )
      vs   )
Andrew Miller &)   Scil Fac.
Woods Lackey, Secy.)   This day Came the plaintiff by atto. & it appearing there has been two nichols returned in this case

and the Defendant being Solemnly called came not.

It is therefore considered by Court that the plaintiff recover against Defendant in Debt in the ScB.Fac. mentioned together with his Costs by him about his suit in his behalf expended & the Deft. in Mercy &c.

264. Robert McCulley)
       vs   )
Samel Eakin &   )
Henry McCulley   ) This day came the plaintiffs by their Attorneys & the
                   plaintiffs Demurror to the Defendants plea being argued and Nature deliberation had thereon

It is therefore considered by court that the plea aforesaid and the Matters therein contained are not Sufficient in Law to barr the plaintiffs action.

A Power of Attorney from Josiah Danforth to James Wilson was acknowledged in open court by said Danforth the Subscriber thereto wherefore It is admitted to Record Let it be registered.

Ordered by court that John Finley be administrator of the Estate of John Johnson Decd. he having given bond with approved Security. as the Law directs.

245. Josiah Danforth)
       vs   )
John Johnson   ) On motion of the plaintiff by Attorney It is ordered
                   by court that the Suit Stand renewed against John
Finley the Defendants Administrator by his consent.

265. Josiah Danforth)
       vs   ) Attach.
John Finley   ) This day came the plaintiff by Atto. & filed his
                   Decl. & the Defendant not appearing tho Solemnly
called

It is therefore considered by Court that the plaintiff recover against the Defendant such damages as he hath Sustained by occasion of the Said Intestates non performance of his assumption in the Decl Mentioned which damages are to be enquired of at our next Court.

John Gardiner Esquire came into open court & resigned his commission as Such Therefore Let the Same be certified to the next General Assembly.

Court adjourned till court in course 9 Oclock

                                   Jas. Gillespy, P. J.

266. Blank

267.   At a court of pleas and quarter Sessions begun & held for the County of Blount at the Court House in Maryville on the fourth Monday of September 1810

                        Present

James Gillespy, George Ewing & John Waugh, Esquires Justices

Andrew Cowan Deputy Sheriff of the County aforesaid returned our writ of Venire to him directed executed on the following persons to wit

1. John Hickland	5. Wm. McKenney	9. John Eddington
2. William Henderson	6. Richard Williams	1o.Jno. Edmonds
3. James Singleton	7. Reuben Charles	11. Josiah Payne
4. John Gould	8. George Cope	12. James Houston
13. James Douglass	14. David Wilson	15. Alex Hartt

A Deed of conveyance from William Maclin to John Montgomery for Six hundred twenty nine & three fourth acres of Land was proven in open Court by Charles Donahoo & James Berry witnesses thereto wherefore it is admitted to record Let it be registered.

268.   Robert McCulley Administrator)
of Robert Eakin Decd.   )
         vs   )   Debt.
Samuel Eakin & Henry McCulley)   This day came the Defendants by their
                                 Attornies & withdrew the pleas by them
Mformerly plead in this cause and on motion of the plaintiff by his Attorney the Defendants were solemnly called came not but made default whereby the plaintiff therein against them remaineth Altogether unexpended.

It is therefore considered by court that the plaintiff recover against the Defendants one hundred & twenty SixDollars & thirty six cents the debt in the declaration mentioned together with fourty five Dollars & fourty Eight cents the amount of Damages by them sustained by occasion of the detention of the Same from which the Defendant prayed an appeal to the next circuit court.

A Deed of conveyance from Robert Tedford to John Montgomery for Two hundred & twenty two acres of land was acknowledged in open court by said Tedford the subscriber thereto
Wherefore it is admitted to Record Let it be registered

269.   William Cox & Co.   )
Assinee of Robert Strain)
         vs   )   This day came the parties by their attornies
William Steward   )   and thereupon came a Jury (to wit.)

1. Thomas Cooper	5. Robert Tedford	9. James Houston
2. Samuel Weir	6. James McKenny	10. John Edmonds
3. Joseph Sloss	7. William Ewing	11. George Cope
4. Benja. Harbert	8. James Douglass	12. William McKamy

who being elected tried and Sworn the truth to speak upon the issue joined upon their Oaths Do say the Defendant hath not paid the Debt in the Declaration mentioned & they assess the plaintiff damages to Nine Dollars & Seventy Seven Cents besides Costs.
It is therefore considered by Court that the plaintiff recover aganist the Defendant Fifty Nine Dollars & twenty five Cents the Debt in the Declaration Mentioned together with the Damages afore-

said in form aforesaid assessed & his costs by him and about his suit
in this behalf expended & the Said Defendant in Mercy &c.

370.   David Caldwell & Thomas Henderson   )
        Administrators of Thomas Weir &   )
        Elizabeth Weir his wife Administratrix) Appeal
                        vs   ) This day came the parties by
        John Waugh   ) their attornies and thereupon
                                                  came a Jury to wit the same Jury
as in the case of William Cox &c. Against William Steward who were elec -
ted sworn & well & truly to try the matter in controversy do Say they
find for the plaintiff & assess their Damages to Fifteen Dollars & Eight
Cents besides costs
            It is therefore considered by Court that the plaintiff
recover against the Defendant the Damages aforesaid as by the Jury aforesaid assessed & their costs by them about their suit in his behalf expended & the Said Defendant in Mercy &c rule for New trial made absolute

        Josiah & John Nichol Assinee)
        of Baker & Russell   )
                    vs   )
        John Wallace   ) Appeal
) This day came the parties by their attornies
                                      and thereupon came a Jury (to wit) the same
Jury as in the case of Cox. & Co. vs. Steward who were elected tried and
sworn well and truly to try the matter in controversy upon their oaths
do say they find for the plaintiff & assess their damages to Forty Seven
Dollars & three cents besides costs.

271.   It is therefore considered by court that the plaintiff recover
        against the Defendant Forty Dollars & Seventy Eight Cents the damages
        as by the Jury in form Aforesaid Assessed & their costs by them about
        their Suit in this behalf expended & the Said Defendant in Mercy &c.

        Robert Taylor Assinee)
        of W. H. James Wood)
                vs   )
        Josiah Danforth   ) Debt
) This day came the parties by their Attornies
                               & thereupon came a Jury to wit the same Jury
as in case Cox & co. Against William Steward who being elected tried
and Sworn well & truly to try the issue Joined upon their Oath Do say
the Defendants hath not paid the Debt in the Declaration Mentioned
& they assess the plaintiffs damages by Occasion of the detention to S
Seven Dollars & twenty Seven Cents besides Costs
            It is therefore considered by Court that the plaintiff
recover against the Defendant Fifty four Dollars & forty six cents the
Debt in the Declaration Mentioned together with Seven Dollars &twenty
seven cents the damages aforesaid as by the Jury Aforesaid assessed
& his costs by him about his suit in this behalf expended & the said
Deft. in Mercy &c.

272.   Charles Baker for the use   )
        of W. Harriss   )
                vs   )
        William McMahan & David Brown) Court & Enquiry
                                       This day came the plaintiff by his
                                       Attorney and thereupon came a Jury

to wit the same as in the case Cox & co. vs Steward who being elected
tried tried & sworn the truth to enquire of damages in this cause upon
their Oaths do say the plaintiff hath sustained damages by occasion of
the Defendants breach of their covenant in the declaration mentioned to
the amount of Sixty four Dollars & thirty Six Cents besides costs.

It is therefore considered by court that the plaintiff
recover against the Defendant Sixty four Dollars & Ninety Six cents
the damages aforesaid as by the Jury aforesaid as by the Jury aforesaid
assessed & his costs by him about his suit in this behalf expended &
the said defendant in mercy.

William Cox & Co.)
    vs   ) Covt.
John Ryder   ) This day came the parties & thereupon came a Jury to
               wit the same Jury as in the case of Cox & Co. vs

273.

Steward Steward who being elected tried and sworn the truth to speak
upon the issue Joined upon their Oaths do say the Defendant hath not
kept and performed his covenant with the plaintiff but hath broken the
same in manner & form as the plaintiff against him hath complained &
they assess the plaintiffs damages by occasion of the non preformance
of that covenant to Eighty one dollars & Fifty five cents besides costs

It is therefore considered by Court that the plaintiff recover against the Defendant his damages aforesaid as by the Jury aforesaid assessed & his suit in this behalf expended & the said Defendant
in Mercy & c.

William Cox Assinee)
of Robert Strain)
    vs   ) Debt
Reuben Charles) This day came the parties by their Attornies &
             thereupon came a Jury to wit the same Jury as in
the case of Wm. Cox & Co against Wm. Steward who being elected tried
and sworn the truth to speak upon the issue Joined upon their Oaths do
say the defendant hath not paid the debt in the Declaration mentioned
as the plaintiff hath complained & they assess the plaintiffs damages
to Nine Dollars by Occasion of the detention of that debt besides costs

274.

It is therefore considered by court that the plaintiff recover against the defendant Sixty Dollars the debt in Declaration mentioned together with nine Dollars his damages aforesaid as by the Jury
aforesaid assessed & his costs by him about his suit in this behalf
expended & the said Defendant in Mercy &c.

Barcley McGhee   )
    vs   )
John McCullock & Thomas McCullock) Covt.
             This day came the parties by their
             Attornies & thereupon came a Jury
to wit the same Jury as in the case of William Cox & Co. against William
Steward who being elected tried and sworn well and truly to try the issue Joined upon their Oath do say the Defendant hath not Kept & preformed his covenant with the plaintiff but hath broken the same in manner and form as the plaintiff against him hath complained and they assess the plaintiff damages by occasion of the Defendants non preforr-
mance of that covenant one hundred & thirty Seven Dollars & Seventy
three Cents besides costs.

It is therefore considered by court that the plaintiff re-

275.   cover against the Defendant one hundred & twenty seven Dollars & seventy
three cents the damages aforesaid as by the Jury aforesaid assessed together his costs by him about his suit in this behalf expended & the
said defendant in Mercy &c.

An instrument of writing purporting to be the last will & Testament
of Thomas Cooper Senr. Decd. was produced in open court & proven by
John Tedford & Thos. Cooper Senior Robert Cooper & James Cooper were ap
pointed Executors of said will were qualified accordingly.

Court adjourned till tomorrow morning 9 Oclock

276.   Tuesday September 25th26th 1810

Court met according to adjournment

Present

James Gillespy, William Davidson, William Lowry, Joseph Alexander,
& Robert McCulley, Esquires Justices present

A Power of attorney from Mary Clendening, Charles Clabough Betsy
Clabough formerly Betsy Clendening Polly Clendening Nancy Clendening
& John Clendening to John McGhee was proven in open court by Mathew Gar-
rett & Zarobell Langston two of the subscribing witnesses thereto
Whereupon It is admitted to Record

Justices Present

William Gillespy, Joseph Alexander, Robert McCulley Esquires

Thomas M. Clarke)
      vs   ) Detuins
John Miller   ) This day came the parties by their attornies & there-
                  upon came a Jury to wit.

1. William Gay   5. Abraham Utter   9. Richard Williams
2. John Boyd   6. Abraham Wallace   10. Jno. Edmonds
3. John Nail   7. John Norwood   11. Jas. Douglas
4. Andrew Kenneday   8. John Hickland   12. Geo. Cope

277.   who being elected tried and sworn the truth to speak upon the issue
Joined upon their Oaths do say the Defendant hath not detained the horse
in the Declaration Mentioned as the Defendant in pleading hath alleged
            It is therefore considered by court that the plaintiff
take nothing by his bill but for his false clamour be in mercy & that
the Defendant go without day and recover against the plaintiff his
costs by him about his defense in this behalf expended From which
Judgment the plaintiff prayed an Appeal to the Honorable Circuit
Court to be holden for Blount County at the Court House in Maryville
on the first Monday of February next.

John B. Cusack   )
      vs   )
Holbert McClure & Securities) This day came the plaintiff by Enoch Par-
                               sons Esquire his attorney

moved for Judgment againstHolbert McClure & his Securities which Motion when argued was overruled.

278.   It is therefore consideredby Court that the plaintiff take nothing by his Motion but for his false clamour be in mercy & that the Defendant go and recover against the plaintiff the costs of this motion.

Ordered by court that John Waugh William Gault & Johh Walker Esquire Settle with Richard Williams & John Gamble Executors of John Williams Decd. & report the Settlement to this court.

On motion of Robert Wilson ordered by court that George Fox be bound to said Wilson until he arrives at the age of twenty one years and Indentures were executed accordingly.

A Settlement of the Estate of John Williams Decd. was returned to Court & filed

A Deed of conveyance from Richard Ramsey to peter Brickey for —————— was acknowledged in open court by said Richard Ramsey the Subscriber thereto wherefore
It is ordered to record Let it be registered.

Ordered by Court that James McClannahan be constable for the County of Blount he having given bond with Hugh Kelsoe & Wm Lowry his Security and was qualified as the law directs.

279: Martin Rorex)
        vs   ) Debt
Andrew Jackson) This day came the parties by their Attornies and thereupon came a Jury (to wit)

1. John Gould   5. Thomas Henderson   9. James McClannahan
2. Reuben Charles   6. John Carson   10. Holbert McClure
3. James Houston   7. David Coldwell   11. John Ryder
4. Samuel Montgomery   8. William Samples   12. Henery Coyle

who being elected tried and Sworn the truth to speak upon the issue Joined upon their oath do say the Defendant hath not paid the debt in the Declaration mentioned and they assess the plaintiffs damages by occasion of the Detention of that debt to Seventeen Dollars & Eighty five cents besides Costs.
It is therefore considered by court that the plaintiff recover against the Defendant the Debt in the Declaration mentioned together with seven Dollars & Eighty five cents his damages aforesaid as by the Jury aforesaid Assessed & his costs by him about his suit in this behalf expended and the said Defendant in Mercy &c.

280. Andrew Jackson)
         vs   )
Benjamin Dowell) This day came the plaintiff by Jacob Peck Esquire his Attorney & thereupon came a Jury to wit the same Jury as in case Rorex Against Andrew Jackson who were elected tried and sworn truly to enquire into facts in this cause do say that Andrew Jackson the plaintiff in this case was Security for the Defendant Benjamin Dowell on a Bond on which Judgment was this day entered in fa-

vour of Martin Rorex against Andrew Jackson for one hundred & twenty
seven Dollars and on motion of the plaintiff by his Attorney Aforesaid
and on the facts as found by the Jury aforesaid and in pursuance of
the Statutes in this case made & provided

It is considered by court that the plaintiff recover a-
gainst the Defendant one hundred& twenty seven Dollars it being the a-
mount of the Judtment & eleven Dollars sixty two ½ a half cents recovered
against the Said Andrew As Security for the Said Benjamin together with
eleven Dollars & fifty the costs of this Motion & the said Defendant
in mercy & C.

A Bill of sale from William Lowry to Abraham Wallace for two hundred & forty four acres of Land was acknowledged in open court by said
Lowry the Subscriber thereto wherefore

It was admitted to Record Let it be registered.

281.　　A Bill of Sale from William Lowry to Abraham Wallace for four negroes was acknowledged in open court by William Lowry the subscriber
thereto wherefore

It is admitted to Record Let it be registered.

A Settlement of the Estate of James Young Deceased was returned to
court & filed

Court adjourned untill tomorrowmorning 9 Ocloc,

282.　　Wednesday 26th September 1810

Court Met according to Adjournment

Present

Joseph Alexander, John Reagen & Robert McCulley Esquires

A lease of Land from Cornelus Alexander to John Montgomery for the
use of Jane Alexander his wife was proven in open court by James Houston
one of the subscribing witnesses thereto

Wherefore It is admitted to Record Let it be registered

Josiah Danforth vs John Finley Administrator of) John Jonston Decd.	Case　　W. of Enquiry This day came the plaintiff by his Attor- ney & thereupon came a Jury (to wit.)

1. Samuel Thompson	5. Samuel Donahoo	9. John Edmonds
2. Robert McMurry	6. John Gould	10. Josiah Payne
3. James Cook	7. William McKamey	11. James Houston
4. Samuel Mitchell	8. Richard Williams	12. James Douglass

who being elected tried and sworn well & truly to enquire of damages
in the case upon their Oath do say they assess the plaintiffs damages
to Sixty Dollars & Twenty five cents besides costs

It is therefore considered by Court that the plaintiff re-
283.　　cover against the Defendant Sixty Dollars & 25, cents the damages aforesaid as by the Jury aforesaid assessed & his costs by him about his

suit in this behalf expended & the Said Defendnat in Mercy &c.

Thomas N. Clarke)
    vs   ) This day came the plaintiff & filed his reasons &
John Miller   ) entered into bond with securities for the prosecu-
               tion of his appeal with effect by him payed yester-
day in this case & the same was granted accordingly.

      A Report of the Guardianship of William Gamble was returned recei-
ved by Court & filed.

      Ordered by Court that Samuel George William Davidson & John Waugh
Esquires be commissioners to Settle with Martha Martin Administratrix
of Warnor Martin Dedd

      A report of the settlement of the Commissioners appointed to settle
with Martha Martin Administratrix of Warnor Martin Decd. was returned
recrived & filed.

284.   William Gardenehire Assinee)
              vs   ) Case
    David Hendley   ) This day came the parties by their Attornies
                   and thereupon came a Jury (to wit.)

1. Joseph Hickland   5. William Moore   9. John Norwood
2. George Cope   6. Silas George   10. Thomas Bell
3/ William Davidson   7. Samuel McGaughey 11. James Strains
4. Samuel McConald   8. Samuel Thompson   12. Holbert McClure

who being elected tried and sworn well and truly to try the issue Joined
and thereupon came the plaintiff with the Article on which he founded
his suit with William Scott a witness thereto all of which he produced
as Evidence in this cause & the Defendant by his attorney moved to Set
the proof aforesaid aside on account of a raxure appearing on the face
of the aforesaid article which motion when argued was sustained to which
Judgment of the Court the plaintiff by Attorney tendereda Bill of Execution which was as follows to wit In this cause the plaintiff produced
285.   a note of hand purporting to be signed by the Defendant in the words
and figures following to wit
              For value received I promise to pay Adam Sherrill ar order
twh hundred and Sixty five Dollars in Horses the twenteeth of June
1807
    Test   David Henley
        Nine Mile Creek
        William Scott 22 April 1807
        which note of hand the 1st day of October 1807 has been assigned to
the plaintiff William Scott the subscribing witness to the note proved
on oath he saw the said David Henly Sign & deliver the note to said
Sherrell at the time stated in the note that the that the Assignment
was in the hand writing of Sherrell at the time stated that the mark ex
er raxure following the words at in the note he could not say whether
it was so when the note was Signed or not nor by whom made nor when and
further stated there was another article under the hand and Seal of
the said Sherrell and Henley executed and delivered at the same time
which last mentioned article recited the whold contract and the place

of payment of the property stated in the note and also stated that the property mentioned in the note was by the agreement of the parties to be paid at Nine Mile at Henleys own house but could not say whether that

286. was mentioned in the note was signed

Upon which Statement of the witness Scott John McCampbell Esquire attorney for the Defendant objected to the note being permitted by the court to go as evidence to the Jury alledging there was proofff proof of an erasure in the before Statement of Scott and by the court inspecting the paper of which openion were the court saying the refure appeared to have done with different Ink and withheld the note declared on by the plaintiff from the Jury upon the objection before Stated and after the note had been read to the Jury

To which openion of the court the plaintiff by Enoch Parsons his counsel excepts in law and prays the court to Sign this his bill of exception which was read. signed & sealed by the Court and ordered to be made a part of the Record in Said Course

                    Wm Davidson
                    John Tedford
                    Wm. Gault

and the Jury aforesaid upon their Oath aforesaid do say the Defendant did not assume upon himself in manner & form as the plaintiff hath declared as in pleading he hath alleged

It is therefore considered by court that the plaintiff take nothing by his bill but for his false clamour be in Mercy &c. & that the

287. Defendant go without day and recover against the plaintiff his costs by him in this behalf expended & c.

On the motion & petition of Martha Martin widow and elect of Warnor Martin Decd.

It is ordered that a Summons issue to the Sheriff of this County commanding him to summons twelve good and lawful men of said county to go on the land the said Warnor was in possession at the time of his decease and lay off and assign unto the said Martha Her dower in the lands of her said husband decd.

Charles McCallister Assinee)
of Nely McDonnald   )
     vs   ) appeal
Walter Trimble   ) This day came the parties by their attornies and thereupon came a Jury to wit

The Same Jury as in the case of Gardishere Assinee vs David Hendley who being sworn they find for the plaintiff and assess his damages to twenty nine dollars & four cents besides his costs

It is therefore considered by court that the plaintiff recover against the Defendant Twenty Nine Dollars & four cents his dam-

288. ages aforesaid as by the Jury aforesaid assessed & his costs by him about his suit in this behalf expended and the said Defendant in Mercy

          Court adjourned till tomorrow morning 9 Oclock

          Thursday Morning 27th September 1810

          Court met according to Adjournment

          Present

James Gillespy, William Lowry, William Davidson & John Reagan Esquires Justices present

Ordered by court that James Curry be allowed out of the poor money in the Treasury Six Dollars for every three months yet to come that he may keep and take care of William Carter one of the poor of this County and it was ordered by court that the clerk issued a certificate accordingly as the money spedfyed in this order may become due.

289.
Charles McCollester Assinee)
of Nely W. McDonnald)
   vs) appeal
Walter Trimble) This day came the parties by their Attos.
              and thereupon came a Jury (to wit.)

1. James McFear   5. Joseph Weldon   9. John Gould
2. William Armstrong   6. Joseph Black   10. William McKenny
3. William Boggertt   7. Samuel Camron   11. Richard Williams
4. Thomas O'Conner   8. John Hickland   12. John Edmonds

who being elecped tried and sworn well & truly to try the matter of controversey upon their Oaths do say they find for the plaintiff and assess his damages to Twenty Eight Dollars & Sixty two cents besides costs
It is therefore considered by court that the plaintiff recover against the Defendant Twenty Eight Dollars & Sixty two cents his damages aforesaid as by the Jury aforesaid assessed & his costs by him about his suit in this behalf expended & the Defendant in mercy &c.

290.
A Bill of Sale from Joshua Freeman to James Pearce for a negro woman & child was proven in open court by Andrew Norris one of the subscribing witnesses thereto wherefore the same was admitted to Record Let it be registered.

Robert McCulley)
   vs)
Samuel Eakin & Henery) This day came the Defendant by their attorney
McCulley) & moved to file reasons for the appeal by them
          heretofore Bond with two Sufficient securities
for the prosecution of same with effect which when argued was not granted

John McCauley & William Barnes who were summoned by the Sheriff as Jurors and Solemnly called came not
It is therefore considered by court that for such their contempt they be fined -------? a half cents each

On motion & affidavit of Joseph Black Junior It is ordered by Court that a certificate issue to Joseph Black Senr. for his attendance as a Juror six days.

300.
Joseph Irwin)
   vs) appeal
Richard G. Waterhouse) This day came the parties by their attornies &
         thereupon came a Jury (to wit.)

1. George Cope   5. James Straine   9. Thomas Hunter
2. Josiah Payne   6. Robert Straine   10. Robert Thompson

3. James Houston	7. Thomas Cooper	11. Joseph Hartt
4. James Douglas	8. William Wallace	12. David Coldwell

who being elected tried and sworn well and truly to try the matter of
controversey upon their oaths do say they find for the Defendant

It is therefore considered by court that the plaintiff
take nothing but for his false clamour be in Mercy & co. & that the defendant go without day and recover against the plaintiff his costs by
him about his defence in this behalf expended

301.

Alexander Patterson)
vs) Debt
James Kendrick & William Kendrick) This day came the Defendants by their
Attorney and relinquished the plea
by them in this cause and the Defendants being solemnly called came not
but made default

It is therefore considered by court that the plaintiff recover against the Defendant the debt in the declaration mentioned and
the damages sustained by occasion of the detention of the same & the
costs by him in this behalf expended & the said Defendant in Mercy & c.
The plaintiff orders a stay of Execution untill the first of December
next.

302.

A Deed of conveyance from Samuel McGaughey to Josiah P. Smith for
two hundred & forty acres three Rods & seven poles of Land was acknowledged in open court by said McGaughey the subscriber thereto wherefore It is admitted to record Let it be registered

Dorcas Wyley Administrator)
of Robert Wyley Decd.)
vs) Debt
John Wilson) This day came the parties by attornies
and thereupon came a Jury (to wit.)

1. William McKenny	5. John Hummell	9. John Edmonds
2. John McGhee	6. Joseph Wilson	10. Saml. Frazier
3. John Martin	7. Joseph Black	11. Wm. Glass
4. John Finley	8. Richard Williams	12. William Finley

who being elected tried and sworn the truth to speak upon the issue upon their oath do say the defendant hath not paid the Debt in the Declaration mentioned nor any part thereof as the plaintiff against him
hath complained and they assess the plaintiff damages to Sixteen Dollars & Eighty Cents besides costs.

303.

It is therefore considered by court that the plaintiff recover against the Defendant Seventy Dollars the Debt in the Declaration
& Sixteen Dollars & Eighty cents the damages sustained by occasion of
the detention of the Same & his costs by him about his suit in this behalf expended and the said Defendant in mercy &c.

John Gibson)
vs)
George Campbell & David Campbell) Appeal This day came the parties by their
attornies & thereupon came a Jury
to wit the same jury as in the case of Wyley against Wilson who being

elected tried and sworn well and truly to try the matter of controversy upon their Oath do say they find for the plaintiff & assess his damages to Forty Seven Dollars Forty six and a half cents besides costs.

It is therefore considered by court that the plaintiff recover against the Defendant Forty Seven Dollars & Forty Six and a half cents by him about his suit in this behalf expended & the said Defendant in Mercy &c.

304.

Friday 28th September 1810

Court met according to Adjournment

Present

James Gillespy, William Gillespy & Joseph Alexander Esquires Justices

State)
vs)
Hugh Cunningham) It appears in this case the Defendant was bound in Recognizance in the sum of two hundred Dollars for the said Hugh appearance at this court and answering to a charge of the State to be exhibited there & tried and the said Defendant being solemnly called came not.

It is therefore considered by court that he forfeit & pay the Sum of two hundred Dollars the amount of his recognizance aforesaid unless the said Hugh appear at Next Court and shew sufficient cause to the contrary

State)
vs)
Miles Cunningham) It appears in this cause the Defendant was bound in Recognizance as security in the Sum of one hundred Dollars for the faithful appearance of Hugh Cunningham at this court to answer a charge of the State to be exhibited against the Said Hugh and

305.

the said Hugh being solemnly called came not and failing to answer the said charge and the Defendant being solemnly called to bring in the body of the said Hugh and failing to do so

It is therefore considered by court that the Defendant forfeit one hundred Dollars the amount of his recognizance aforesaid unless he appear at the next term of this court and shew cause to the contrary

Love, Chairman of the)
Board of Commissioners)
vs) Appeal
James Trimble) This day came the parties by attornies & the
rule to shew cause to quash & dismiss the
proceedings being argued was discharged thereupon came a Jury (to wit.)

1. Richard Williams   5. James Douglass   9. Robert Maxwell
2. John Edmonds   6. Nathan Ewing   10. Saml. McCullock
3. Josiah Payne   7. Jonathan Weir   11. Richard Kirby
4. James Houston   8. Thomas Coldwell   12. Robert Young

who being elected tried and sworn well and truly to try the matter in

306. controversy upon their oath do say they find for the Defendant

It is therefore considered by court that the plaintiff take nothing but for his false clamour be in Mercy &c. And that the Defendant go thereof without day and recover against the plaintiff his costs by him about his defence in this behalf expended. & C.

Bethia Stephens former wife and relict of John Stephens Decd. came into open court & Voluntarily relinquished her rights of administrating on the Estate of said John Stephens Decd. and on motion of John Stephens Junior administration of the said Estate was granted to him he having given bond with James ~~pexxxxxx~~ pearce & Richard Kirby in the sum of five thousand Dollars for the faithful administration of the same.

Bethia Stephens & William Stephens came into open court and made choice of John Stephens as their Guardian who entered into bond as the Law directs.

Ordered by court that Mathew Wallace Esquire make out a list of the Taxable polls and property in the bounds of Capt Thompson Company
307. & return the same within 25 days to the Clerks Office of this county.

Thomas D. OConner)
  vs   )
David Miller   ) On motion of the plaintiff by Attorney & for rea-
         sons appearing in the affidavit of the said plain-
tiff

It is ordered by court that a commission Issue to Mathew Wallace to take the Deposition of Isaac Upton residing in the Cherokee Nation && without the courts of this State with giving the Defendant fifteen days previous notice of the time & place of taking the same whose deposition is to be read at the trial of this Court in behalf of the plaintiff

An Instrument of writing purporting to be the last will & Testament of Hugh Weir Senr Decd. was produced in open court & proven by Joseph Alexander & Robert Young the subscribing witness thereto & John James one of the Executors therein appointed was qualified accordingly.

John Lowry   )
  vs   )
Archibald Trimble) This day came the parties by their attornies &
         the defendants surrender to the plaintiffs De-
claration being argued was overruled

It is therefore considered by court that the plaintiff recover against the Defendant such damages as he hath sustained by occasion. of the Defendants non preformance of his Covenant in the Declaration mentioned which damages are to be enqyired of by a Jury
308. at next court until which time this cause is continued.

William Armstrong)
  vs   )
Joseph Wilson) This day came the parties by their attornies &
         thereupon the Defendants Demurrer to the plaintiffs
declaration being argued and the matter of Law arising thereupon

It seems to the court here that the declaration aforesaid

& the matters therein contained are sufficient in Law to maintain the plaintiffs action

It is therefore considered by court that the plaintiff recover against the Defendant the damages he hath sustained by occasion of the Defendants non preformance of his covenant in the Declaration mentioned but because those damages are unknown to this court it is ordered that the same be enquired of by a Jury at next court until which time this cause is continued.

399.   James Moore)
      vs   ) Covt.
Aaron Allen) This day came the parties by their Attornies & the Defendants demurrer to the plaintiffs declaration being argued was overruled

It is therefore considered by court that the plaintiff recover against the Defendant such damages as he hath sustained by Occasion of the Defendants non preformance of his covenant in the Declaration mentioned which are to be enquired of by a Jury at next court until which time this cause is continued.

A Deed of conveyance from Robert Garrett & Elizabeth Garrett his wife to Samuel Maynard and a letter of Attorney contained in said Deed of conveyance from Robert Garrett to Henry H. Norwood and Thomas Harris Junior was duly proven in open court by the oaths of Enoch Parsons & Jacob Peck subscribing witnesses thereto who say they saw the said Robert Garrett & Elizabeth Garrett his wife sign seal & heard them acknowledge the same by their act and Deed for the purposes therein expressed the said Elizabeth being turely examined as the Law directs by James Gillespy presiding Justice &c.

310.   David Coldwell   )
      vs   )
John Lowry John Waugh   ) Debt
Adam Safley & Henry Parrott) This day came the parties by their attornies & thereupon came a Jury (to wit)

1. John Gould   5. Jacob Frank   9. John Strain
2. William McKamey   6. John Coldwell   10. John Glass
3. George Cops   7. Gavin Black   11. Alexander Harris
4. James Pearce   8. John Wilson   12. David Eagleton

who being elected tried and sworn well & truly the issue Joined upon their Oaths do say the Defendant hath not paid the Debt in the Declaration & they assess the plaintiffs damages by occasion of the detention of that Debt to Seventeen Dollars besides costs

It is therefore considered by court that the Plaintiff recover against the Defendant one hundred Dollars the debt in the declaration mentioned together with Seventeen Dollars the damages aforesaid as by the Jury aforesaid assessed & his costs by him about his suit in this behalf expended & the Defendants in Mercy &c.

311.   David Coldwell   )
      vs   )
John Lowry John Waugh   ) Debt
Adam Safley & Henry parrott) This day came the parties by their attornies & thereupon came a Jury (to wit.)

the same Jury as in the last case except James Dougless in place of John Wilson who being elected tried and sworn the truth to speak upon the issue Joined upon their Oath do say the Defendants hath not paid the Debt in the Declaration mentioned & they assess the plaintiffs damages to nineteen Dollars besides costs.

It is therefore considered by Court that the plaintiff recover of the Defendant one hundred Dollars the Debt in the Declaration mentioned together with Nineteen Dollars his damages aforesaid as by the Jury aforesaid and his costs by him about his suit in this behalf expended & the said Defendant in Mercy &c.

312.   Peter Hoyle)
              vs   )
        John Licans)   This day came the plaintiff by John Wilkinson Esquire his
                        Attorney & Moved for Judgment against the Defendant & It
appearing by an Execution in favour of William Logan against the said John Licans & peter Hoyle & the receipt for the same that the said Peter had satisfied the Same as Secutity for the said John Licans amounting to one hundred & one Dollars & Eighty Six cents principle & Interest.

It is therefore considered by Court that the plaintiff recover against the Defendant one hundred & one Dollars & Eighty Six cents the amount as appears to be paid by the said Hoyle as Security as aforesaid together with the costs of this motion & the said Defendant in Mercy & c.

Court adjourned till tomorrow morning 9 Oclock

313.   Saturday 29th September 1810

Court met according to Adjournment

Present

James Gillespy, Andrew Bogle, Mathew Wallace & Robert McGulley Esquires Justices present

Josiah Danforth)
        vs   ) attachment
Amos Edwards   ) This day came the plaintiff by Attorney & filed his
                    Declaration & the Defendant being attached by his
goods & chattles Lands & Tenaments to overule the plaintiff in the sum of Twelve thousand five hundred Dollars and he being solemnly called came not but made default.

It is therefore considered by Court that the plaintiff recover against the Defendant Twelve Thousand five hundred Dollars the Debt in the Declaration Mentioned together with Six thousand Seven hundred & Eighty one Dollars & twenty five Cents the damages sustained by occasion of the detention of the same & his costs by him about his suit in this behalf expended & the Defendant in Mercy &c.

314.   John Tipton by his Guardian)
        Jacob Moore   )
                    vs   )
        William Tipton, Executor of) Petition for distribution share of Estate
        Benjamin Tipton   ) This day came the plaintiff by Attorney &

on his Motion the Deft. was Solemnly called came not
It is therefore ordered that the petition be taken for confessed & the matters thereof be decreed accordingly and that the same be set for hearing expended & contd.

John Finley)
    vs
Saml. Donahoe) This day came the plaintiff & dismissed his suit & the Defendant agrees to pay the costs of the same.
It is therefore considered by court that the plaintiffs suit be dismissed & that the defendant pay the costs of the same.

Saml Frazier)
    vs   ) certiorari
Mathew Wallace) This day came the parties by their attornies & thereupon came the plaintiffs Rule to dismiss the writs of certiorarie & Supersidias was argued was sustained
315. It is therefore considered by Court that the plaintiff recover of the Defendant his costs by him about his suit in this behalf expended & the defendant in Mercy &c.

Samuel Frazier)
    vs   )
Mathew Wallace) Ordered by court that writs of certiorari & Supersidias issue according to the Defendants petition James Gillespy Robert McCulley & Aaron Bogle Esquires

Thos. D. Oconner)
    vs   )
David Miller) On motion of the plaintiff by attorney to take out of courts the Deeds on which he substituted this suit which Motion when argued was granted

Thomas D. O'Conner)
    vs   )
David Miller) This day came the plaintiff by Attorney & Moved to take out of court the Deed on which he substituted this suit which motionwhen argued was granted

316. Samuel Frazier)
    vs   )
Mathew Wallace) on motion of the Defendant & because It appears to the court here that there is no Justice to whom writs can issue he who tryed the cause having remained from the State
It is therefore ordered by Court that writs issue to the Clerk of this court to transmit the papers in this cause to our next Court & that the same be ready for hearing at the next Term of this Court.

Jacob Coyle)
    vs   )
William Schrimsher) It appears in this case on Motion of the plaintiff by Jacob Peck his attorney that the plaintiff obtained an Execution against the Defendant for the sum of Twenty four Dollars Debt & costs which execution was returned to Court levyed on a tract of Land

tract of land

It is therefore considered by Court that the Land on which the aforesaid Execution was leveyed be exposed to Sale agreeable to Law to satisfy the sum aforesaid together with the costs of this Motion

Ordered by court that John B. Cusack be fined Ten Dollars & Samuel Houston Five Dollars for commiting a contempt to this court in their view is disorderly riotously with an assemby of Melitia annoying the Court with the noise of a Drum and with force preventing the Sheriff and officer of the Court in the discharge of their duty and with force distubbing theGood order of said Court and abusing their Sheriff and demeaning themselves against the peace and dignity of the State

Ordered by court that John B. Cusick be fined Twenty Dollars for committing a contempt to this court in their view is aſ disorderly manner with an assembly of Malitia annoying the Court with the noise of **318.** aſ Drum and disregarding the Commands of their Sheriff.

Court adjourned till court in course
James Gillespy
presiding Justice

319. December 24, 1810

At a Court of pleas & quarter Sessions began & held for the County of Blount at the court house in Maryville on the fourth Monday of December 1810
Present

James Gillespy, Wm. Gillespy, John Tedford, George Ewing & Wm. Davidson Esqrs.

Andrew Cowan Deputy Sheriff of the county aforesaid returned our writ of Venire to him directed executed on the following persons (to wit.)

1. James Hammel	5. Isom Adams	9. David Coldwell
2. Alexander Ford	6. Alexander McClanahan	10. Alex. Malcum
3. Charles McClure	7. John Edmondson	11. Mashack Tipton
4. Samuel Ross	81 Joseph Hartt	12. Wm. Glass

Robert McCurdy summoned constable

The inventory of the Estate of John Stephens Decd. returned & filed

On motion administration of Wm. Hannahs Estate Deceased was granted Jean Hannah John Houston & Joseph Alexander they entering into bond & security ware qualified as the law directs.

320. Josiah Danforth }
vs } Attachment
Archibd Lackey } In this case the plaintiff having obtained an execution against the Estate of the Defendant & the Constable Charles Donahoo returned that he had levyed the same on one thousand acres of Land theproperty of Archibald Lackey laying on

Tennessee River including the plantation of Alex Kelly & Others

On motion of the plaintiff by Attorney Ordered that the aforesaid land be exposed to Sale agreable to Law.

A Deed of Conveyance from Burtin pride to John Biggs for four hundred acres of land was acknowledged in open court by said pride the subscriber thereto & admitted to record let it be registered.

A Deed of conveyance from Burton Pride to John Torbet for two hundred & Nineteen acres of land was acknowledged in open court by Burtin pride the subscriber thereto & admitted to Record let it be registered

On motion of Mashedk Upton he was appointed constable & entered into bond with John Lowry & James McClanahan security was qualified accordingly

321.　　　　Hugh Pugh returns as taxable 757 acres of land

Nancy Scott Admitx)
　　　vs　　　　）
John Wilkinson &　） Covt.
Samuel McGaughey　) This day came the parties by their attorneys &
　　　　　　　　　　the plaintiff Demurra to the second & fourth pleas
of the Defendant & the matters of law arising thereon & being argued it seams to the law then that the pleas aforesaid & the Matter therein contained are not sufficient in law to barr said plaintiff from his sd Action & that the Sd. Demurrar is sustained.

Alexander paterson)
　　　vs　　　　　）
Wm Kendrick &　　） Debt
James Kendrick　　) This day came Joseph Patty who was summoned a
　　　　　　　　　　garnishee in this case deposeth & saith　that
he gave his note to William Kendrick one of the defendants for one hundred & sixty six dollars & sixty six & two third cents due the 25th day of September 1810 & that if he had not assigned said note which he believes he has not to somebody else he owes him that payable in horses to be valued by John Cox & David Law at John Coxes house & to be valued equal to a brown horse let sd. Kendrick have last foal at eighty dollars & also eighty four cents payable the same way & no more & that he Knows of no other person owing the Defendant anything

322.　　　　　　　　Therefore it is considered by court that the property aforesaid be condemned in the hands of the garnishee to go to the payment of the Judgment & costs in the above suit & if it amounts to more that the ballance be refunded to the Defts.

　　John Tipton by Jacob Moore)
his Guardian Complxx complaint)
　　　　vs　　　　　　　　　　）
Wm. Tipton, Executor of Benjamin) petition for a distribution show
Tipton, Deceased　　　　　　　) of the sd. Benjamins personal
　　　　　　　　　　　　　　　　　Estate
　　Whereas on or about the month of February 1807 Benjamin

Tipton the father of the complainist departed this life in Blount
County Just having made his last will & Testament & therein appointed
Wm. Tipton of Knox County & Samuel Tipton of Carter County his Executors and the said Wm. Tipton one of the Executors afterwards in Blount
County proved sd William took upon himself the execution thereof and
whereas by the petition of sd complaintist pled in our sd court at
August sessions & which was then taken an confessed as the Defendant
failed to answer the same that the said complaintist is indebted to one
tenth part of the personal Estate of sd Benjamin Tipton Dedd. as his
distributive shaw and that sd Estate amounted to the sum of one thous-

323. and Dollars

Wherefore it is now ordered adjudged & Decreed by our sd
Court that the sd plaintiff recover of the sd. Defendant the sum of
one hundred Dollars & the further sum of three dollars the Interest on
said sum from the filing of the petition to this date and that the sd.
plaintiff recover against the sd. Defendant his costs in this behalf
expended & sd Daft. in Mercy &c.   Credit by ———— 59.25

Court adjourned till tomorrow 9 Oclock

Tuesday 25 of December 1810

Court met according to Adjournment

Present

James Gillespy, Wm. Davidson & John Waugh, Esqrs.

A Deed of conveyance from Saml Cowan Sheriff of Blount County to
James Dunlap was acknowledged in open court by sd. Cowan the subscriber
thereto & admitted to record let it be registered

324. A Deed of Morgage from Andrew Kenedy to George Ewing, Robert McTeer
Carson Coldwell & John Gamble for three hundred & thirty one acres of
land was acknowledged in open court by Andrew Kenedy the subscriber
thereto & admitted to record let it be registered

A Deed of conveyance from Adam Kuns & Mary his wife & Robert Murrin & Cathrine his wife to George Kilenger was acknowledged in open
court by Adam Kuns & Robert Murrin & John Waugh & Wm. Davidson to of
the acting Justices in sd.County who was appointed to take the privey
examination of Mary Kuns & Cathrine Murrin do certify that they freely
& voluntarily & without any scortion on the part of their respective
husbands acknowledged the syning & sealing the same wherefore it is
ordered by court that the same be admitted to Record

325. Nancy Scott Admitx　　　　　}
　　　　vs　　　　　　　　　　　}
John Wilkinson & Saml. McGaughey) This day came the parties by their at-
　　　　　　　　　　　　　　　　torniss ahd thereupon came a Jury

(to wit.)

1. Henry McCully	5. Wm. Logan	9. John Duncan
2. John Murphy	6. James McTeer	10. James Hamble
3. Robert Murrin	7. Holbert McClure	11. Charles McClure
4. George Irwin	8. James McGinley	12. Joseph Hartt

who being elected tryed & sworn the truth to speak on the issue Joined
upon their Oaths do say the Defendant hath not Kept & preformed their
covenant but the same hath broken in manner & form as the plaintiff a-
gainst them hath complained neither have they paid the money as in the
pleading they have alleged by reason of which breaches & further they
assess the plaintiff damage to one hundred & eighteen dollars & forty
one cents besides costs

        It is therefore considered by court that the plaintiff re-
cover of the Defendant the damage aforesaid as by the Jury aforesaid
assessed & the Costs by him about his suit expended & the sd Defendants
in Mercy &c.

326.   John Lowry   )
            vs   )   Case
    Charles McCormack)   This day came the parties by their Attornies & there-
                        upon came a Jury (to wit.)

1. Patrick Culton	5. James Strain	9. Elias Debusk
2. Aaron Beaty	6. Thomas Cooper	10. William Hicks
3. John Holoway	7. Wm. Wallace	11. Stephen Graves
4. Hezikiah Posey	8. James Dunlap	12. David Caldwell

who being elected tried and sworn the truth to speak on the issue Joined
upon their oaths do say the Defendant did assume on himself in Manner
& form as the plaintiff against him hath complained and they assess
the plaintiff damage by occasion of the non preformance of the asumpset
to one hundred & forty dollars thirty six & a half cents besides costs

        It is therefore considered by Court that the plaintiff re-
cover of the Defendant the damages aforesaid as by the Jury aforesaid
assessed & his costs by him about his suit in this behalf expended &
the said Deft. in mercy.

327.   William Armstrong)
            vs   )   Covt. Enquiry
    Joseph Wilson   )   This day came the parties by their attornies & there-
                        upon came a Jury (to wit.)

1. Robert Hurrin	5. Halbert McClure	9. Charles McClure
2. George Irwin	6. James McGinley	10. Joseph Hartt
3. Wm. Logan	7. John Duncan	11. Hugh Weir
4. James McTear	8. James Hamel	12. Alex Malcum

who being elected tryed & sworn well & truly to enquire of damages in
this case do say the plaintiff has sustained damage by occasion of the
Defendants Breach of his covenant to the Amount of one hundred & eighteen
dollars & forty one cents besides his costs.

        It is therefore considered by court that the plaintiff re-
cover of the Defendant the damages aforesaid as by the Jury aforesaid
assessed & his costs by him about his suit in this behalf expended &
the sd Defendant in Mercy &c.

    A Deed of trust from John Lowry to Hugh S. White John McCampble
& Robert King in trust for Jon. & Ro. Gamble Junr of the city of Rich-
mond was proven in open court by John Nicol & James Berry two of the

subscribing witnesses thereto & admitted to record let it be registered

328. William Finley)
     vs   ) certiorari
James McTear) This day came the parties by their attornies & there-
               upon came a Jury to wit

1. George Tedford	5. Hezekiah posey	9. Elias Debusk
2. patrick Culton	6. Thomas Cooper	10. William Hicks
3. Aaron Beaty	7. William Wallace	11. Stephen Graves
4. John Holaway	8. James Dunlap	12. George Dillard

who being sworn well & truly to try the Matter in controversy upon their
oaths do say they find for the Defendant
It is therefore considered by Court that the plaintiff
take nothing by his false clamour be in Mercy & c. & that the defendant go thereof without day & recover against the plaintiff his costs
by him about his suit in this behalf expended &c.

Elisa E. Moore & Mary Moor came into court & being over fourteen
years of age Chase Elizabeth Moor Guardian to Seyinah McPheebes Evelina
Moor & William Moore & the sd. Elizabeth Moor entered into bond in the
sum of ten thousand dollars for the faithful performance of sd trust
with William Aylett Alex Moor her security adjourned till tomorrow 9
Oclock

329.   Court met according to Adjournment

           Present

Andrew Bogle, George Ewing & John Regan Esquires

On motion of James Turk & the consent of those who had the case
of John James an infant under the age of twenty one years which sd
John was bound by indentures to sd Turk.

It is ordered that sd indenture be canceled & made void & the sd.
John James be discharged from sd service.

Samuel Love & Co.)
     vs   )
John Caruth   ) This day came the plaintiff by Enoch Parsons Esquire
              his Atforney & suggests to thiscourt that an execu-
tion issued in favour of him against the Defendant for the sum of forty
seven dollars Debt & costs which was returned to Court by Charles Donahoe Constable no property to be found in my county & levyed on a tract
of land in sd County lying on the waters of Crooket Creek where William Morrison now lives.
        It is therefore considered by court that the sd land be
exposed to sale or so much thereof as will be of value sufficient to
satisfy sd. Debt & Costs together with the costs of this motion as the
law directs The above Judgment & costs pd to M. parsons.

330.   XXXXXXXXXX

330. Isaac Wright)
   vs   )
  John Caruth) This day came the plaintiff by Enoch Parsons his Attor-
           ney & suggests to this court that an execution issued
in favour of him against John Caruth for the sum of seventeen dollars
& sixty two cents debt & costs which is returned to this court by
Charles Donahoo constable no personal property to be found in my county & leveyed on a tract of land in sd County laying on the waters of
Crocket creek whare William Morison now lives
     It is therefore considered by court that said land be
exposed to sale or so much thereof as will be of value sufficient to
satisfy sd, debt & costs together with the costs of this Motion the
above Judgment & costs pd to Mr. parsons.

Hance Russells Adms)
   vs   ) Appeal
John Waugh by their) This day came the parties by their Attornies
attornies   ) & thereupon came a Jury

1. Joseph Hartt	5. William Taylor	9. Abrah Wallace
2. Charles McClure	6. James Irwin	10. Robert Boyd
3. James Strain	7. John P. Harris	11. John Eagleton
4. Wyat Elliot	8. Benj. Wallace	12. Johh McAley

who being elected tried and sworn the truth to speak do say they find
for the Defendant

331)
332) Blank

333.   It is therefore considered by Court that the plaintiff take nothing by their false clamour but be in Mercy &c. & that the Defendant go
thereof without day & recover against the plaintiff his costs by him
about his suit in this behalf expended &c.
    On which Judgment & verdict the plfts pray an appeal filed
their Reason & entered into bond as the law directs & to them it was
granted.

   A Deed of conveyance from Samuel Cowan Sheriff of Blount County to
John Nicl for a tract of land not Known was acknowledged in open court
by sd. Cowan the subscribing Witness thereto and admitted to Record let
it be registered.

   A Deed of gift from Robert Warren to Wm. B. Warren for a negro
boy named John Was proven in open Court by Thomas Rankin & James Se-
vier the subscribing witnesses thereto & admited to record let it be
registered.

      Court adjourned

334. Edward Sharp)
   vs   ) Certiorari
  John Sharp) This day came the parties by their Attornies & there-
        upon came a Jury (to wit.)

1. David Coldwell	5. Carson Caldwell	9. Jonathan Tipton
2. James Hamel	6. James Syms	10. John Black
3. John Gamble	7. James McNutt	11. John Hickland
4. Samuel Henry	8. Jacob Frush	12. John Clayton

who being elected tried and sworn the truth to speak on the matter in controversy do say they find for the plaintiff & assess his damages to eleven dollars & costs.

It id therefore considered by court that the plaintiff recover of the Defendant the damages aforesaid as by the Jury aforesaid assessed & his costs by him about his suit in this behalf expended & the sd. Deft. in mercy &c.

On motion of Hopkins Lacy administration was granted him on the Estate of William Maclin Deceased who entered into bond with John Reagan James Kenny Wm. Kenny

335.   William Hicks Natt B. Buckhanan & Carson Coldwell his securities & was qualified accordingly.

Ordered by court that the clerk be allowed for the years 1809 & 1810 one hundred & twenty Dollars for his Exofice services

Ordered that the Sheriff of this county be allowed for the years 1809 & 1810 one hundred & forty dollars for his Exofice services

336.   Court met according to adjournment

Present

James Gillespy, Joseph Alexander & William Davidson Esquires

A Deed of conveyance from Samuel Cowan Sheriff of Blount County to Joseph Danforth for a tract of land the quantity not Known was proven in open court by John Wilkinson & John Gardiner to of the witnesses thereto & admitted to record let it be registered

A Deed of conveyance from Samuel Cowan Sheriff of Blount County to Josiah Danforth for a tract of land the quantity not known was proven in open court by John Wilkinson & John Gardiner two of the witnesses thereto & admitted to record let it be registered.

A Power of attorney from James Hanna to Joseph Calaway was proven in open court by James Calaway & Joseph McFadin two of the subscribing witnesses thereto & admitted to record let it be registered.

A Bill of Sale from Nathaniel Cox to John Cox for two negros was proven in open court by Anbros Cox & Richard Norris the witnesses thereto & admitted to record let it be registered.

337. Edward Sharp)
           vs   ) certiorari
      John Sharp) In this case on motion of Enoch parsons Attorney for the
                        defendant a rule was granted him to shew cause why a new

trial should be granted

Samuel Bowman)
  vs   ) Appeal
Thomas Henderson) This day came the parties by their Attornies and
        thereupon came a Jury (to wit.)

1. David Coldwell	5. Charles Hicks	9. Jeremiah Hammontree
2. James Hamel	6. Hugh Weir	10. Andrew Rody
3. James Donahoo	7. John Holaway	11. James Pearce
4. John Duncan	8. Joseph McFadien	12. Holbert McClure

who being elected tried and sworn the truth to speak on the matter in
controversy do say they find for the plaintiff & assess his damage to
ten dollars & twenty five cents besides his costs.

   It is therefore considered by court that the plaintiff recover of the Defendant his damages aforesaid as by the Jury aforesaid
assessed & his costs by him about his suit in this behalf expended &
the sd Defendant in Mercy &c.

  In the above case on Motion of the Deft by his attorney a rule was
granted him to show cause why a new trial should be granted.

338. John Lowry)
   vs   ) Covt & writ of Enquire
 Archibald Trimble) This day came the parties by their Attornies and
        thereupon came a Jury (to wit.)

1. Alex Malcom	5. Archbd. Maxwell	9. John Watson
2. Charles McClure	6. James Clark	10. Adam Warfill
3. Ransomperry	7. John Cox	11. Wm. James
4. Stephen Graves	8. Philip Fouts	12. Richd Chandler

who being elected tried and sworn well & truly to enquire of damages in
this case do say the plaintiff hath sustained damage by occasion of
the Defendants breach of covenant to the amount of Sixty dollars besides
his costs

   It is therefore considered by Court that the plaintiff recover of the Defendant the damages aforesaid as by the Jury aforesaid
assessed & his costs by him about his suit in this behalf expended & the
sd. Deft. in Mercy &c.

  A Deed of conveyance from James Moor to Charles Hicks for one hun-
dred& twenty nine acres of land was acknowledged in open court by James
Moor the subscriber thereto & admitted to record let it be registered.

339. Ordered by court that the clerk issue to Joseph Henderson a Certificate of his Moral Standing since ha had resided in the county of
Blount

  Ordered by court that James Gillespie & John Gillespie Esquires be
commissioners to settle with the Administrators of Hance Russell Deceased

James Moore)
    vs   ) Covt & writ of Enquire
Aaron Allin) This day came the parties by their attornies & thereupon
              came a Jury to wit

1. Ambros Cox	5. John Duncan	9. John Holaway
2. David Coldwell	6. Charles Hicks	10. Jeremiah Hammontree
3. James Hebel	7. Hugh Weir	11. Andrew Rody
4. James Donahoo	8. Joseph McFaedon	12. Halbert McClure

who being elected tryed & sworn well & truly to enquire of the damages
in this case do say the plaintiff hath sustained damages by occasion
of the Defendants breach of covenant to one hundred & one dollars & forty eight cents besides his costs.

        It is therefore considered by court that the plaintiff re-
cover of the Defendant one hundred & one dollars & forty cents the damages aforesaid as by the Jury aforesaid assessed & the sd. Defendant
in Mercy &c.

        Ordered that the following Justices return a list of the taxable
property in the several companies alotted by them (Viz.)

Capt. Dixons	Company	Henry Franks
" Buchanans	"	Joseph Alexander
" Houstons	"	John Tedford
" Beatys	"	George Ewing
" Allens	"	Robert McCulley
" Gardiners	"	Andrew Bogle
" Thompsons	"	Matt. Wallace
" Foresters	"	John Gillespy
" Hendersons	"	Wm. ~~kuckay~~ Lowry
" Wheelers	"	Wm. Davidson
" Davis	"	John Walker
" Ousack	"	Jessee Wallace

Jurors to March Court John Clayton Sam. Gould Samuel Saffle Robert Murrin
Robert McGhee, Senr., John May, Elias Debusk, John Woods, George Snider
Henry Bondm Junr. James Adams, Washington Allen & Wm. Finley

        The inventory of the Estate of James Greenaway presented in court
& ordered to be filed

                Court adjourned till tomorrow 9 Oclock

341.   Court met according to adjournment

                  Presnet

    James Gillespie, John Walker, George Ewing & John Waugh Esqrs

    A Deed of conveyance from Samel Love to Andrew Kennedy for three
fourth of an acre of land in the town of Maryvile was proven in open
court by Samuel Smith one of the witnesses thereto

A Deed of conveyance from Andrew Kennedy to John Nicol for three fourth of an acre of land with the appartinances was acknowledged in open court by sd Kenedy the subscriber thereto & admitted to record let it be registered.

A Deed of conveyance from William Colman to Thomas McFee for eighty six Acres of land was proven in open court by John Gardiner & Jacob Pick the subscribing witness thereto and admitted to record let it be registered.

342.   Ordered that William Brice Christopher ------? John Ried Samuel Alexander James Lackey Junr. William Reid & William Cagle be a Jury of View to lay out mark & report a road from Archer Johnstons to Greenaway Mills.

Andrew Gamble)
    vs   )
Andrew Evins &) In this case It appears to us on Motion of Enoch parsons
Charles Evins) esquire the plaintiff obtained an execution in our sd.
               Court against Andrew Evins George Ewing & Thomas Mc-
Cullock sixteen Dollars & fifty eight Cents & the sd. Andrew Evins Willing to Avail himself of an act of Assembly relative to the stay of execution entered into bond together with Charles C. Evins his security agreably to sd law But failing to comply with the request of Sd. bond
        It is therefore considered by court that the plaintiff recover of the Defendant of Andrew & Charles Evins security as aforesaid sixteen dollars & eighty three cents the amount of the aforesaid execution together with the costs of prescuting this motion & the sd. Defts. in Mercy &c.

343.   Elizabeth Steele)
Admtx. of Joseph)
Steele Deceased) In this case it appears to us on motion of John Wal-
    vs   ) ker esqr. the plaintiff obtained an Execution in our
Andrew James &) sd. court against Andrew James & Others for the sum
Joseph Wilson) of fourteen Dollars forty one cents & the sd. Andrew
          Willing to avail himself of an act of Assembly relative to the stay of Executions entered into bond together with Joseph Wilson his security agreable to sd law but failing to comply with the requests of sd. bond
        It is therefore considered by court that the plaintiff recover of the Defendant & their security Joseph Wilson fourteen dollars & forty one cents the amount of the aforesaid execution together with the costs of prosecuting this Motion & the Defts in mercy &c.

State   )
    vs   ) Sire Facus
Miles Cunningham) This day came the partievs by their Attornies & the
           Defendants attorney moved to quash the Sire faces &
dollen argument being had thereon & Mature deliberation the motion was overruled

State   )
    vs   )
Miles Cunningham) Security for Hugh Cunningham Fire Facias.

In this case ordered by court that the forfetures be set aside on payment of costs.

State)
vs) Sire Facias
Hugh Cunningham) In this case ordered by court that the forfeture be set aside on payment of costs.

State)
vs) Indictment
Hugh Cunningham) In this case the defendant being charged on the bill of Indictment plead not guilty and Afterwards withdraws his former plea & saith he is guilty in Manner & form as in the Indictment against him is alleged & puteth himself on the Mercy of the Court.

It is therefore considered by court that he pay five Dollars for the use of the County & pay the costs of this prosecution & May be taken & c.

345. State)
vs) Indictment A. B.
Jesse Vaughn) This day came as well the Solicitor as the Attorney for the Defendant & the Defendant by his Attorney moved for to be discharged & for reasons it appearing to the Court
It was ordered that the proceedings be dismissed & the Defendant discharged.

346. On Motion Administration of the Estate of James Smith Deceased is allowed to James Houston who entered with Wm. Alyatt & John Gardiner his securities in the sum of one thousand Dollars & was qualified as the law directs.

Elizabeth Kirkpatrick came into Court & relinquished his right of Administration on the Estate of Thomas Kirkpatrick & Administration was grant to Joseph Hart with the will examined which was proven & he entered into bond in the sum of one thousand Dollars with John Lewis & John Tedford his security & was qualified as the law directs.

Wm Robertson)
vs)
Wm Johnston) This day came the plaintiff by his Attorney & moved for a rule to dismiss the certiorari & to him it was granted.

347. On motion the Administration was granted to Hopkins Lacy on Wednesday last he resinded It appearing to the court that the sd Wm. Maclin had made a will in writing & sd Will was proven in open Court & proven by the oath & David Cunningham & Betsey Hill two of the witnesses thereto & admitted to record & Thomas McCurry John Montgomery John Wilkinson & Hopkins Lacy appeared in open court & took on themselves the Execution of sd Will being a Majority of those appointed in sd will & ware qualified accordingly & Benjamin C. Parker & Joseph Aver & Wm. Montgomery the other Executors did not appear.
It is therefore ordered by Court that the sd Hopkins

Lacy have the bond and entered into with his securities out of the clerks office

```
State          )
    vs         )   Demurra
Miles Cunningham)   Sire Facias
```

This day came as well the Attorney for the State as the Defendant by his attorney & the Defendant Demurra to the sire facias being sollemnly argued & Mature deliberation being had thereon

It is considered by court that the Demurra be sustained & the Defendant bedischarged

348.
```
Daniel Bess  )
    vs       )
Wm. Stuart & )
John Trimble )
```
In this case on motion of John Gardiner Esqrs. it is suggested to this court that an execution issued from Wm Gault Esquire in favour of the plaintiff against Wm. Stewart & John Trimble for fifteen dollars & sixty one & a half cents Benjamin Irwin returned no goods & chattles to be found in my country leveyed on a tract of land on Nine Mile whereon John Trimble lived.

It is therefore considered by court that the said land or so much thereof as will of value sufficient to satisfy sd Debt & costs be exposed to sale to satisfy sd. Debt & costs with the costs of this Motion.

Orderedthat Andrew Bogle John Walker & John Regan Esqrs. be commissioners to settle with Wm. Tipton Executer of the Estate of Benjamin Tipton Decd.

```
Josiah Danforth)
    vs         )   Ejectment
Smnel Frazier  )

Amos Byrd Do. )
    vs        )   Do.
James Dyal    )

Do.    )
  vs   )  Do.
Wm. Gay)
```

349.
```
Josiah Danforth)
    vs         )   Do.
Isaac Brooks   )

Do                 )
vs                 )  Do.
Jonathan Timberman )

Do             )
vs             )  Do.
Edward Buchanan)
```

Do   )
vs   ) Do
James Weir)

Do   )
vs   ) Do
Abraham Ghormley)

By consent of parties In the above cases the cases are contd. & the plaintiff is put under a rule to give security on Wednesday of next term or the above cases will be dismissed.

Henry & Lendenbarger)
      vs   )
Lowry & Waugh   ) In this case on motion of the plaintiff by his
                       Attorney a commission was awarded him to take
the deposition of sundry persons in the City of Baltimore by giving the Defendant thirty days Notice of the time & place

Samuel Bowman   )
      vs   )
Thomas Henderson) In this case there was a rule entered for a New trial
                   & made absolute & this cause is continued

50.   A Deed of conveyance from Samuel McCulloch to James Gillespie for three hundred & thirty seven Acres of land was proven in open court by John Wilkinson the subscribing witness thereto & admitted to record let it be registered.

A Bill of Sale from Samuel Cowan to James Gillespie for three hundred & thirty seven acres of land was acknowledged in open court by Samuel Cowan the subscriber thereto & admitted to Record let it be registered.

Ordered that Micheal Robertson be overseer of the road from James Denhams to Greenways Mill and aply to squire Fouts for a list of hands to work

Ordered that George Montgomery be overseer of the road from the hill at John Glass field to within half of a mile of Mr Caps & Wm. Lowry supply a list of hands to work.

Ordered that Brice Blair be overseer of the Road from where George Montgomery stops to the Tellico Road & Wm Lowry supply a list of hands to work.

By consent of the parties by their Attorneys the Court ordered all the cases take new stand on the Debt entered to be continued on the Clerks rule Docket to next Court.

Court adjourned to Court in Course

James Gillespy P. J.

Monday 25, March 1811

353.   At a court of pleas and quarter Sessions began & held for Blount
County at the court house in Maryville on the fourth Monday of March
1811

                    Present

          James Gillespy, John Tedford & John Reagin Esquires

          Andrew Cowan Esquire deputy Sheriff of the county aforesaid re-
turned our writ of Venire to him directed executed on the following
persons to wit

1. John Clayton	6. Henry Bond	11. John Farbet
2. George W. Allen	7. John Eagleton	12. John McReynolds
3. William Henry	8. Samuel Davidson	13. Wilson White
4. Joseph Stukes	9. Mathew Hanna	14. Martin McFear
5. John McGhee	10. James Henry	15. Felix Kennedy

Josiah Danforth   )
          vs   )
Wm. Sherrell & Little Sims)
Sims his securities   )   On motion of Josiah Danforth by John Gar-
                                      diner his Attorney to enter Judgment on a
stay bond taken by William Francis Sheriff of Rhea County & Little &
Sims securities It appearing to the court that the time for which said
stay was taken has expired It is therefore considered by court that
Judgment be entered against said defendant William Sherrill & Little &
Sims his securities for the sum of thirty two dollars & seventeen
cents. and a half the amount of the original Judgment besides the
costs of this Motion & the defendants in Merfy &c.

353.

          Joseph R. Henderson & James McCample took the Oaths of Attorney
& were admitted to practice in this court.

          A Morgage from Thomas Moor to Frances Henderson & Josiah John-
ston for a Negro girl named Nancy was proven in open court by George
Tedford a witness thereto & admitted to record let it be registered

          A Deed of conveyance from Aaron Beaty to James Beaty for eighty
eight acres of land was acknowledged in open court by Aaron Beaty the
subscriber thereto & admitted to record let it be registered.

          A Deed of conveyance from James Beaty to Aaron Beaty was acknow-
ledged in open court by James Beaty the subscriber thereto & admitted
to record let it be registered

          Ordered by court that Joseph Alexander be allowed till next court
to make return of the tax list of Capt Buchanans Company

William Regans Admists)
          vs   ) Appeal
Wm. Green & John Lowry) This day came the parties by their attorneys

& thereupon came a Jury to wit.

1. John Coayton
2. Wm. Henry
3. John McGhee
4. John Eagleton

5. Jonathan Tipton
6. John Norwood
7. Robert Housten
8. John Black

9. Mathew Hannah
10. James Henery
11. John McRanalds
12. Wilson White

356.

who being elected tried and sworn the truth to speak on the Matter in dispute do say they find for the plaintiff & assess their damages to sixteen dollars & Ninty five cents besides costs.

It is therefore considered by court that the plaintiff recover of the Defendant their damages aforesaid as by the Jury aforesaid assessed & their costs by them about their suit in this behalf expended & the sd. Deft. in Mercy &c.

John Lowry)
vs   ) Judgment for Security
Wm. Green) This day came the plaintiff by Enoch parsons his Attorney

& thereupon came a Jury to wit the same Jury as in the case Wm. Regans Administrator against Wm. Green & John Lowry who were elected tryed & sworn well & truly to enquire into facts in this case do say that John Lowry the plaintiff in this case was security for the defendant on a bond on which Judgment was this day entered in favour of the Adms of Wm. Regan Deceased for sixteen dollars & ninty five cents debt & damages & Nine dollars & forty three cents costs.

On motion of the plaintiff by his attorney aforesaid Y on the facts as found as by the Jury aforesaid and in pursuance of the Status in this case made & provided

It is therefore considered by court that the plaintiff recover of the Defendant sixteen Dollars & ninty five cents It being the amount of the Judgment recovered against the sd John as security for the sd. William as also the further sum of nine Dollars & forty cents recovered for costs & charges together with the costs of this Motion & the sd Defendant in Mercy &c.

John McGhee   )
vs   )
Miles & David Cunningham) This day came the plaintiff by his Attorney
as well as the Defendants in their proper person & the Defendant acknowledged the plaintiffs Action for one hundred & seventeen dollars & sixty six cents debt & damages besides the costs.

355.

It is therefore considered that the plaintiff recover of the Defendant one hundred & seventeen dollars as by them aforesaid confessed together with his costs by him about his suit in this behalf expended & the sd Defendants in Mercy &c.

Wm. Trige surviving Executor)
of Wm. King deceased & with)
James King the other Executor)
assines of John Bull   )
vs   ) Covenant
George Montgomery & Wm.   ) This day came the parties by ▓▓▓ At-
Montgomery.   ) tornies and thereupon Came a Jury The
) same Jury as in the case Reagans Admrs

vs. Green & Lowry who being elected tried and sworn the truth to speak
on the issue Joined Do say the Defendants hath not Kept & preformed
their covenant but the same hath broken to the damages of the plaintiff ninty two dollars & fifty one cents

It is therefore donsidered by Court that the sd. plaintiff
recover of the defendant the sum of Ninty two dollars & fifty one Cents
the damages as by the Jury aforesaid Assessed together with his costs
by him About his suit in this behalf expended & the sd. defendant in
Mercy &c.

Wm. Cox)
)
  vs   ) appeal
)
John Bible) This day came the parties by their attorneys & thereupon came
           a Jury (to wit)

1. Alexander Ford	5. Wm. Forester	9. Jessee Rhea
2. Samuel Eakin	6. Thos Campble	10. Wm. Rooper
3. Charles Lockhart	7. Wm. Robertson	11. Aaron Waller
4. William McGaughey	8. Carson Caldwell	12. John McGhee

356.   who being elected tryed & sworn thetruth to speak on the matter in
dispute do say they find for the plaintiff & assess his damages te
thirty two dollars seventy two & three fourth cents besides costs
4   It is therefore considered by Court that the plaintiff
recover of the defendant thirty two dollars & seventy two cents the
damage aforesaid as by the Jury aforesaid Assessed & his costs by him
about his suit in this behalf expended & the sd. Deft. in Mercy &c.

Thomas Henderson & David Cold-)
well & Betsy Russell adms. of)
Hance Russll, Decd.   ) Appeal
)
        vs   ) This day came the parties by their At-
) tornies & thereupon came a Jury The
John Gould & John Lowry   ) same Jury as in the case Cox vs Bible

who being elected tryed & sworn the truth to speak on the matter in
dispute Do say they find for the plaintiff & assess his damage to fifty
dollars & Ninty three cents besides costs.
        ↓   It is therefore Considered by Court that the plaintiff re-
cover of the Defendant fifty dollars & Ninty three cents the damage as
by the Jury aforesaid Assessed together with his costs by them about his
suit in this behalf expended & the said Defendants in Mercy &c.

McCulloch & Poor Assinee)
of John Lowry   )
)
        vs   ) Appeal
)
John Wallace   ) This day came the parties by their Attorneys
                           & thereupon came a Jury to wit The same Jury
as in the case Ragans Administrators against Green & Lowry All but Aaron
Beaty & William Williams in place of John McGhee & Wilson White who be-
357.   ing elected tryed & sworn the truth to speak on the matter in dispute
        do say they find for the plaintiff & assess their damage to twenty two
dollars & eighty cents besides costs.
        It is therefore considered by Court that the pl[...] re-
cover of the Defendant twenty two dollars & eighty cents the d[...] as
by the Jury aforesaid assessed to gether with his costs by him About

his suit in this behalf expanded & the sd. Defendant in Mercy &c.

Prichet & Shall Assinee of
James Trimble
    vs   Appeal
Thomas McCullock   This day came the parties by their attornies
& thereupon came a Jury to wit The same Jury
as in the case McCulloch & poor against John Wallace who being elected
tryed & sworn the truth to speak on the Matter in dispute do say they
find for the plaintiff & assess their damage to forty five dollars &
forty cents besides costs.

    It is therefore considered by Court that the plaintiff recover of the Defendant the sum of forty five dollars & forty cents as
by the Jury aforesaid assessed together with the costs by him about his
suit in this behalf expended & the sd. defendant in Mercy &c.

Baker & Russle)
    vs   )   Certroria
Archbd. Lackey)   This day came the parties by their Attorneys & thereupon came a Jury (to wit.) The same Jury as in the
case prichet & Shall against Thomas McCullock. Who being elected tryed
& sworn the truth to speak on the Matter in dispute do say that they
find for the plaintiff & assess their damages to twenty eight dollars
& fifty cents besides costs

358.   It is therefore considered by Court that the plaintiff recover against the defendant Archibald Lackey & his security John Lowry
& Josiah Gamble the sum of twenty eight dollars & fifty cents the damage as by the Jury aforesaid assessed together with the costs by them
about yheir suit in this behalf expended & the sd. Defendants in Mercy

John Hannah)
    vs   )
Robert Gault)   This day came the plaintiff by his attorney as well as
the defendant in his proper person & the plaintiff dismisses his suit & the Defendant confesses Judgment for all costs except the plaintiffs attorneys for which the plaintiff assumes to pay.

    It is therefore considered that the plaintiff suit be
dismissed & that Judgment for costs go agreable to the above confession

Andrew Miller)
    vs   )
Edward Tul   )   In this case it appears that James P. Chisholm summons
a witness in behalf of the plaintiff & being sollemnly
called came not but made default

    It is therefore considered by court that he forfeit accordingly to act of assembly unless he appear at next court & shew
sufficient reasons

Do)
vs)
Do)   In this case the parties appearing by their attorneys & the plaintiff not being ready for trial it is considered by court that he
be non suited whereupon on motion of the plaintiff by his attorney a
389. rule is granted him to shew cause why the non suit should be set aside.

Lowry & Waugh)
  vs   )
Robert J. Henry) This day came the parties & with the consent of the
             parties & assent of the court this case is continued
to next court.

Henry & Lingenbarger)
  vs   )
Lowry & Waugh   ) This day came the parties & with the consent of
             the court this cause is continued to next court

Thomas Thompson)
  vs   )
Andrew Ferguson) This day came the plaintiff as well as the Defendant
             in this proper person & the plaintiff dismisses his
suit & the defendant confesses Judgment for all costs.
         It is therefore considered by court that the plaintiff
suit bedismissed & that Judgment for costs go agreable to the above confession.

         Court adjourned till tomorrow 9 Oclock

360.   Tuesday 26th March 1810

         Court met according to Adjournment

               Present

    James Gillespy, Robert McCulley & Joseph Alexander Esquires Justices

Elihu Emery Assinee & c   )
for the use of Francis Willitt)
  vs   )
Isaac Wright   ) This day came the plaintiff by attorney
                & moved for Judgment agt. the Defendant
on a bond taken by the Sheriff for the prison bounds & thereupon came
the Defendant into open court & confessed Judgm for three hundred &
thirty Six Dollars & Eighty cents the amount of the Ca. La. for which
said bond was taken.
         It is therefore considered by court that the Sheriff re-
cover of the Defendant aforesaid Three hundred & thirty Six Dollars &
Eighty cents the amount as stated in the Case aforesaid confessed together with the costs of this Motion & the Said defendant in Mercy &.

    A Deed of conveyance from James Beaty to James McNutt for twenty
seven Acres of land was acknowledged in open court by said Beaty the subscriber thereto and admitted to Record Let it be registered

Samuel Bowerman)
  vs   )
Thomas Henderson) On motion of the Defendant by Attorney It is ordered
             by Court that a commission de benne issue to John
Waugh & James Gillespy Esquires or either of them to take the deposition
of David Cowan to be read as evidence at the trial of this cause in
behalf of the Defendant.

On Motion Administration of the Estate of James Houston Decd. was granted to pheba Houston William McClung & John Houston who together with Mathew Wallace & Samuel Houston entered into & acknowledged their bond for for five thousand Dollars.

A Bill of Sale from Andrew Kennedy to John Montgomery for a negro yellow named Abel was proven in open court by James Berry & David Russle the witnesses thereto whereupon the fine was admitted to record Let it be registered.

An Inventory of the Estate of James Smith Deceased fild

362. Barnes Hollaway)
            vs   )
      Colmon Knight) This day came the plaintiff into open court & dismissed his suit and thereupon came Joseph Hollaway into court and confessed Judgment for the costs.
              Wherefore It is considered by court that the said suit be dismissed and that the plaintiff go without day and recover of the said Joseph Hollaway his costs by him about his suit in this behalf expended &c.

      Morrison for the use of Baker)
                  vs   )
      David Brown & ----? McMahan) This day came Hugh Hackney who was summoned a Garnishee in this cause and being sworn deposith & saith that he gave a note for seventy five Dollars payable in cotton or cattle on Christmas day next to David Brown & that he owes him nothing more nor did he at the time he was summoned a Garnishee in this case & that the said deponent further says that he Knows of no person owing the defendant anything nor did he at the time he was summoned as Garnishee in this case.

363. John Keys   )
            vs   )
      William Maclin Decd.) On motion of the plaintiff by Attorney It is ordered by court that a Scb, facias issue to the Executors of the Defendant to recover the said cause in their name to which Judgment the Defendants Attorney tendered a Bill of Exception to the court which was signed & filed.

A Deed of conveyance from James Montgomery to Alexander Hail for two hundred & seventy one acres of Land was proven in open court by John Montgomery & John Norwood the witnessed thereto wherefore the sum was admitted to Record Let it be registered.

An Inventory of the Estate of James Houston Decd. was returned to court confirmed & filed and an order of Sale of the personal Estate was granted.

Ordered by Court that the fines heretofore to wit at September Term 1810 assessed against Captain John D. Cusack & Samuel Houston be remitted and that the money be refunded to them.

364.   Ordered by court that the personal Estate of John Stephens Decd. be exposed to Sale agreably to Law.

Ordered by Court that John Walker, William Geult & John Waugh Esquires be commissioners to settle with William Gillespy Guardian to Margaret Porter & report to this court.

Ordered by Court that William Davidson John Walker & Jessee Wallace settle with the Administrator of John Hess Decd.

Ordered by Court that a writ of Hobeas Corpus Issue directed to William Young to bring into Court an orphan child by him unlawfully detained so that this court may do what of right ought to be done According to Law.

365.   Court met according to adjournment.

Present

James Gillespy, William Davidson & John Reagen Esquires Justices.

A List of Sales of the Estate of William Maclin Decd. was returned to court & filed.

A Bond from John Lowry Attorney to Christian Kisor was produced in open court and the said John Lowry Attorney the obliger in Said Bond Appeared in open court and acknowlidged that he did Sigh Seal and deburr Said bond for the purpose therein expressed on the 26 day of March 1811 conditional to make to said Christian a title to one hundred & Ten Acres of land lying & being in the county of Rockbridge in the State of Virginia on the North branch of James River wherefore the same was admitted to Record & Ordered to be Registered.

Robert Eakin)
    vs   )
Robert McCulley) This day came the plaintiff by Attorney & on his petition moved to record the Letters of Administration granted to the Defendant on the Estate of Robert Eakin Decd. which Motion after Argument is continued untill tomorrow for the court to advise

366. Hezekiah Possy   )
    vs   )
Benjamin Kilbourn) On motion of the Defendant & for sufficient reasons appearing in his affidavit a commission de-bene esse is awarded him to take the deposition of Samuel McCulloch & John Louder with giving the plaintiff five days previous Notice of the time & place of taking the same & that the commissioners issue to Joseph Alexander & John Waugh or either of them

Ordered by court that James Gillespy & John Waugh Esquires Settle with the administrators of the Estate of Hance Russell Decd.

Justices present James Gillespy John Reagan & George Ewing Esquires

Samuel Bowerman)
    vs   ) Appeal
Thomas Henderson) This day came the parties by their attornies & thereupon

came a Jury to wit

1. Robert Houston
2. Robert Cooper
3. John Houston
4. William Robinson
5. William Eakin
6. William Rooker
7. Wilson White
8. James Henry
9. Mathew ~~Ixkix~~ Hanna
10. John Eagleton
11. Wm. Henery
12. John Clayton

who being elected tried and swon5 well & truly to try the matter in controversy and because they cannot agree on resputed form rendering their verdict untill tomorrow

267. Samuel Bowerman)
vs) Appl.
Thomas Henderson) In this case it appears Andrew Cowan was Security for the Defendant prosecuting his said Appeal with effect & the defendant here in open court leased this sd. Andrew & entered into bond with Barcley McGhee Jacob Peck & William Cox his security for the prosecution of Same.

Court adjourned till tomorrow Morning 9 Oclock

368. Thursday 28th March 1811

Court met according to Adjournment

4 Present

James Gillspie, Wm. Gillespie, John Regan & Wm. Davidson Esqrs.

James McClanahan who had the appoihtmenr of Constable in this county resigned his appointment

Alexander McClanahan was appointed in his room who entered into bond with Hugh Kelsoe & John Trimble his securites as the law directs.

Robert McMurry)
vs)
James McClanahan) In this case on motion of the Defendant a sufficient awarded Him directed to John Waugh Esquire to take the deposition of ~~firmxixy~~ Samuel Beal to be read in evidence in this cause by giving the plaintiff five days notice of the time & place.

369. Arch Johnston)
vs)
Jacob Prush & James Martin) This day came the parties by their attornies and thereupon came a Jury to wit.

1. John McGhee
2. Robert Montgomery
3. James Weir
4. Hugh Kelsoe
5. Peter Snider
6. John McNeely
7. James McClanahan
8. Samuel Weir
9. Richd. Trotter
10. Charles Hood
11. John McRaynolds
12. John Finley

who being elected tried and sworn the truth to speak on the matter in dispute do say they find for the plaintiff & assess his damage to

Eighteen dollars & forth eight cents besides co sts.

It is therefore considered by court that the plaintiff recover of the Defendant eighteen Dollars & forty eight cents the damages aforesaid as by the Jury aforesaid assessed & the sd. Defendant in Mercy & c.

John Sharp)
vs)
Robert Bell) This day came the plaintiff by Attorney and it appearing to the satisfaction of this court that the plaintiff obtained an execution against the Defendant for the sum of five Dollars & sixty eight cents Debt & costs before John Waugh Esquire which was returned to court by Samuel Cowan Sheriff Levyed on the land that the Defendant lives on

It is therefore considered by court that the aforesaid Land or so much thereof as will be sufficient to satisfy the Debts & Costs of this Motion be exposed to Sale agreable to Law

370.   David Dearmond)
vs)
Robert Cooper) On motion of E. parsons Esqr It appears in this case that the Defendant aforesaid on Execution before Samuel George Esquire for the sum of Ten Dollars Thirty Seven & a half cents Debt & costs against the Defendant which Execution was returned to court by William Fagg no property found Levyed on the land whereon the Defendant now lives

It is therefore considered by court that said land or so much thereof as will be sufficient to satisfy the Debt & costs aforesaid together with the costs of this Motion be exposed to sale Agreably to law pd. Dearmond 5 Dollars pd. Gillespie 3 Dollars

Samuel Bowman)
vs)
Thomas Henderson) This day came the parties by their Attorneys & the Jury who were yesterday respited from rendering their verdict do say they find for the plaintiff & assess his damage to thirteen dollars & Ninty five cents besides costs.

It is therefore considered that the plaintiff recover of the Defendant aforesaid thirteen dollars & ninty five cents the damage as by the Jury aforesaid Assessed & the Defendant in Mercy &c. & on which Verdict & Judgment aforesaid the Defendant prays an appeal to the circus court for Blount County files his reasons & enteres into bond with security as the law directs & to him it was granted.

371.   Wm. Cox)
vs) Appl.
John Bible) This day came the parties by their attornies & thereupon came a Jury (to wit.)

1. Wm. Rocker   5. John Eagleton   9. Wm. Long
2. Wilson White   6. Wm. Henry   10. Alex. Gamble
3. James Henery   7. John Clayton   11. Samuel Blackburn
4. Mathew Hannah   8. Robert Boyd   12. Wm. McGaughey

who being elected tryed & Sworn the truth to speak on the matter in dispute do say they find for the plaintiff & assess his damages to thirty five dollars & forty to cents besides costs

It is therefore considered by court that the plaintiff recover of the defendant thirty four dollars & forty two cents the damage aforesaid as by the Jury aforesaid assessed together with his costs by him about his suit in behalf expended & the sd. defendant in Mercy &c.

James Hall ⎞
　　vs　　⎟ appeal
Reuben Charles⎠ This day came the plaintiff by his attorney as well as the defendant in his proper person & the defendant acknowledges the plaintiff cause of action for thirty eight dollars & twenty four cents damage as by the Defendant aforesaid confessed together with his costs by him about his suit in this behalf expended & the sd Deft. in Mercy &c.

William Brant ⎞
　　vs　　⎟ Appel
James McClanahan⎠ This day came the parties by their Attorneys & thereupon came a Jury the same Jury as in the case Cox vs. Bible who being elected tryed & sworn the truth to speak on the matter in dispute do say they find for the plaintiff & assess his damage to ninteen dollars sixteen & two third cents

372.

It is therefore considered by Court that the plaintiff recover of the Defendant the damages aforesaid as by the Jury assessed & sd. Deft. in Mercy &c. rule for new trial made aboslute.

Wm. Houston ⎞
　　vs　　⎟ Debt.
Andrew Kennedy⎠ This day came the parties by their Attorneys & thereupon came a Jury (to wit.)

1. James Hammontree
2. John Smith
3. John McGhee
4. James Weir
5. Hugh Kelsoe
6. Peter Snider
7. James McClanahan
8. Saml. Weir
9. Richd Trotter
10. Charles Head
11. John McConald
12. John Finley

who being elected tryed & sworn the truth to speak on the issue joined do say the Defendant hath not paid the Debt in the Declaration Mentioned nor any part thereof & by reason of the detention of said debt we assess the plaintiffs damages to twenty three dollars sixty two & a half cents besides costs

It is therefore considered by Court that the plft. recover of the Defendant the debt in the Declaration Mentioned together with the damages as by the Jury aforesaid assessed & the sd. Deft. in Mercy &c.

Wm. Regans Administrators ⎞
　　　　vs　　　　⎟ appl
Andrew Evins & Mashec Tipton⎠ This day came the parties by their Attorneys & thereupon came a Jury to with the same Jury as in the Case Cox vs Bible who being elected tryed & sworn the truth to speak on the matter in dispute do say they find for the plaintiff & assess their damage to sixteen dollars & fifty six cents besides costs

373.

It is therefore considered by Court that the plaintiff recover of the Defendant Sixteen dollars & fifty six cents as by the Jury aforesaid assessed together with their costs by them about their suit in this behalf expended & the sd. Defendant in Mercy &c.

Wm. Regans Administrators)
       vs) appl
Saml. McGaughey & Miles Cunningham)   This day came the parties by their
                attorneys & thereupon came a Jury
to wit the same Jury who being elected tryed & sworn the truth to speak on the matter in dispute do say they assess the plfts. damages to twenty seven dollars & sixty three cents besides costs

      It is therefore considered by court that the plaintiff recover of the Defendant twenty seven dollars & sixty three cents the damages aforesaid as by the Jury aforesaid assessed together with his costs about his suit in this behalf expended & the sd defendant in Mercy &c.

Wm. Regans, Adms.)
     vs)
Samuel McGaughey &) Appl.
David Coldwell   ) This day came the parties by their Attorneys &
               thereupon came the same Jury as above who being
elected tryed & sworn the truth to speak on the matter in dispute do say they find for the plaintiffs assess his damage to twenty eight dollars & thirty eight cents besides costs.

      It is therefore considered by Court that the plaintiff recover of the Deft. the damages aforesaid as by the Jury aforesaid assessed & the Deft. in Mercy &c.

374. Wm. Regans Adms.)
     vs)
Coldwell, Evins & Cannon) This day came the parties by their attorneys
               & thereupon came a Jury to with the same
Jury as before who being elected tryed & sworn the truth to speak on the matter in dispute do say they find for the plaintiffs assess his damage to thirty five dollars & thirteen cents besides costs.

      It is therefore considered that the plaintiff recover of the Defendant thirty four dollars & thirteen cents the damage aforesaid as by the Jury aforesaid assessed & the Deft. in Mercy &c.

Wm. Regans adms.)
     vs)
John Lowry & John Waugh & George Berry) This day came the parties by
               their attorney & thereupon came
a Jury the same Jury as above who being elected tryed & sworn the truth to speak on the matter in dispute do say they find for the plaintiff & assess his damage to forty six dollars & twenty one cents besides costs

      It is therefore considered by Court that the plaintiff recover of the Defendant the damage aforesaid as by the Jury aforesaid & the Defendant in Mercy &c.

John McGhee)
   vs-) Appl.
Archibald Lackey) This day came the parties by their attorneys & thereupon came a Jury (to wit) the same Jury as in the case
Houston against Kennedy who being elected tryed & sworn the truth to speak

on the Matter in dispute do say they assess the plaintiff damage to thirty nine dollars & seventy five & a half cents besides costs

It is therefore considered by court that the plaintiff recover of the Defendant thirty nine dollars seventy five & a half cents the damage as by the Jury aforesaid assessed & the defendant in Mercy &c.

375. Wm. Trigg surviving Executor of Wm. King decd. & Joint Assinee) with James King the other Executor of John Null)
vs) Appl.
James Edmondson & John Gould) This

day came the parties by their Attorneys & thereupon came a Jury the same Jury as above who being elected tryed & sworn the truth to speak upon the matter in dispute do say they assess the plaintiff damage to nineteen dollars & seventy six cents

It is therefore considered by Court that the plaintiff recover of the Defendant Nineteen dollars & seventy six cents the damage aforesaid as by the Jury aforesaid assessed together with his costs by him about his costs by him about his suit in this behalf expended & the sd. Defendant in Mercy &c.

Hance Russells Administrators)
vs)
Joel Wallace & William Wallace) This day came the parties by their attornies and thereupon came a Jury to wit the same Jury as above who being elected tried & sworn well & truly to try the matter in controversy upon their oaths do say they find for the plaintiff and assess their damages to Forty Nine Dollars & forty cents besides costs.

It is therefore considered by court that the plaintiff recover of the Defendant forty Nine dollars & forty cents their aforesaid as by the Jury aforesaid assessed & their costs by them about their suit in this behalf expended & the defendant in Mercy &c.

376. Jonathan Trippett)
vs) Appl
Lowry & Waugh) This day came the parties by their Attorneys & thereupon came a Jury to wit the same Jury as before who being sworn well & truly to try the Matter in controversy upon their came a jury to wit the same Jury as before who being sworn well & truly to try the matter in controversy upon their oaths do say they find for the plaintiff & assess his damage to Thirty three Dollars Twelve & a half cents besides costs

Wherefore It is considered by Court that the plaintiff recover of the Defendant Thirty three Dollars twelve & a half cents together with the costs of this suit & the said Defendant in Mercy &c.

John Rankin)
vs) Appl
John Waugh) This day came the parties by Attornies and thereupon came a Jury (to wit) the same Jury as in the case above who being elected tryed & sworn well & truly to try the matter in controversy upon their oaths do say they find for the plaintiff & assess his damages to Thirty five dollars & twenty five cents besides the costs

Therefore It is considered by court that the plaintiff recover of the Defendant Thirty five Dollars & twenty five cents his damages aforesaid as by the Jury aforesaid Assessed & his costs by him about his suit in this behalf expended & the Defendant in Mercy &c.

An Inventory of the Estate of Geofrey pate Decd. was returned to Court & filed and an order of the Sale granted.

377. Montgomery & Walker Edmors)
      of Samuel Reid   )
                vs   )   Appeal
      John Gould & Samuel Hogg)   This day came the parties by their Attornies
                                         & thereupon came the same Jury as in the
last case do say they find for the plaintiff and assess their damages to nineteen Dollars & thirty eight cents besides costs
      It is therefore considered by Court that the plaintiff recover of the Defendant Nineteen Dollars & thirty Eight cents the damage aforesaid as by the Jury aforesaid assessed & their costs by them about their suit in this behalf expended & the Defendant in Mercy &c.

      James P. H. Porter)
                vs   )   Appeal
      Reuben Charles   )   This day came the parties by their attornies and
                              thereupon came a Jury to wit the same Jury as a-
bove who being sworn Do say they find for the plaintiff & assess his damages to fifty three Dollars & thirty cents besides costs.
      It is therefore considered by court that the plaintiff recover of the Defendant fifty three Dollars & thirty cents the damage aforesaid xxxxx assessed & his costs by him about his suit in this behalf expended & the said Defendant in Mercy &c.

378. Blank

379. White & Henderson)
                vs   )   Appeal
      Joseph Welden   )   This day came the parties by their attornies & there-
                              upon came the same Jury as in the case Cox vs Bible
who being sworn & c do say they find for the plaintiff & assess his damages to thirty four dollars & one cent besides Costs It is therefore considered by court that the plaintiff recover of the defendant thirty four Dollars & one cent but the damages aforesaid as by the Jury afore said assessed & their costs by them about their suit in this behalf expended & the said Defendant in Mercy &c.

      Brice Blair)
                vs   )   Appeal
      John Gould)   This day came the parties by their attornies and there-
                        upon came a Jury to wit the same Jury as in the case Cox
vs.

380. John Rankin   )
                vs   )
      John Lewry & John Waugh)
      David Bussell & James)   Debt.
      Gillespie   )   This day came the parties by their attornies

& thereupon came a Jury to wit the same Jury as in the last case
who being elected tried & sworn well & truly to try the issue
upon their oaths do say the defendant hath not paid the Debt in the
declaration mentioned & they assess the plaintiff damage yet unpaid
by occasion of the detention of that Debt to forty four Dollars &
Seventy cents besides costs.

It is therefore considered by court that the plaintiff
recover of the Defendant one hundred & forty Dollars the Debt in the
Declaration mentioned together with forty four dollars & Seventy cents
his damages aforesaid yet unpaid by the Jury aforesaid assessed & his
costs by him about his suit in this behalf expended & the said Defendant in Mercy &c.

Baker & Russell)
vs) Appl
William Maclin) This day came the plaintiff into court & dismissed
his suit

It is therefore considered by court that the plaintiffs
suit be dismissed & that the Defendant go without day and recover of
the plaintiff his costs by him about his defence in this behalf expended & c.

381.   Fredrick Jordon)
vs) Case
Lowry & Waugh) This day came the parties by Attornies & thereupon
came a Jury to with the Same Jury as in the case Cox
against Bible who being elected tried and Sworn well & truly to try the
issue joined upon their oath do say the Defendants did assume upon
themselves in Manner & form as the plaintiff hath complained & they
assess the plaintiff damages by occasion of the non performance of
that assumption to Two hundred & twenty one Dollars & twenty cents
besides costs

Therefore It is considered by court that the plaintiff
recover of the Defendant Two hundred & Twenty one dollars & twenty
cents the damages aforesaid as by the Jury aforesaid assessed & his
costs by him about his suit in this behalf expended & the said Defendant in Mercy &c.

Love & Luttrell)
vs) Sci. Fac.
Andrew Russell) This day came the plaintiff by attorney & moved for
Judgment against the Deft for ninety five Dollars
& Ninty two cents the debt in the Declaration mentioned and the plaintiff not appearing to defend the Same or show any reasons to the contrary

It is therefore considered by court & that the plaintiff
recover of the Defendant ninety five Dollars & ninety two cents the
382.   amount as stated in the Sire Facias aforesaid together with the costs
of this suit & the said Defendants in Mercy &c.

Baker & Russell)
vs) Appel
John Wilkensen) This day came the plaintiff and dismissed his suit
& the Defendant confessed Judgment for the amount
of the costs

It is therefore considered by court that the plaintiffs

suits be dismissed & that the defendant pay the costs agreable to the aforesaid Confession & be in Mercy &c.

Wm. Reagan Administrators)
      vs   ) Appeal
John Clark & Samuel McCullock) This day came the plaintiff by his at-
                       torney & dismissed their suit
       It is therefore considered by court that the plaintiffs suit be dismissed & that the Defendant go without day & recover of the plaintiff his costs by them about his suit in this behalf expended &c.

Wm. Regans Admors)
      vs   ) Appl.
George Smith & David White) This day came the plaintiff by their At-
                    torney & dismissed their suit
       It is therefore considered by court that the plaintiffs suit be dismissed & that the Defendant go thereof without day and re-cover of the plaintiff their costs by them about their suit in this behalf expended.

Wm. Regans Admors)
      vs   ) Appl.
Wm. Gay & Adam Dunla;) This day came the plaintiffs by their Attor-
                  ney & dismissed their suit
       It is therefore condisered by court that the defendant go without day thereof & recover of the plaintiff their costs by them about their suit in this behalf expanded &c.

383. Wm. Regans Administrators)
          vs   ) Appl.
Morgan Edwards & Nathan Farmer) This day came the plaintiff by their
                          Attorney into court & dismissed their
suit
       It is therefore considered by court that the Defendant go without day & recover of the plaintiff their costs by them about their suit in this behalf expended

Wm. Macklin)
      vs   ) Case
Ambrose Briand) This day came the defendant by his Attorney and the
               plaintiff failing to prosecute
       It is therefore considered by court that sd. suit stand abated that the Defendant go without day.

Robert McMurry)
      vs   ) Case
Rebecka Ried) This day came by consent of the parties & report of
             Court is continued to next court.

Micheal Earhart)
      vs   )
George Cagle) This case was continued on affidavit of the Defendant
             to next court

John Jackson)
vs) Appl
Lowry & Waugh) This day came the plaintiff & dismissed his suit
It is therefore considered by court that the suit be dismissed & that the defendant go without day & recover of the plaintiff their costs &c.

Court adjourned till tomorrow 9 Oclock

Friday 29th of March 1811

Court met according to Adjournment

Present

James Gillespie John Waugh & Matt Wallace Esquires

A Deed of conveyance from Robert Bill to Jonathan Henderson for one hundred & eighty eight acres of land on the waters of Crooked Creek was acknowledged in open court by the sd. Robert Bill the subscriber thereto & admitted to Record Let it be registered.

White & Wilson)
vs) Certiorari
Samuel McGaughey) This day came the plaintiff by their attorneys
& moved to dismiss the writs of certiorari & supersidious & on sollemn argument & mature deliberation being had thereon the writs of certiorari & supersideous was dismissed & a provendo awarded to the Justice & that the defendant pay the costs &c.

Prichet & Shall)
vs)
Wm. Macklin) This day came the plaintiff by attorney and suggested the plaintiffs oath at December Septem,
1810 moved for a Sci. facies to issue directed to the Executors of the defendant to the Executors of the defendant to appear and shew cause why the Same should not be received in their name if any they can.
It is therefore considered by court that an Sci facius issue to the Said Executors to appear at our next court & shew cause if any they can why the Said suit should not be received in their names.

Prickett & Shall)
vs) Appl
William Macklin) This day came the plaintiff by attorney & having suggested to court the death of the defendant at
December session 1811
Moved for a Sci facias to issue directed to the Defendants Executors to appear at next court & shew cause if any they can why the said suit should not be received in their name.
It is therefore ordered by court that a Sci. facias issue directed to the defendants Executers to appear at next court and shew cause if any they can why the same Should not be received in their name.

Stephen Hair)
vs   ) appl
Wm. Maclin) This day came attorney & the defendants death being formerly suggested at December Session 1810 Moved for a sire facias directed to the Executors for the defendant to appear and shew cause if any they can why the same should not be recrived in their name.

It is therefore considered by court that a Sci. Facias issue accordingly

386. William L. Lewis)
vs   ) Appl
William Maclin) This day came the plaintiff. by attorney & the Defendants death having been formerly suggested moved for sire facias directed to the defendants Executors to appear and shew cause if any they can why said suit should not be received in their name

It is therefore ordered by court that a Sire facias issue accordingly.

John Brown)
vs   ) appl.
Wm. Macklin) This da came the parties by their Attorneys & agreed that this suit should be received.

It is therefore ordered by court that the causestand receivedagainst the Executors & continued

John McGhee)
vs   ) appl
John Krimble) this day came the parties by their aattornies and thereupon came a Jury to wit

1. Robert Bell   5. Wm. Greenaway   9. Matt Hannah
2. John Holaway   6. David Coldwell   10. John McRanolds
3. Wm. Barnes   7. William Henry   11. Wilson White
4. Alex Hartt   8. John Eagleton   12. Wm. Rooker

Stephen Hair)
vs   ) Appl.
Wm. Macklin) This day came the plaintiff by Attorney & the defendants death being formerly suggested At December Session 1810 moved for a sire facias directed to the Executors for the defendant to appear and shew cause if any they can why the same should not be received in their name.

It is therefore considered by Court that a Sci facias issue Accordingly

386. William L. Lewis)
vs   ) Appl
William Maclin) This day came the plaintiff by Attorney & the Defendants death having formerly suggested moved for sire facias directed to the defendants Executors to appear and shew cause if any they can why said suit should not be received in their name.

It is therefore ordered by court that a Sire facias issue accordingly.

John Brown)
    vs   ) Appl.
Wm. Mackling) This day came the parties by their Attorneys & agreed
            that this suit be received

          It is therefore ordered by court that the cause stand re-
ceived against the Executors & continued

John McGhee)
    vs   ) Appl
John Trimble) This day came the parties by their attorneys & there-
         upon came a Jury to wit

1. Rovert Bell	5. Wm. Greenway	9. Matt Hannah
2. John Holaway	6. David Coldwell	10. John McRanolds
3. Wm. Barnes	7. William Henery	11. Wilson White
4. Alex Hartt	8. John Eagleton	12. Wm. Rooker

who being elected tryed & sworn the truth to speak on the matter in
dispute do say they find for the plaintiff & assess his damages to
387. thirty nine dollars fifty six & a half cents besides costs

         It is therefore considered by court that the plaintiff
recover of the defendant thirty nine dollars fifty six & a half cents
his damages aforesaid assessed together with his costs by him about his
suit in this behalf expended & the sd Defendant in Mercy & c.

Jacob Danforth)
    vs   ) Case
John Lowry) This day came the parties by their Attornies & there-
         upon came a Jury (to wit.)

1. John McGhee	5. Samuel Harris	9. Jeremiah Hammontree
2. James Henry	6. John Harris	10. Barnes Holloway
3. John Toel	7. James Duglas	11. Wm. Gay
4. Edwd Buchanan	8. John Holloway	12. Reuben Charles

who being elected tryed & sworn the truth to speak on the issue Joined
do say the defendant did assume upon himself in Manner & form as the
plaintiff against him hath alleged & for the mon preformance of such
assumpsit they assess the plaintiffs damages to two hundred & eighty
six dollars eighty seven & a half cents besides costs

         It is therefore considered by court that the plaintiff
recover of the Defendant the damages aforesaid as by the Jury aforesaid
assessed & their costs by him about his suit in this behalf expended
& the sd. Deft in mercy &c.

388. Wm. Cox   )
      vs   ) Appl
George Coops) This day came the parties by their attornies and there-
         upon came a Jury to with the same Jury as above

who being elected &c. do say they find for the plaintiff & assess his
damage to eleven dollars & thirty six cents besides costs

It is therefore considered by court that the plaintiff recover of the Deft eleven Dollars & thirty six cents the damages aforesaid as by the Jury aforesaid assessed together with his costs by him about his suit in this behalf expended & the sd. Deft. in Mercy &c.

John Nicol Assinee)
vs) Debt
John McCullock, Samuel Mc-) This day came the parties by their attornies
cullock, Thomas McCullock) and thereupon came the same Jury as above
who being elected tryed & sworn the truth
to speak on the issue Joined do say the defendant have not paid the debt
nor any part thereof as in pleading they have alleged & for the detention of which they assess the plaintiff damage to twenty one dollars
& fifty cents besides costs

It is therefore considered by court that the plaintiff recover of the defendants ————— dollars & ——— cents the debt in
the declaration mentioned together with twenty one dollars & fifty cents
his damages as by the Jury aforesaid assessed together with hiscosts
by him about his suit in this behalf expended & the sd Deft in Mercy &c

On motion of David Russell who was bound to keep a publick house
in the town of Maryville Entered into bond with John Montgomery & Andrew
Thompson his securities as the law directs.

389. Josiah & John Nicol)
vs) Debt
William Wallace) This day came the parties by their attorneys &
thereupon came the same Jury as above who being
elected tried & sworn the truth to speak on the issue Joined do say
the defendant hath not paid the debt in the declaration & they assess
the plaintiff damage by accasion of the detention of that debt to sixteen dollars & three cents besides costs

It is therefore considered by court that the plaintiff
recover of the Debt dollars the debt in the Declaration Mentioned together with sixteen dollars & three cents the damages aforesaid as by
the Jury aforesaid assessed & his costs by him about his suit in this
behalf expended & the said Defendant is in Mercy &c.

Administrators of)
Hance Russell)
vs)
Moses Keywood) In this case Robert Rhea & John Rhea were summoned
witnesses in behalf of the Deft & tho sollemnly
called came not but made default.

It is therefore considered by court that for this default
they forfeit & pay to the defendant the sum of one hundred & twenty
five dollars unless they appear at next court & shew sufficient reasons
to the contrary.

Robert McCall)
vs)
Samuel McGaughey) This day came the plaintiff by his attorney & having
filed his declaration & the Defendant being Sollemnly
called came not but made default & no pleading filed
It is therefore considered by court that the plaintiff re-

of the Defendant the debt in the two hundred & twenty dollars the Debt yet unpaid costs together with ten dollars & ninty one Cents damages yet unpaid which the plaintiff hath sustained by occasion of the detention of the debt aforesaid together with the costs by him about his suit in this behalf expended & the Deft in Mercy &c.

Robert Steel)
    vs   )   certiorari
Andrew Agnew) This day came the parties by their attorneys & there-
           upon came the same Jury as above who being elected &c
do say they find for the plft & assess his damage to thirty seven dollars & forth five cents besides costs

        It is therefore considered by court that the plaintiff
recover of the Deft. thirty seven dollars & forty five cents the damage aforesaid as by the Jury aforesaid Assessed together with his costs
by him about his suit in this behalf expended & the sd. Deft. in Mercy

John Walker   )
    vs   )
Solloman McCampble &)   Debt
Greenbury Edwards   (This day came the parties by their attos. & there-
           upon came the same Jury as above who being elec-
ted tried & sworn the truth to speak on the issue joined do say that the
defendant hath not paid the debt in the declaration Mentioned & they
assess the plft damage by occasion of the detention of the same to sixteen dollars & ninty six cents besides costs

        It is therefore considered by court that the plft recover
of the Deft. the Debt in the declaration mentioned together with sixteen dollars & ninty six cents the damage as by the Jury aforesaid assessed & his costs by him about his suit in this behalf expended & the
Defts in mercy &c.

371. John Nicol)
        vs) Appl.
    Wm. Long) This day came the parties by their atternies & thereupon
           came the same Jury as above who being elected &c do say
they find for the plaintiff & assess his damages to twenty one dollars
& thirty four cents besides costs

        It is therefore considered by court that the plaintiff re-
cover of the defendant & his securities Samuel Steel, Robert Young &
John Wilkinson twenty one dollars & thirty four cents the damages as
by the Jury aforesaid Assessed together with the costs by him in this
behalf expended & the Deft. in Mercy &c.

Alexander paterson   )
      vs   )
Wm Kendrick & James Kendrick) this day came the parties by their at-
               tornies & thereupon came the same
Jury as above who being elected tryed & sworn the truth on the issue
Joined do say the Defendant hath not paid the Debt in the Declaration
mentioned nor any part thereof by occasion of the detention of which
debt they assess the plaintiff damage to nine dollars besides costs

        It is therefore considered by court that the plaintiff
recover of the defendant the Debt in the Declaration mentioned & the

damage aforesaid as by the Jury aforesaid assessed together with the Costs by him about his suit in this behalf expended & the said Defendant in Mersy &c.

392.   Adam Saffley Assinee)
of John Thornbury   )
            vs   )   Appeal
Alexander Harris   )   This day came the parties by their Attornies &
                             thereupon came a Jury to wit the same Jury as before who being elected and sworn well and truly to try the matter in controversy upon their oaths do say they find for the plaintiff and assess his damages to forty six dollars & forty Six cents besides costs

            It is therefore considered by court that the plaintiff recover of the defendant & Charles Donahoo his Security his damages aforesaid as by the Jury aforesaid assessed & his costs by him about his suit in this behalf expended & the said defendant in Mersy &c.

John Nigel)
        vs   )   Appeal
John Glass)   This day came the parties by attornies & thereupon came
                a Jury to with the same Jury as before who being elected and sworn well and truly to try the matter in controversy upon their oath do say they find for the plaintiff & assess his damages to Nineteen Dollars & Ten cents whereupon came the plaintiff by attorney and moved for Judgment against Jonathan Trippett & Steward Montgomery his securities Nineteen Dollars & ten cents the damages aforesaid as by the Jury aforesaid assessed together with the costs of this suit and the said defendants in mercy &c.

393.   Charles Henry   )
            vs   )
James Hollaway &)   Appeal
Nevins Hollaway)   This day came the parties by their Attornies and
                    thereupon came a Jury to with the same Jury as in the case John McGhee against John Trimble except Robert Cooper & William Eakin in place of John Hollaway & David Coldwell who being elected tried and sworn well and truly to try the matter in controversy upon their oaths do say after having retired some time to make up a verdict that they cannot agree

            Therefore with the consent of the parties a mistrial is ordered

Easter Finley)
        vs   )   Appeal
Samuel McCullock)   This day came the parties by their attornies & thereupon came a Jury to with the same Jury as in the case Jacob Danforth against John Lowry who being elected and sworn well and truly to try the matter in controversy Do say they find for the plaintiff & assess his damage to Sixty Dollars & twenty five cents besides Costs

            It is therefore considered by court that the plaintiff recover against the defendant Sixty Dollars & twenty five cents his damages aforesaid as by the Jury aforesaid assessed & his costs by him about his suit in this behalf expended & the defendant in Mercy &c.

                Court adjourned till tomorrow 9 Oclock

394.

Saturday 30th of March

Court met according to Adjournment

Present

George Ewing, Andrew Bogle & Wm. Davidson Esqrs

On motion of Miles Cunningham a leave was granted him to keep a publick house in the town of Maryville who entered into bond & with Charles Donahoe & John Thornbury agreable to law

Archibald Trimble)
vs) Fi Fal
Samuel Finley) On motion of Enoch parsons for the plaintiff the rule entered by the defendant to quash the plaintiffs execution was discharged

James Regan Assinee)
vs) Demurra
Edwards & Legg) Overruled by consent & writ of enquire awarded & continued to next court

White & Henderson)
vs) Certiorari
James Lusk) on motion of the plaintiffs Enoch parsons their attorney & for reasons appearing to the court the writs of certiorari & supersideous are set aside
It is therefore considered by court that the plaintiff recover of the defendant & his security John Lowry the sum of forty nine dollars & fifty nine cents damage together with their costs by them about this suit in this behalf expended & the sd Deft in Mercy &c.

395. Robert McCamey)
vs)
James McClanahan) On motion of the plft by his attorney & by consent of the parties a commission was awarded him to George Ewing & John Walker Esquires to take the deposition of Robertson Montgomery by giving the defendant five days notice of the time & place of taking the same to be read in Evidence in this cause

Robert Eakin)
vs) petition
Robert McCulley) This day came the plaintiff by his attorney & moved to amend his petition in this case & have it granted do not quash said petition.

made
Jenney Russell a minor orphan came into court & made a choice of Thomas Henderson as his guardian who entered into bond with Enoch parsons his security in the sum of one thousand dollars for the faithful discharge trust reposed in him

On motion of Barclay McGhee he was appointed Guardian of Barclay Russell a minor orphan under fourteen years & entered into bond with David Goldwell his security in the sum of one thousand dollars for the

20 Mcv 1811

faithful discharge of the trust reposed in him

On motion of Thomas Weir he was appointed guardian for sally Russell a Minor orphan under fourteen years & entered into bond with Banner Shields his security in the sum of one thousand dollars for the faithful discharge of the trust reposed in him.

396. Nancy Galbourn)
   vs   ) petition Habes Corpus
Wm. Young   ) This day came the parties by their attornies & sollem argument being had there-in & Mature deliberation.

   It is therefore considered by court Child specified in sd. Habeas Corpus be commited to the care of Wm. Young till next court & that Nancy Galbourn is not the person to which said child should be commited to take care of & that the sd. Nancy take nothing by her false writ & the defendant go without day

   A Bill of sale from Adam Sofley to John Nicol for a negro boy named Frank was acknowledged in open court by Adam Safley the subscriber thereto & admitted to record let it be registered

Robert Gault & James Houston)
   vs   )
John Lowry, John Waugk & others) In this case Andrew Cowan Deputy
           Sheriff returned our writ of Copeas
----------? executed on John Lowry, John Waugh, Hugh Kelsoe, Wm. Davidson & the rest not found
   It is therefore ordered by court that an Abes Writ issue against David Craig John Craig George Colville Joseph Colvill & James Martin returnable to our next court

Wm Armstrong)
   vs)
Joseph Wilson) In this case Saml. Johnston who was appearance bail
       for the Deft surrendered the defendant in discharge of himself & the plaintiffs attorney prays him in custody.

397.   Ordered by court that John Waugh Esquire make out and return to our next court & complete list of the taxable polls & property in the bounds of Capt. John B. Cusacks Company.

   Ordered that the clerk and orders to the defent Justices who have not returned the tax lists to this court agreeable to the orders of last Court

   John Thomas an orphan child now of the age of fourteen years & three months was bound to Samuel Houston to learn the blacksmith trade & entered into indentures as the law directs

   In this suit Josiah Danforth on Judgment against James Dial Isaac Brooks Jonathan Timberman Edward Buchanan & Abraham Ghormley the Defendants by their attorneys offered their pleas & court give to the three days of next term to give security to file their pleas

Samuel Cowan Sheriff & Collector for Blount County returned
the following grants of tax as not listed for xxikxxreturn

Stockley Donelson & others	Tennessee River	1000
Samuel Weir		700
W. Lackey, Tennessee River		1000
Hugh & Archibald Lackey	Tennessee River	1000
Hannah Chamberlain	Houlston	1000
Archibald Lackey	Tennessee	1000
Wm Hutton	Bakers Creek	1200
John Cowan & others	Nine Mile	640
John & James Cowan	Tennessee	640
Mortens heirs	Nine Mile	640
Joseph Weir	Xxkxxxxxx Pistol Creek	640
Stockley Donelson	Holston & Tennessee	20000

398.

supposed to be so much to which the claim

James V. Lackey	Little River	1500
Robert Wilson	Nine Mile	400
Wm. Lackey	Holston	1000
Alex Kelley	Holston	600

It is therefore ordered by court that the clerk publish the
same in the Knoxville Gazet & that Judgment be entered up against sd.
tracts of land respectively for the double taxes & charges severally
thereon & that the Sheriff expose sd tracts of land to sale agreable
to law or so much thereof of each tract as will be sufficient to
satisfy sd. tax & costs & charges

Robert Gault & James Houston)
        vs   )
John Lowry & others   ) In this case the writ was returned exe-
                             cuted on John Lowry John Waugh Hugh Kel-
soe & Wm Davidson the rest not found
        It is therefore ordered that an ——— writ issue for the
others & this cause is continued

                                James Gillespy
                                presiding justice